CRIMINAL JUSTICE RESEARCH SOURCES

THIRD EDITION

ROBERT L. O'BLOCK

 anderson publishing co.
2035 reading road
cincinnati, ohio 45202
(513) 421-4142

CRIMINAL JUSTICE RESEARCH SOURCES
Third Edition

ISBN 0-87084-665-5

Library of Congress Catalog Number 92-70236

Kelly Humble *Managing Editor*   *Project Editor* Elisabeth Roszmann

ACKNOWLEDGMENTS

This volume is an attempt to incorporate all major sources of information available to the student of criminal justice. I would like to thank my colleagues and students for reviewing the initial stages of this work and for their helpful comments and suggestions.

I would like to thank Professor Richard Schaffer, J.D., LL.M., Livian Lawrence, Janet Pointdexter, Boyd Overman, Kelly McRae, Kelly Welburn, Krist Culp, Eric Rice, Marsha Jackson, Twana Hudson, Blair Hall, James Currier, Kathleen Kempinger, Donald Penland, Mike Rowland, Kris Rose and Michael DeChene of the NCJRS, Victoria W. Schneider of the Inter-University Consortium for Political and Social Research, Nancy Holsenbeck, Jennifer Van Horn, Linda Brewer, Jason Berry, Amy Phipps, Hobart Owen and Renee Killelea.

INTRODUCTION

Criminal Justice Research Sources is a carefully compiled, comprehensive handbook of criminal justice research sources, designed with the objective of making criminal justice research less frustrating, more efficient, and more complete. Many students feel that the typical library is very complex and they may only be familiar with the card catalog, the *Reader's Guide to Periodical Literature*, and a few major criminal justice journals. As a result, term papers and theses are written without students having the benefit of other major sources of information, and they may not be able to find enough specific information on their research topic in basic sources.

From the author's own professional experiences and those of many of his colleagues, it is a disappointing but documented fact that students have actually stated they cannot find material on such major topics as police patrol, community-based corrections, white-collar crime, female offenders, etc. It is highly unlikely that the inadequacies of any library would account for this inability by the student to locate material on these major topics. It is more likely a result of students not knowing where or what to look for, or not being aware that there are many different sources available to them.

When the needs of students are met through the use of this handbook, professors will also benefit. They will be relieved of the time-consuming responsibility of locating or referring students to appropriate sources, and can expect more thorough and complete research papers. Students claiming they "cannot find a thing in the library on. . . . ." will become rare in criminal justice departments that use this resource book. At the same time, students will gain an understanding of, and appreciation for, the holdings of any particular library. Knowledge of the literature, especially that which is available in one's library, is something students should begin acquiring during the first year of college. This text was written so that it can be clearly understood by the first-year student while being comprehensive enough to assist the junior, senior, or graduate student.

This handbook has been designed to be of value as a major reference text to any criminal justice course that requires outside assignments—from annotated bibliographies to major research projects. It also addresses the importance of information that can be obtained from private and community service agencies. Thus, students using this handbook literally will have hundreds of sources at their fingertips. The great majority of these sources have been annotated to further expedite the literature search. Each chapter of the text includes a descriptive introduction that explains the importance and uses of the particular category of information sources being described. The major components of a research paper are also described in an appendix.

This work has been set up as though students were being taken through the steps of a literature search. The most likely place students will begin to search, aside from their textbooks, is the card catalog, followed by several other sources of books, and then perhaps journals. This will assist students with their preliminary search, and should facilitate the entire research process and help maintain the student's interest in the project.

FOR THE PROFESSOR

Some professors will find that their libraries do not have many of the basic reference works in criminal justice. This book can serve as a guide to the types of material that should be included in the criminal justice holdings. While we all have libraries with limited budgets, librarians tend to be very conscientious persons who want to build thorough collections. A meeting between the criminal justice faculty and the library director can be very beneficial. Librarians will want to add to their collection, but they need to know what types of material to add and need to have a prioritized list of those items. Further, many items listed in the chapter on the National Criminal Justice Reference Service (NCJRS) are available free of charge; other items described in the Government Documents chapter can be obtained at a nominal cost.

Criminal Justice Research Sources was also written with the objective of compiling into one easy-to-use source, a comprehensive collection of materials that can be of assistance to criminal justice students when gathering information for reports, term papers, and research projects. Many students, through no fault of their own, are simply not aware of the many bibliographies, directories, encyclopedias, periodicals, abstracts, indexes, computerized literature search services, and other materials and services that are at their disposal in libraries. Of course, it must be kept in mind that the larger the library, the more materials a researcher will have access to. Some of the materials described in this book are very expensive, and smaller libraries simply do not have the budgets or the room for them. Therefore, sources may not be directly available in every library, but can usually be obtained through such services as interlibrary loans. If uncertainty exists about the holdings of a particular library, the reference librarian should be consulted for information and assistance. Being aware of the materials that exist in the criminal justice area is a major step toward effective research.

FOR THE STUDENT

Students sometimes experience a feeling of helplessness when they first walk into the reference department of the library. Where do you go first? What library materials should you look for first? When should you ask the reference librarian for help and what information can you supply about the material in question to make his or her job easier? What are some sources outside the library that might supply the needed information? This handbook will help you with these questions. It will also help you spend your time more wisely, because there are a number of other things college students would rather do than stumble around an unfamiliar library. Most importantly, your research should be thorough and you will have the added advantage of turning in a higher quality paper.

The descriptions and listings of various sources of information pertinent to criminal justice takes the chance out of finding sources and you will no longer have to depend upon "just happening to run across" a particular publication. Therefore, students, use this sourcebook to its fullest!

CONTENTS

The Research Process

CHOOSING THE INVESTIGATIVE TOPIC

The student who has a topic assigned to him or her by the professor will be relieved of the responsibility of the first step in research—that is, selection of the subject. However, many college students, particularly graduate students, are at liberty to choose their own research problem. This selection is perhaps the most important step in the research effort and it should be made with familiarity of the criteria for selection of a research topic. There are several criteria for this selection, and although there are no rules that will guarantee the suitability of the topic, the researcher should utilize certain criteria for guidance and choose the topic accordingly.

Criteria for Selecting a Research Topic

1. Choose a topic you are interested in. Don't be impulsive in your selection. Give the topic careful consideration and if it's one that you know very little about, read up on it. Otherwise you could find out too late that you're not really interested in what you chose. Bear in mind, however, that too much personal interest can be a limitation; strong opinions, biases, and prejudice can work against you. Be alert to your own convictions and don't let them influence the outcome of your research in any way. Maintain an objective outlook to avoid value judgments on your chosen topic.

2. The topic should be sufficiently original so that the research effort is not a duplication of the work of others. If you are working on a thesis or dissertation this is especially important, because you are expected to find out if similar studies have already been carried out.

3. The topic should be amenable to research. Many topics are of great interest and can be thoroughly discussed, but cannot be researched to provide objective evidence. For example, the question "Should juvenile offenders work in a community setting rather than going to jail?" is very general and is a somewhat philosophical issue—not easily subject to scientific determination with extensive experiments. If we rephrased this question and oriented the research toward determining a specific criterion pertaining to the original broad question, such as "What antisocial behaviors, if any, are demonstrated by juvenile offenders serving their sentence in community work settings as opposed to those sentenced to jail?", our research topic would be more realistic and testable. Conclusions could then be drawn from the results of this question to help answer the first question of what should happen to juvenile offenders.

4. The problem should be significant enough so that the results of the research will add knowledge to the field of criminal justice. There are many significant problems to which the field needs solutions, and researchers should not waste time on insignificant topics that lack the potential to advance the science further. In fact, documenting the significance of your study is essential to a

sound research proposal. Concerns to consider that will assist you in selecting a research problem with significance include:

(1) practical problems encountered by practitioners in criminal justice,

(2) criminal justice problems or procedures that are under active attack by the media, practitioners, or theorists, and

(3) emerging problems that have not yet been researched.

5. The research problem must be specific. A research topic that proposes to document the whereabouts of every handgun ever manufactured in the United States would indeed add to

the knowledge of the field, but it is definitely not a feasible study. Another example of an unfeasible study would be to describe terrorist attacks in foreign countries. You would be inundated with literature and would still be sitting at the library table going over terrorist attacks of just one country while the rest of your classmates graduated. To avoid this, limit the subject further, which may take several steps. The initial step in such a process is to perform preliminary scans of the literature, so as to restrict the topic to a manageable form.

PUTTING THE EVIDENCE TOGETHER

Once the research problem has been selected, the researcher is ready to act as detective and investigate the literature sources. Some tips and clues to help in this investigation are listed below.

Tips and Clues

1. Don't let the number of information sources cited in this handbook, or the number of sources available in your library overwhelm you. If your topic has been wisely selected and its scope is sufficiently refined or narrowed, your literature search should not be overwhelming.

2. The extent of your information search will depend upon your research project. If you're writing an undergraduate term paper, as opposed to a thesis or dissertation, for example, you can be more selective of the information sources you choose to evaluate. You may have more than enough material for the backbone of a term paper on your topic if you stick to the major works published in the field. To learn more about the major works, you many only have to search the card catalog and a few indexes and abstracting services covering the major journals in the field. Thesis and dissertation candidates, on the other hand, will need to get their picks and shovels ready because they will have a lot more digging to do. If you're working on a graduate project, you should make your information search as comprehensive as possible. This involves

checking out all forms of publications likely to provide information on your research problem. In essence, the term paper student will rarely be expected to evaluate *all* the pertinent information sources, although as many of the relevant outstanding works as possible should be identified and used as the foundation for the paper. The thesis or dissertation student will be expected to use a wide variety, if not all of the information sources relevant to his or her topic.

3. If the available literature proves to be too voluminous, perhaps the topic is not specific enough and needs to be narrowed.

4. If the literature is too scant, perhaps you need to broaden the scope of your topic.

5. Don't feel discouraged if you have to broaden or narrow your topic. Some preliminary reading and research is often necessary before a topic is adequately defined.

6. Make some determination as to the period of time represented by your information search. Some topics, such as victim compensation, witness assistance programs, and community-based corrections are fairly new and literature concerning these topics will have been published

within the last few years. Other topics, such as drug smuggling and canine-assisted patrol, are older, and literature addressing these subjects will span many years. Do not automatically rule out the older studies. They will usually have a great deal to offer in terms of historical background and provide insight into significant developments that influenced the "state-of-the-art" as it is today. If you think the older sources have relevance to your topic, then you should extend your search far enough back to cover these sources. The current relevant sources should also be assessed.

7. Keep a complete bibliographic record of each literature source that you read, paraphrase, or quote. Each source should be recorded separately on a 3" x 5" card. Don't rely on odd pieces of paper, shopping lists, or class notes because these might be misplaced. Cards are ideal for this purpose because each source can be alphabetized and rearranged as needed. The author, title of the publication, location and name of the publisher, date of publication, and inclusive page numbers should be recorded.

8. Notes that you think will contribute to the research paper should be made on larger cards. These cards should note the author, title, and exact page number of the material used, but additional information is not necessary because the 3" x 5" cards should detail the complete bibliographic citation.

9. Brief notes summarizing the main theme or points of the source should be sufficient during the preliminary search of the literature. A brief sentence describing each paragraph of an article, for example, should be enough to remind you of the bulk of information presented in each paragraph, which is a good way to remember the contents of the entire article. If direct quotations are made, be sure to include the exact page number, because this information will be needed when footnoting the source. This is a frequent oversight that causes a lot of trouble later — you either have to go back to the library and look up the source again, or turn your paper in without the page number and hope your professor doesn't notice.

10. When beginning the first rough draft of the paper, write something based on your preliminary research and keep writing. This rough draft can be amended later, and it is more important to maintain a thought pattern than to interrupt for editing.

11. A revision with added information and documentation will be needed after the rough draft is written.

12. Do not use long quotes unless the passage is absolutely necessary to the content of the paper, or its meaning would be distorted if paraphrased.

13. Always give credit to sources of information cited. Failure to do so could result in charges of plagiarism, which is the use of another's materials as one's own. Paraphrasing another's ideas or patterns of thought without referencing the work is a common form of plagiarism.

14. Try to use a variety of sources so that the report is not limited to information gathered exclusively from books, encyclopedias, or dictionaries.

15. Look carefully at the references cited by books, articles, and other publications. They can be excellent sources of information, although some of these references may be older than desired.

16. Unless it is a proposal for a study to be done in the future, write the paper in the past tense.

17. Make sure you thoroughly understand your topic.

18. Always use complete sentences.

19. Attempt to keep in mind what the reader of the paper will be looking for.

20. If you must refer to yourself in the paper, use such terms as "the researcher," "the investigator," or "the writer," but avoid referring to yourself as "I."

21. Let the research paper sit for awhile after an initial draft is completed. Then read it aloud. There will probably be well-written parts and portions that are choppy, redundant, or meaningless. A revision will be necessary.

22. Always make a carbon copy or photocopy the final paper before turning it in to the professor. Some departments do not return papers to the students so you will want to have an extra for your files, and there is always the possibility the paper could be lost before it is graded.

23. Do not hesitate to request the services of the librarians. They are experts at locating information and can be immensely helpful.

PRESENTING THE EVIDENCE

As with the detective's report of a crime, the researcher must prepare a clear, written report of his findings. In a short time after beginning your investigation and search of the literature, you may have a large amount of information without really knowing how to present it in an organized written form. Studying the notes made in the preliminary review of the literature should be the first step. Determine if your topic should be restricted or narrowed. Then make a preliminary but detailed outline of divisions and subdivisions derived from your notes. There will likely be gaps in this outline that will need to be filled by additional and more thorough reviews of the literature. After these inadequacies have been compensated for, the first draft can be written. As mentioned previously, it is important to maintain a thought pattern when writing this first rough draft, so don't worry about editing the paper at this point.

The exact style, format, and content of the paper will depend upon requirements set forth by the professor, department, or university. Many professors, for example, will require the use of a certain style manual, while others will leave the choice of style to the student. In some colleges and universities, the style manual is determined by departmental policy. Be aware of any type of required style manual before beginning the research paper, otherwise you could spend a lot of time and effort only to have your project disqualified for noncompliance. The content and purpose of the paper will also vary according to various other requirements and conditions. For example, an undergraduate research paper will generally differ in scope and purpose from a graduate research paper, and the basic elements of a research paper may or may not be pertinent to the undergraduate research project, depending upon the course objectives and the individual instructor's requirements.

THE RESEARCH PAPER

Part One

Introduction. The introduction is a broad overview of the problem to be studied. It should acquaint the reader with the nature of the subject matter and briefly point toward the scope and dimensions of the topic to be discussed. It should also serve to attract and stimulate the reader's interest in the paper. The first sentence should state the essence of the study, i.e., "This study was undertaken to . . . ." Brief documentation is necessary. The introduction should be between one and three pages in length and should conclude with a smooth transition to the statement of the problem.

Statement of the Problem. The statement of the problem should be a concise sentence, which identifies the goal of the study and sets the direction for the study. It must be carefully and clearly described so that there can be no misunderstanding concerning the exact subject matter and the question the research hopes to answer. The statement of the problem serves as the basis from which the purpose of the study is drawn.

Statement of Purpose. The statement of purpose should tell the reader the reason for the study. A statement of the problem will not suffice for a statement of purpose. The statement of purpose should be concise and tell the reader exactly what is to be achieved. Many studies will have more than one purpose and each purpose should be addressed individually.

Significance of the Study. This is a very important section, which should clearly present the need for the research as well as describe the expected benefits that might be made available as a result of the research. The need for the study should be documented by presenting quotes or paraphrasing statements made by authorities in the field that reflect their authoritative opinion as to the need for further research in that particular area. All such statements must be fully footnoted. There should also be a concluding paragraph or sentence to the significance of the study.

Theoretical Framework. The contents of the theoretical framework should support the statement of the problem through a brief discussion of various theories proposed by others that relate to the research topic. This section should give structure to the study by making explicit the relationship of various theories and principles to the facts of the problem. For example, "This study is based on the theoretical frameworks of Doe, who maintained that aggression in humans has a direct effect upon job performance, and Smith, who proposed that empathic ability influenced interaction with other persons, and Johns, who stated that perceived power and authority among law enforcement personnel was always higher than actual or given power and authority." (These theories are fictitious). Further discussion and elaboration of the supporting theoretical frameworks is now in order. In other words, how the theories relate to the problem of identifying reasons for breaches of the exclusionary rule should be explained.

Hypothesis. Depending upon the type of research, hypothesis may or may not be appropriate. The hypothesis is a statement of relationship to be tested. The specific prediction of expected outcome of the study is stated. Hypotheses in the null form are simply statements of no relationship. Generally, rationale or reasons for the particular outcome predicted by the researcher, whether a statement of relationship or a statement of no relationship, will be required. Historical research projects will not have hypotheses but will ask questions that need to be resolved by the results of the study. Descriptive studies may or may not require hypotheses or null-hypotheses, but experimental studies will always require a declaration regarding relationship, and it is this declaration that the study is testing. (For more information on the different types of research studies, consult the references cited in the "Collecting Original Data" section of this handbook.) Our sample research study of the causative factors of violation of the exclusionary rule by police officers is a descriptive study that seeks to identify relevant data and does not require a hypothesis.

Definitions and Terms. This section is sometimes optional but if included should define all unclear, ambiguous, or newly coined terms used in the study because these terms have the potential of being unfamiliar to or misinterpreted by the reader. Exclusionary rule, police officer, and violation are all examples of terms used so far which should be defined. Persons outside the field of criminal justice who may read the paper cannot be expected to know the meaning of exclusionary rule, and *police officer* and *violation* used in this sense are rather vague or broad terms that the writer should clarify. Exactly what is meant by *police officer*, for example, should be clearly stated, otherwise there may be confusion as to whether other law enforcement officers such as auxiliary police officers, or probation and parole officers, and even deputy sheriffs, are included.

Limitations. A limitation is the recognition of a variable that has bearing on the study but which the researcher cannot control. Some limitations will be apparent at the beginning of the study. Others, such as unreturned questionnaires, will not become apparent until after the data has been collected. This section is for the protection of the researcher, and to help ensure the quality of the study. If the investigator has done a good job in recognizing weaknesses of the study, no one can say that this or that has not been considered, or that the validity of the results of the study and the conclusions that can be drawn are questionable.

Delimitations. Delimitations are variables having a bearing on the study that the researcher does control. Unlike limitations, they are not weaknesses of the study, but should be recognized, because they still affect the results. Examples of delimitations are the period of time involved in the study, the subjects studied, and even the literature and other information sources available for review. For example, if you wanted to restrict your study of violations of the exclusionary rule to only full-time police officers, or violations of the rule by male police officers only, these are delimitations and should be listed as such. The literature available for review is listed as a delimitation because usually this review is limited to materials available from one or two libraries and possibly a few other outside sources. However, the investigator cannot be expected to review everything ever written on his research topic, and the sources the researcher does choose to utilize are assumed to be good ones that will not be a weakness to the study.

Assumptions. Assumptions are statements accepted as universal truths that have application to the study. If we're doing a descriptive study of violations of the exclusionary rule, for example, we're assuming that there have been documented cases that will be available for examination.

Part Two

Review of Literature. The review of literature summarizes pertinent problems, methods, and findings of other investigators. Proper documentation with footnotes *must* be given. The writer's analysis as to strengths, weaknesses, agreements or disagreements with other findings is applicable here. The literature review is a very important component of your study and you do not want to cloud it with improperly conducted, biased, or poorly written studies. Before proceeding with the review of literature, take a few moments to read the following questions for critiquing research studies.

What information is valuable in the work?

What method of research was used to carry out the study?

What statistical tool was used to measure the data?

What were the specific procedures for gathering data?

Who conducted the research study?

Were the research results affected by limitations or delimitations?

Is the research report presented in such a way that it could be replicated?

Is the research tool reliable?

Does the researcher present conclusions based on the results of the study?

Has the researcher avoided interjecting his or her opinions and biases into the study, except where permissible, as in the review of literature?

The review of literature for your study would consist of background information on the subject in a synthesized manner as well as citing studies relating to the topics. In most cases this part should be organized into major subdivisions and conclude with a summary of the review of literature.

Part Three

Research Design. The research design should begin with an introductory paragraph, briefly restating the goals of the study and briefly describing, in general terms, what was done. Sub-headings should be used to identify the elements comprising the research design and each of these elements should be described in precise detail so that another person could set up and carry out the study in exactly the same manner. Where appropriate, describe each of the following elements:

A. Sample. Describe the population on which the study was based, tell how the sample was derived, and the procedure for randomization. For example, if you studied 100 violations of the exclusionary rule, you would need to explain exactly how these particular violations were chosen out of the total sample population. Did you pick every fourth one on record, or did you use another sampling technique? From where did you derive the sample—one large police department or several small departments? For additional information on sampling techniques, consult one of the many research books cited in Chapter 2, "Collecting Original Data."

B. Controls. What controls or conditions were maintained constant for one group that were varied for another? How were your control group and experimental group derived? Did you use the "double blind" technique?

C. Tool. Describe the instrument used to gather the data (questionnaire, interview, test, observation checklist, etc.). Indicate whether the tool was developed by the researcher or if it was a standardized tool. Describe the method of development and the method used to establish validity and reliability. Standardized tools are fully described in The Mental Measurement Yearbook (see Chapter 2, "Collecting Original Data," under the sub-heading, "Reference Books").

D. Procedure for data collection. Describe exactly how you went about obtaining the information that you have. Did you mail a separate questionnaire to each person in your sample group, or did you go before your sample population in person and explain the questionnaire? Did you follow up on unreturned questionnaires mailed? If you observed, in what way did you observe?

E. Statistical analysis. Indicate the statistical design you used to treat the data collected.

Part Four

Presentation and Analysis of Data. This section should describe, present, illustrate, and analyze the data obtained. Charts, graphs, and tables, in addition to the written description of the data, are appropriate to help illustrate the results. Data should be examined and presented according to any subgroups identified within the sample population so that differences, if any, in the responses of subgroups can be identified and compared. Any significant differences should be examined singularly, with a step-by-step analysis of treatment of the data. This part should conclude with a summary of significant values.

Bibliography

The bibliography should list all of the sources of information used for the preparation of the paper. This includes references used but not cited as footnotes in the body of the paper. For arrangement of the bibliography, consult the required form and style manual of your professor or department. If there is no required manual, one of the following style manuals will provide additional information on manuscript and footnote format and preparation:

American National Standards for Writing Abstracts. (New York: American National Standards Institute, 1979).

The Chicago Manual of Style, 13th edition, revised and expanded. (Chicago: University of Chicago Press, 1982).

The Complete Guide to Citing Government Documents: A Manual for Writers and Librarians. (Bethesda, MD: Congressional Information Service, Inc., 1984).

Form and Style in Thesis Writing, Campbell and Ballou. (Boston: Houghton-Mifflin, 1978).

Form and Style: Theses, Reports, Term Papers. (Boston: Houghton-Mifflin, 1990).

A Handbook for Scholars, Mary-Claire van Leunen. (New York: Random House, 1978).

A Manual for Writers of Term Papers, Theses, and Dissertations, Fifth edition, Kate L. Turabian. Revised and expanded by Bonnie Birtwistle Honigsblum. (Chicago: University of Chicago Press, 1987).

Mastering APA Style: Instructors Resource Guide. Mastering APA Style is designed to test students' weaknesses on APA's points of style in their writing before they begin that research paper, allowing the professor to concentrate on course material. The *Instructor's Resource Guide* contains 8 multiple-choice mastery tests, correction keys, and answer sheets, along with informative instructions. An essential resource, *Mastering APA Style: Instructor's Resource Guide,* enables students to polish their writing skills as they gain a thorough knowledge of the *Publication Manual of the APA,* Third Ed. (Washington, DC: American Psychological Association, 1990).

Mastering APA Style: Student's Workbook and Training Guide. Mastering APA Style: Students Workbook and Training Guide is the source students need to improve their writing skills. Designed and student-tested for self-study, this book begins with a writing evaluation test followed by exercises with identifiable errors. As they work through the exercises, students learn correct applications of the *Publication Manual of the APA, Third Ed.* This valuable educational workbook will help students reduce style errors in future research and term papers, improve their grades, and allow them to master APA style. (Washington, DC: American Psychological Association, 1990).

MLA Handbook: For Writers of Research Papers, Theses, and Dissertation, Third Edition. (New York: Modern Language Association of America, 1988).

NEA Style Manual for Writers and Editors. (Washington, DC: National Education Association, 1962).

Prentice-Hall Handbook for Writers, Glenn H. Leggett, et al. (Englewood Cliffs: Prentice-Hall, 1988).

Publication Manual of the American Psychological Association, Third Edition. Key information on the preparation of manuscripts for publication. The third edition introduces new and reorganized material, clearly defines the requirements of APA style for the preparation of manuscripts submitted for publication, and includes a sample single-experiment paper. You will find information on the process of publication from organizing, writing, and typing the manuscript to submitting the manuscript and handling the accepted article. The *Publication Manual* describes the APA journal program and publication policies and provides checklists to help authors assess their manuscripts. (1983)

The Random House Handbook, Fourth Edition, Frederick Crews. (New York: Random House, 1983).

Style Manual: Guide for the Preparation of Reports & Dissertations, Martha L. Manheimer. (New York: Dekker, 1973).

Words Into Type, Marjorie Skillen and Robert Gay, (Eds.). (Englewood Cliffs, NJ: Prentice-Hall, 1986).

Writing for Social Scientists. How to Start and Finish Your Thesis, Book, or Article, Howard S. Becker. With a Chapter by Pamela Richards. (Chicago: University of Chicago Press, 1986).

2

Collecting Original Data

DESCRIPTIVE AND HISTORICAL RESEARCH

The two most common types of research done by students are descriptive and historical research. Historical research is done by reviewing archival data. The examination of historical data is relatively easy for students who have access to collections of records. However, there are methodological dangers to accepting historical information as fact. The researcher, for example, may not know how the information was collected and thus the reliability of aggregate data could be suspect. Likewise, historical information, for example in personal diaries or writing, may reflect the biases of that individual's perspective and therefore not portray reality accurately.

Descriptive research usually involves looking at the class characteristics of a group or subgroup of a specific category. For example, the attitudes of black police officers on a certain subject. This delineation is a depiction, portraiture, or illustration and quantification of the subject's quality or qualities.

Because there are more methodological problems associated with experimental research as well as cost factors and the need for random sampling of representational groups, students usually opt for descriptive or historical research projects. The following are offered as some basic guidelines to follow in the collection and examination of data by students.

Many students, particularly those working on a thesis or dissertation, will have the opportunity to collect original data for their research project. A variety of data collection techniques are available, such as observation, surveys, mail questionnaires, and interviews. But before data collection commences, you should be very familiar with your data collection method in order to avoid the many types of sampling errors, and to make certain that the collection process transpires as smoothly as possible. For example, if you are planning to interview, make sure to avoid questions that could be answered by searching other easily accessible sources. There are also some guidelines that you should follow if you are using observation as your data collection technique. Failing to adhere to the correct procedures for data collection could make your data invalid and unreliable.

In addition to following the correct procedures, there may be several permission forms that will need to be filled out and accepted before your research project can get under way. Colleges and universities usually have written guidelines and requirements that students must abide by, in addition to a committee that approves research proposals. Academic advisors should be consulted regarding any existing regulations, and clearance or permission should be granted well in advance of when the actual data collection process begins. In most cases permission must also be obtained from cooperating agencies such as correctional institutions, police departments, halfway houses, state hospitals, schools, and so forth, that will contribute directly to the research project. These agencies generally have standardized regulations regarding their participation in research projects, which sometimes means that students must make changes in their original research proposal in order to stay within the realm of these guidelines. This is why it is extremely important to obtain permission early. Just in case a proposal is not acceptable, there will be time to revise it according to the agency's or university's specifications. Also, students should not expect to present their proposal one day and collect the data the next day, as usually there will be "red tape" in obtaining the needed permission. If a student intends to collect data by interviewing inmates of a correctional institution, for example, the proposal must first be approved by the criminal justice department and perhaps a university committee. Then the proposal should be discussed with an administrator of the correctional institution. This discussion will provide the student with an idea of the institution's requirements and expectations. Permission should then be obtained in writing, provided the proposal meets the designated requirements.

Students will generally be asked to furnish information about the basic nature of their research, the significance of their study, the exact method of data collection (observation, interviewing, etc.), the approximate amount of time required to complete the data collection, possible complications or adverse effects to subjects as a result of participating in the study, and the agency will generally request that results of the research be provided to them.

REFERENCE BOOKS

There are a number of sources that detail scientific procedure in the collection, presentation, and analysis of data. Among many useful references are the following examples:

Adult Learning: Psychological Research and Applications. Michael J.A. Howe (ed.). (London, New York: Wiley, 1977).

Basics of Qualitative Research, Anselm Strauss and Juliet Corbin. (Newbury Park, CA: Sage Publications, 1990).

Case Study Research: Design and Methods. Robert Y. Yin. (Newbury Park, CA: Sage Publications, 1989).

Categorical Longitudinal Data. Jacques A. Hagenaars. (Newbury Park, CA: Sage Publications, 1990).

Computer Simulation Applications: An Introduction. Marcia Lynn Whicker and Lee Sigelman. (Newbury Park, CA: Sage Publications, 1991).

Criminal Justice Research in Libraries: Strategies and Resources. Marilyn Lutzker and Eleanor Ferrall; foreword by Edward Sagarin. (Westport, CT: Greenwood Press, 1986).

Decision Research: A Field Guide. John S. Carroll and Eric J. Johnson. (Newbury Park, CA: Sage Publications, 1990).

Doing Field Research. John M. Johnson. (New York: The Free Press, 1978).

The Essence of Social Research. Charles Lachenmeyer. (New York: The Free Press, 1973).

Ethics and Values in Applied Social Research. Allan J. Kimmel. (Newbury Park, CA: Sage Publications, 1988).

Experiencing Fieldwork. William B. Shaffir and Robert A. Stebbins. (Newbury Park, CA: Sage Publications, 1990).

Foundations of Behavioral Research. Third Edition. F.N. Kerlinger. (New York: Holt, Rinehart, and Winston, 1986).

Fundamental Research Statistics, Second Edition. John T. Roscoe. (New York: Holt, Rinehart, and Winston, 1975).

Fundamentals of Criminal Justice Research. Robert S. Clark. (Lexington, MA: Lexington Books, 1977).

Heuristic Research. Clarke Moustekas. (Newbury Park, CA: Sage Publications, 1990).

Integrating Research: A Guide for Literature Reviews. Harris M. Cooper. (Newbury Park, CA: Sage Publications, 1989).

Interviewer's Manual. (Ann Arbor, MI: Survey Research Center, Institute for Social Research, 1976).

An Introduction to Social Research, Second Edition. H.M. Blalock, Jr. (Englewood Cliffs, NJ: Prentice-Hall, 1982).

Introduction to Social Research, Third Edition. Sanford Labovitz, Robert Hagedorn. (New York: McGraw-Hill, 1981).

Investigative Methods. James D. Scott. (Reston, VA: Reston Publishing, 1978).

Investigative Methods. Art Buckwalter. (Boston: Butterworth, 1984).

Investigative Methods in Library and Information Science: An Introduction, John Martyn, F. Wilfred Lancaster. (Arlington, VA: Information Resources Press, 1981).

Investigative Social Research. Jack D. Douglas. (Beverly Hills, CA: Sage Publications, 1976).

Linking, Auditing and Meta-Evaluation: Enhancing Quality In Applied Research. Thomas A. Schwandt and Edward S. Halpern. (Newbury Park, CA: Sage Publications, 1988).

The Mental Measurements Yearbook. Oscar K. Buros. (1938- .) Indexes, describes and evaluates thousands of tests used in research projects.

Methods for Policy Research. Ann Majchrzak. (Newbury Park, CA: Sage Publications, 1984).

The Modern Researcher, Fourth edition. Jacques Barzun and Henry F. Graff. (New York: Harcourt Brace Jovanovich, 1985).

Observing the Law: Field Methods in the Study of Crime and the Criminal Justice System. George McCall. (New York: The Free Press, 1978).

Obtaining Citizen Feedback: The Application of Citizen Surveys to Local Governments. Kenneth Webb and Harvey Hatry. (Washington: Urban Institute, 1973).

The Paradigm Dialog. Egon G. Gruba. (Newbury Park, CA: Sage Publications, 1990).

Participatory Action Research. William Foote Whyte. (Newbury Park, CA: Sage Publications, 1990).

Photographing the Self. Robert C. Ziller (Newbury Park, CA: Sage Publications, 1990).

Practical Sampling. Gary T. Henry. (Newbury Park, CA: Sage Publications, 1990).

Psychological Research, Fourth edition. Arthur B. Bachrach. (New York: McGraw, 1981).

Qualitative Evaluation and Research Methods. Michael Quinn Patton. (Newbury Park, CA: Sage Publications, 1990).

The Research Almanac, Second edition. Nancy Polette. (O'Fallon, MO: Book Lures, 1986).

The Research Craft: An Introduction to Social Science Methods, Second edition. John B. Williamson, et al. (Boston: Little, Brown and Company, 1982).

Research in Education, Sixth edition. John W. Best, James V. Kahn. (Englewood Cliffs, NJ: Prentice-Hall, 1989).

Research with Hispanic Populations. Gerardo Marin and Barbara Vanoss Marin. (Newbury Park, CA: Sage Publications, 1991).

Research Methods in Criminal Justice. Jack D. Fitzgerald, Steven M. Cox. (Nelson-Hall, 1986).

Research Methods in Criminal Justice and Criminology. Frank E. Hagan. (Macmillian Publishing Co., 1989).

Research Methods in Criminology and Criminal Justice. Edwin S. Johnson. (Englewood Cliffs, NJ: Prentice-Hall, 1981).

The Sampling Survey: Theory and Practice. Donald Warwick and Charles A. Lininger. (New York: McGraw-Hill, 1975).

Secondary Research: Information Sources and Methods. David W. Stewart. (Newbury Park, CA: Sage Publications, 1984).

Social Statistics Without Tears. Allan G. Johnson. (New York: McGraw-Hill, 1977).

Standardized Survey Interviewing: Minimizing Interviewer-Related Error. Floyd J. Fowler, Jr. and Thomas W. Mangione. (Newbury Park, CA: Sage Publications, 1989).

Survey and Opinion Research: Procedures for Processing and Analysis. John A. Sonquist and William C. Dinkelberg. (Englewood Cliffs, NJ: Prentice-Hall, 1977).

Survey Research. Charles Backstrom and Gerald Hursh. (Macmillan, 1981).

Survey Research by Telephone, Second edition. James H. Frey. (Newbury Park, CA: Sage Publications, 1989).

The Survey Research Handbook. Pamela L. Alreck, Robert E. Settle. (Homewood, IL: Richard D. Irwin, 1985).

Survey Research Methods. Earl R. Babbie. (Belmont, CA: Wadsworth Publishing, 1990).

Survey Research Methods, rev. ed. Floyd J. Fowler. (Newbury Park, CA: Sage Publications, 1988).

Survey Sampling. Leslie Kish. (New York: J. Wiley, 1965).

Telephone Survey Methods: Sampling, Selection and Supervision. Paul J. Lavrakas. (Newbury Park, CA: Sage Publications, 1987).

Understanding Research in the Social Sciences: A Practical Guide to Understanding Social and Behavioral Research. Curtis Hardyck and Lewis Petrinovidh. (Philadelphia: Saunders, 1975).

Writing Research Papers, Fifth edition. James D. Lester. (Glenview, IL: Scott, Foresman, 1987).

DISSERTATION AND THESIS ABSTRACTS

Theses and dissertations can provide a very significant contribution to a research project because they are assumed to provide original knowledge of research that is of value to a particular field of study. Master's theses and doctoral dissertations are listed in special bibliographies, so they cannot be located unless one of these bibliographies is consulted.

The Analysis of Public Policy: A Bibliography of Dissertations, 1977-1982. Compiled by John S. Robey. (Westport, CT: Greenwood Press, 1984). The *Analysis of Public Policy* is a current annotated bibliography covering the doctoral work done primarily in the United States, and to a lesser extent in Canada and Great Britain, in a number of specific areas of academic concern. It offers a systematic and thorough guide to the recent research findings of over one thousand English-language dissertations selected from those reported in *Dissertation Abstracts International.* Public policy-making in sixteen fields of concentration is represented, including state and local administration, agricultural policy, civil and women's rights, taxation, education, housing, energy, judicial, military, welfare, foreign policy, and international trade.

Comprehensive Dissertation Index. An annual publication consisting of five volumes. The first two volumes abstract selected dissertations pertaining to the Sciences (biology, chemistry, agriculture, health, physics, engineering, mathematics, earth sciences, environmental sciences). Volumes three and four contain selected abstracted dissertations relating to the Social Sciences and Humanities (education, fine arts, library science, communications, music, psychology, anthropology, business and economics, geography, history, language, law and political science, philosophy, religion, sociology). Volume five consists of an author index. (Keywords appear in bold-faced type in the title of dissertations.) (Ann Arbor, MI: University Microfilms International).

Criminal Justice and Law Related Titles: A Dissertation Bibliography. Contains a selected listing of over 1,300 doctoral dissertations and 145 master's theses relating to the field of criminal justice, and related law titles. (Ann Arbor, MI: University Microfilms International).

Dissertation Abstracts International. The most comprehensive source for doctoral dissertation abstracts written in the United States. Divided into two sections: Section A — the Humanities, and Section B — the Sciences. Abstracts of doctoral dissertations submitted by more than 400 cooperating institutions in the United States, Canada, and Europe are included. Keyword title and author indexes are published each month and cumulated annually. Bibliographic entries are classified and arranged alphabetically by important keywords in the title, which makes up the keyword title index. (Ann Arbor, MI: University Microfilms International).

Section A includes five broad subject categories of Communication and the Arts, Education, Language, Literature, and Linguistics, Philosophy, Religion and Theology, and Social Sciences. The criminal justice student should seek Section A and look in the table of contents under Social Sciences. The word "criminal," for example, will most likely prove to be a very productive keyword in the search for abstracts pertaining to criminal courts, criminal procedure, criminals, etc. Section B includes five broad subject categories of Biological Sciences, Earth Sciences, Health and Environment Sciences, Physical Sciences, and Psychology.

Guide to Lists of Masters Theses. Dorothy Black. (Chicago: American Library Association, 1965.) Lists masters theses written through 1964 at institutions in the United States and Canada. Subject and institutional lists provide access.

Harvard Graduate School of Education: A Bibliography of Doctoral Dissertations, 1918-1987. John W. Collins III and Leslie DiBona. (Westport, CT: Meckler Corporation, 1989).

Higher Education in American Life, 1636-1986: A Bibliography of Dissertations and Theses. Arthur P. Young. (Westport, CT: Greenwood Press, 1988).

Index to Theses Accepted for Higher Degrees in the Universities of Great Britain and Ireland. An annual publication arranged by subject classification. (London: Association of Special Libraries and Information Bureau, 1953-).

Law and Criminology, A Dissertation Catalog. Lists doctoral dissertations pertaining to law and criminology recently published by University Microfilms International. Each entry supplies the author, full title, degree earned, school name, date of degree, number of text pages, citation to DAI or Master's Abstracts, and order number for purchase. Approximately 450 citations are included. (Ann Arbor, MI: University Microfilms International, 1980).

Master's Abstracts. Published quarterly. Provides a selective annotated list of master's theses by students from many United States colleges and universities. (Ann Arbor, MI: University Microfilms International).

Masters Theses in the Pure and Applied Sciences, Vol. 32: Accepted by Colleges and Universities of the United States and Canada. W.H. Shafer. (New York: Plenum Publications, 1989).

Microfilm Abstracts: A Collection of Abstracts of Doctoral Dissertations and Monographs Which Are Available in Complete Form on Microfilm. This publication abstracts dissertations which are available in their entirety on microfilm. (Ann Arbor, MI: University Microfilms, 1938-date).

Research in Institutional Advancement: A Selected, Annotated Compendium of Doctoral Dissertations. Westley A. Rowland and Robert Carbone. (Washington, DC: Coun. Adv. and Supp. Ed., 1986.)

Social Service Review. "Doctoral Dissertations in Social Work." An annual publication since 1954 which provides abstracts of completed dissertations by students of schools of social work with doctoral programs. Dissertations in progress are also listed. (Chicago: University of Chicago Press).

GRANTS

References

Students of any major may be particularly interested in sources of grants. There is always the possibility of having a research project or other academic activity funded, and in some cases, the money may just be waiting. But the secret is knowing where to look for it and how to get it. Several sources exist that can help researchers obtain grants. Many of these sources are described below.

Computerized Data Base for Funding Sources

IRIS is an on-line computerized file containing descriptions of over 3000 funding opportunities from federal agencies, private and corporate foundations, and other not-for-profit organizations. More specifically, the IRIS database contains information on continuing programs for institutions, faculty, and graduate and undergraduate students. These programs support activities such as research, travel, teaching and advanced study. Several restrictions have been placed on the type of funding opportunities included in IRIS. Programs that disburse funds in a limited geographic area are not included, as IRIS is used nationwide. One-time solicitations or requests for proposals (RFP's) are not included because of their short turn-around, making them inappropriate to the design and intended function of IRIS. Also excluded are opportunities that require the recipient to enroll for credit at specific institutions and permanent employment opportunities.

The results of a search of the database are intended to provide sufficient information for the user to identify programs that warrant further consideration as possible sources of support. When conducted in cooperation with, or under the auspices of an office of sponsored programs, the search can provide a firm foundation for further inquiry.

Information for the IRIS database is obtained directly from funding sources rather than from resource books or newsletters, which can often contain out-of-date or misinterpreted data. In addition, whenever notification of program changes are received outside of the usual funding cycle, these changes are immediately incorporated into the database.

Foundation Directory

> Current year's data
> 5,148 records
> Semiannual revision
> The Foundation Center, New York, NY

The *Foundation Directory* provides descriptions of over 3,500 foundations that have assets of $1 million or more or that make grants of $100,000 or more annually.

Foundation Grants Index

> 1973 to the present
> 355,314 records
> Bimonthly
> The Foundation Center, New York, NY

Foundation Grants Index contains information on grants awarded by 400 major American philanthropic foundations, representing all records from the *Foundation Grants Index* section of the bimonthly *Foundation News*. Information on grants given by foundations is useful in determining types and amounts of grants awarded since foundations seldom announce the availability of funds for specific purposes. Approximately 20,000 new grants are added to the file each year.

Grants

Grants is the source of thousands of grants offered by federal, state, and local governments, commercial organizations, associations, and private foundations. All grants included in the database carry application deadlines up to six months ahead. Each entry includes full description, qualifications, money available, and renewability. Full name, address, and telephone number for each sponsoring organization are included when available.

National Foundations

National Foundations provides records of all United States foundations that award grants, regardless of the assets of the foundation or of the total amount of grants it awards annually. As with the foundations included in the *Foundation Directory*, each foundation conforms to the general description of a "nongovernmental, nonprofit organization, with funds and program managed by its own trustees or directors, and established to maintain or aid social, educational, charitable, religious, or other activities serving the common welfare, primarily through the making of grants."

Funding Sources

Annual Register of Grant Support. Subject guide to public and private sources of grant support, with organization, geographic, and personnel indexes. Annual. (Chicago, IL: Marquis Academic Media).

The Complete Grants Sourcebook for Higher Education, Second Edition. David G. Bauer. Profiles of private, corporate, and governmental funding sources with a subject index. Includes helpful tips on writing a successful proposal. (New York: Macmillan, 1985).

Catalog of Federal Domestic Assistance. Many indexes, including agency, subject, applicant eligibility. Entries for programs give funding agency, authorization, objectives of program, types of assistance, uses and use restrictions. (Washington, DC: U.S. Government Printing Office, annual).

Grants in the Humanities: A Scholar's Guide to Funding Sources. William E. Coleman. Especially useful are sections showing a sample proposal and budget. (New York: Neal-Schuman, 1980).

Directory of Research Grants, 1979. William K. Wilson and Betty J. Wilson (eds.). An annual publication which describes over 2,000 private and public research grants in ninety different categories. The "where, when, and how" of securing federal, state, and local governmental grants is described as well as those awarded by foundations, educational institutions, private donors, corporations, and so on. Grants available to graduate as well as undergraduate students are included. The arrangement is by subject areas and each entry includes information on qualifications of the recipients, when and where to apply, the sponsoring agency, amount of money available, and the application deadline. (Phoenix: Oryx Press, 1979).

Directory of Research Grants. Guide to more than 4,000 sources in all areas, with subject and sponsoring agency indexes. May also be searched by computer through the MARS service. (Phoenix: Oryx Press, annual).

The Federal Register. Daily publication providing much information on grant sources, as well as other governmental news. (Washington, DC: U.S. Government Printing Office.) (See Chapter 10, "Government Documents," for additional information on this source.)

Foundation Center National Data Book, Third edition. 2 volumes. Brief information about more than 21,000 non-profit organizations. Arranged by name and state, information given includes total dollar amount of grants awarded for the year, assets, principal officer, etc. Currency of information varies. (New York: Columbia University Press, 1981).

Foundation Directory. Arranged by state, with indexes of field of interest, name of foundation, etc. Brief summary of purpose, financial data, address, and officers. Grant application information. May also be searched by computer through the MARS service. (New York: Foundation Center, annual).

Foundation Grants Index, Nineteenth edition. Comprehensive list of grants of $5,000 or more awarded by private foundations. May also be searched by computer through the MARS service. (New York: Columbia University Press, 1990).

Getting Grants. Craig W. Smith and Eric W. Skjei. Takes the guesswork out of getting grants. It portrays how the grant system works and how it can work for you. (New York: Harper and Row, 1980).

A Guide to Scholarships, Fellowships and Grants: A Selected Bibliography. (Printed by the Institute of International Education, 809 United Nations Plaza, New York, New York 10017).

The International Foundation Directory, Fourth edition. H.V. Hodson (ed.) (Detroit, MI: Gale Research, 1986).

National Data Book, Seventh edition. Brief information about more than 21,000 non-profit organizations. Arranged by name and state, information given includes total dollar amount of grants awarded for the year, assets, principal officer, etc. Currency of information varies. May also be searched by computer through the MARS service. (New York Foundation Center, 1983).

National Endowment for the Humanities. Office of Challenge Grants.

Challenge Grants: Guidelines, Application Instructions, and Administrative Requirements. (Washington, DC: NEH, 1989).

Synopses of Community Demonstration Grant Projects for Alcohol and Drug Abuse Treatment on Homeless Individuals. National Institute on Alcohol Abuse and Alcoholism. (Rockville, MD: The Institute, 1988).

Directory of Financial Aids for Minorities, 1984-1985. Gail Ann Schlachter. Santa Barbara, CA: Reference Services Press, 1984. List of scholarships, fellowships, loans, grants, etc. awarded primarily to minorities.

Directory of Financial Aids for Women, 1985-86. Gail Ann Schlachter. Santa Barbara, CA: Reference Service Press, 1985. 1985/86. Guide to scholarships, grants, awards "designed primarily or exclusively for women."

Grantseeking in North Carolina: A Guide to Foundation and Corporate-Giving. Anita Gunn Shirley. Raleigh, NC: N.C. Center for Public Policy Research, 1985. Funding sources are arranged by size with indexes by funding interest and name. Also includes tips on writing the proposal.

Writing the Proposal

The "How To" Grants Manual: Successful Grantseeking Techniques for Obtaining Public and Private Grants, Second edition. David G. Bauer. (New York: Published for the American Council on Education by Macmillan, 1988).

Grant Money and How to Get It: A Handbook for Librarians. Richard W. Boss. (New York: R.R. Bowker, 1980).

Fund Raising; The Guide to Raising Money From Private Sources, Second edition. Thomas E. Broce. (Norman, OK: University of Oklahoma Press, 1986).

The CISP International Studies Funding Book, Fourth edition. Walter T. Brown, et al. (eds.) (New York: Council on International and Public Affairs. 1986).

How to Get Federal Grants, Third edition. Daniel Lynn Conrad. (San Francisco: Public Management Institute, 1980).

Grants for Libraries: A Guide to Public and Private Funding Programs and Proposal Writing Techniques, Second edition. Emmett Corry. (Littleton, CO: Libraries Unlimited, 1986).

How to Write Successful Foundation Presentations. Joseph Dermer (ed.) (Hartsdale, NY: Public Service Materials Center, 1984).

Fundraising For Nonprofit Institutions. Sandy F. Dolnick (ed.) (Greenwich, CT: JAI Press, 1987).

Plain Talk About Grants: A Basic Handbook. Robert E. Geller. (Sacramento, CA: California State Library Foundation, 1986).

A General Theory of Categorical Grants-In-Aid, 1978. Frederick C. Doolittle.

Grant$ for Arts and Cultural Programs. (New York: Foundation Center, 1986).

Grants for Research and Demonstrations. (Baltimore: Health Care Financing Administration, Office of Research, Demonstrations, and Statistics, 1981).

Grants Magazine; The Journal of Sponsored Research and Other Programs. Quarterly. New York: Plenum, 1978-. Tips in writing and presenting proposals, where to find grant funding. Each issue has an example of a "winning proposal."

The Grant System. John W. Kalas. (Albany, NY: State University of New York Press, 1987).

3

Sources of Books

Most libraries are now computerized to some extent. Many libraries have taken out the old catalog filing cabinets altogether, some have a mix of sources on both manual cards and computers, and a few still use only the card catalog. Students should be aware that in most libraries, only books, monographs, and government documents are in the general catalog. There are many other sources of information in a typical library, including commercial computer data bases, indexes, abstracts, periodicals, newspapers, microfilm, and others.

This chapter on sources of books will start by describing the card catalog. If your library is fully on-line, this information still applies, but think of your computer terminal as an electronic card catalog.

CARD CATALOG

The card catalog will contain most of the books in the library's collection, and is a good starting point for a researcher. However, a word of caution is appropriate here, because it is not a good idea to spend hours digging around a card catalog to begin a literature search. The card catalog will indeed be very helpful, because, depending upon the topic, you will probably find several pertinent books. But in the beginning, just take several minutes to scan the catalog and see what is available, perhaps look up a few books, and then move on to other sources. Books can provide a great deal of detailed information on a topic, but they may not be as valuable as some of the more current sources, such as journals. Later, you may want to return to the card catalog, if it is necessary to broaden the literature search with additional books.

The card catalog is an A-through-Z file of cards, indicating the catalog entries of author, title, and subject of most of the books in the library. Cards are alphabetically arranged and filed under each of these entries. All cards are tagged with a classification or call number, generally in the upper left hand corner of the card. This number indicates the location of the book on the shelf. Fiction books may be arranged alphabetically by author on a shelf, instead of having a call number. Ask a librarian for specific locations of call numbers within the library.

If you want a book by a particular author whose name you know, look under the author's last name. When you find the card representing the book you want, write down the call number and look for the book in the designated location. Authors can be an individual, a society, an institution, or a government department or bureau. You can also find a book if you know the title but not the author. Titles are filed under the first word, excluding *A, An,* and *The.* If you're looking for a certain book but are not sure of the author and title, don't frustrate yourself. Seek the assistance of a reference librarian.

If you're looking for books about a particular subject but don't have any specific books in mind, look under that subject. If you're in doubt about what subject heading to look under (i.e., "Do I look under administration of justice or justice—administration of?") ask the reference librarian for advice. Some libraries distinguish the subjects by red headings or capitalized black headings and some have divided catalogs for author-title cards and subject cards. A list of subject headings contained within a library's card catalog is generally available from the reference librarian upon request. Such a list will provide an overview and general idea of the library's holdings, along with what term or subject headings one should look under. More comprehensive lists of subject headings relating to criminal justice can be found in the following sources:

1. *Library of Congress Subject Headings,* Volume I, 13th edition. (Washington, DC: Library of Congress, 1990.)

2. *Sears List of Subject Headings,* Barbara M. Westby (ed.) (New York: H.W. Wilson Company, 1982.)

3. *National Criminal Justice Thesaurus.* (Washington, DC: National Institute of Justice/National Criminal Justice Reference Service, June 1982.)

Call Numbers

One of two different classification systems will be used by every library. These systems are the Dewey Decimal Classification System and the Library of Congress Classification System. The two systems have different call numbers. Major categories of the Dewey Decimal Card Catalog System are as follows:

000 – 099 – General Works
100 – 199 – Philosophy
200 – 299 – Religion
300 – 399 – Social Sciences
400 – 499 – Language
500 – 599 – Pure Science
600 – 699 – Technology
700 – 799 – The Arts
800 – 899 – Literature
900 – 999 – History

Categories in the Library of Congress Classification System are as follows:

A	—	General Works/Polygraphy	M	— Music
B	—	Philosophy/Religion	N	— Fine Arts
C	—	History/Auxiliary Sciences	P	— Language and Literature
D	—	History and Topography (except America)	Q	— Science
E/F	—	America	R	— Medicine
G	—	Geography/Anthropology	S	— Agriculture/Plant and Animal Husbandry
H	—	Social Sciences	T	— Technology
J	—	Political Science	U	— Military Science
K	—	Law	V	— Naval Science
L	—	Education	Z	— Bibliography and Library Science

Books pertaining to criminal justice are classified under the Social Sciences, are designated by the prefix letters of HV, and will have call numbers ranging from 340 to 360. To find a specific book, consult the card catalog to determine the book's call numbers and proceed to the correct location.

Most academic libraries have, or are in the process of, converting from the Dewey Decimal Classification System to the Library of Congress Classification System. Therefore, there is a good possibility that you will be confronted with the two systems at once, which may be a little confusing. If the desired book is not at the location indicated by the card catalog classification number, check the sorting shelves located in a designated area in the library. If the book still cannot be located, check the circulation desk to make sure the book has not been checked out. If it has not, the library will usually initiate a search for the book. If the book has already been checked out to someone else, it can be reserved and the library will notify you when it is returned.

BOOKS IN PRINT

Books in Print (New York: R.R. Bowker) is an annual publication that lists most available books in any given area of knowledge. It should be used as a supplement to the card catalog of any library because the card catalog contains only the holdings of the library. There will be many more books written on criminal justice than the average library will possess. The 1979-80 edition of *Books in Print* listed approximately 520,000 titles of books in print from 7,800 publishers. Each edition consists of four volumes, the first two of which are arranged alphabetically by author. Volumes three and four are alphabetically arranged by title. Volume four also includes a list of publishers whose books are listed.

Information provided for books listed includes author, title, edition, publisher, and year of publication. *Books in Print* does not include information on out-of-print books, periodicals, government literature, or unpublished research such as dissertations. However, it is an excellent source because it will provide information on the vast majority of books published in criminal justice. Subject headings contained in *Books in Print* that relate to criminal justice include:

crime and criminals	criminal investigation	criminologists
crime in literature	criminal jurisdiction	gangs
crime prevention	criminal justice-administration of criminal law	offenses against the person
criminal anthropology	criminal liability	organized crime
criminal courts	criminal procedure	rehabilitation of criminals
criminal and dangerous	criminal psychology	reparation
criminal intent	criminal statistics	victims of crime

It also includes headings of specific crimes such as gambling, murder, robbery, and so forth. Once book titles and authors are known, you should check to see if the desired books are available in the library or if they can be ordered through interlibrary loan. If so desired, the book could also be ordered and purchased through a bookstore or from the publisher.

Another good source of books is the *Cumulative Book Index* (New York: H.W. Wilson, 1898-). This is a monthly index, listing all new books published in various areas of interest, many of which may not yet be available to academic libraries. Also included are selected government documents. Books are listed by author, title, and subject.

INTERLIBRARY LOAN

If you've become aware of a "perfect" book which you think would greatly contribute to your research, and you break all track records getting to the card catalog only to find your library doesn't have it, don't be disappointed. Use your library's interlibrary loan service. The purpose of this service is to make material not owned by the library available for research. Chances are that another library owns the book and will loan it to your library upon request. In addition to books, other materials such as articles and government documents may be obtained through interlibrary loan. It is very difficult, however, to borrow theses, dissertations, complete issues of journals or newspapers, rare or fragile materials, reserve books, and reference materials.

When using interlibrary loan, you will be required to fill out an interlibrary loan request form, which may be obtained at the reference desk. Undergraduate students are sometimes required to have their request form approved by their faculty advisor. Information needed for the form includes the title, author's full name, publisher, place of publication, date, and the source of this bibliographical information. If the material is part of a series, the series title will also be required. Give the completed form to a member of the interlibrary loan or reference staff. After receiving the request, the library will locate the nearest establishment possessing the material requested. Interlibrary loan material should be requested well in advance of when it will actually be needed, because it takes an average of two weeks, and in some cases up to six weeks, for the order to be filled. Most libraries will notify you by mail when your requested item arrives. Some materials, such as journal articles and newspaper clippings will be photocopied and can be kept by the student. Loans, however, are usually not renewable and can only be kept a maximum of one to two weeks, depending upon the loaning library. There may be a small service charge to cover photocopying, postage, or insurance. Most libraries charge ten cents per photocopied page. There should be a space on the request form to indicate your price limit for photocopying charges.

Libraries participating in the interlibrary loan program have the opportunity to offer their users virtually every book, article, or other material that has ever been written.

Figure 1.1
Typical Interlibrary Loan Request Form

INTERLIBRARY LOAN *BORROWING* REQUEST

_____book _____dissertation _____thesis _____document _____newspaper

PLEASE: 1. USE A SEPARATE FORM FOR EACH ITEM YOU REQUEST.
              2. PRINT NEATLY AND LEGIBLY IN INK.
              3. USE FULL NAMES FOR AUTHOR, TITLE, SERIAL, ETC. DO NOT ABBREVIATE.

Borrower's name_____ Department _____ Phone # _____

Mailing address _____ City _____ State _____ Zip Code _____

Check one: ☐ faculty   ☐ staff   ☐ graduate student   ☐ undergraduate

Faculty signature (required for undergraduates):   _____

Today's date _____ Need by _____ Not needed after _____

NOTE: INCOMPLETE OR INCORRECT INFORMATION CAUSES CONSIDERABLE DELAY IN PROCESSING OF REQUESTS.

Author: _____

Title: _____

Publisher _____ Place _____ Date _____

This edition only _____ ISBN, ISSN, OCLC, or CODEN if known_____

VERIFICATION: PLEASE INDICATE THE SOURCE IN WHICH THE ABOVE REFERENCE WAS FOUND. VERIFICATION IN A STANDARD REFERENCE WORK IS PREFERRED. A LIST OF STANDARD VERIFICATION SOURCES IS AVAILABLE AT THE REFERENCE DESK.

Title _____

Volume _____ Date _____ Page _____ Item #_____

NOTE: I agree to pay charges that may be incurred to obtain this material. Maximum amount _____.

Signature_____ Date_____

Figure 3.1

The NCJRS Criminal Justice
Document Loan Program

An Interlibrary Loan Service

Document Loan Program

The National Institute of Justice/NCJRS (National Criminal Justice Reference Service), an information clearinghouse serving practitioners, researchers, students, and the general public, maintains a collection of nearly 100,000 documents related to criminal justice. It also has an interlibrary loan program.

The collection grows by about 6,000 documents annually and includes such subjects as child abuse, corrections, courts, crime prevention, dispute resolution, domestic violence, drugs and crime, juvenile justice, law enforcement, sexual assault, and victims.

To facilitate research and to improve access to research results, NCJRS makes most items in this collection accessible for a nominal fee to people in the United States and Canada through interlibrary loan.

Borrowing Procedures

- NCJRS lends documents only to other libraries. Contact your local public, academic, agency, or corporate library to borrow documents.
- You must request each document on a separate interlibrary loan form—the standard four-part American Library Association (ALA) form. NCJRS cannot give you the ALA forms but can tell you where to get them. Call NCJRS at the number listed on this page.
- You may borrow documents for up to 6 weeks. Libraries in the Washington, D.C., area may allow you to hand carry loan requests and pick up materials in person from the NCJRS Reading Room; in this case the borrowing period is 4 weeks.
- Renewals must be arranged through the borrowing library.
- NCJRS assesses a $12 charge for each lost or damaged document in addition to the cost of replacing the document.
- NCJRS does not routinely photocopy materials in lieu of lending.

Identifying Documents in the Collection

Each document in the NCJRS collection is identified by a unique accession number—the NCJ number. Be sure to cite this number on the ALA form.

If you are searching for a specific title, the following NCJRS products and services are excellent sources for identifying criminal justice documents and their NCJ numbers:

- *Document Retrieval Index (DRI)*—an annually updated microfiche catalog of the entire NCJRS collection.
- *NIJ Reports*—a bimonthly journal that includes abstracts of the most significant additions to the NCJRS collection.
- *Topical Searches, Topical Bibliographies, and Custom Searches*—listings of abstracts from the 100,000-item data base representing published and unpublished documents in the collection. The accession number shown on these products is the NCJ number. On records retrieved through DIALOG on File 21, the NCJ number is displayed as the DIALOG number before each citation.
- *Index to the NCJRS Microfiche Collection*—access by author, subject, and title to more than 25,000 documents in the collection that are also available on microfiche from NCJRS.

For more information, call NCJRS.

The National Institute of Justice/NCJRS
toll-free number is 800-851-3420;
301-251-5500 from Metropolitan
Washington, D.C., or Maryland.

Many documents can be purchased by writing University Microfilms International, 300 North Reeb Road, Dept. P.R., Ann Arbor, MI 48106.

RESERVE BOOKS

Books for use in specific courses will generally be placed on "reserve" in the library by the professor because they will be in heavy demand by students. Some libraries will designate reserve books by placing a red card in the card catalog. Others will maintain notebooks containing lists of reserve books. These notebooks may be arranged alphabetically by the professor's name, or alphabetically by title of the book. Books on reserve must be obtained from the reserve reading room within the library and are usually circulated for a period of two hours during the day.

BOOK REVIEWS

Book reviews can serve a variety of purposes, but they are basically summaries of another writer's interpretation and opinions of the contents of the original work, and should not be used as a substitute for reading the entire book. Upon comparing a review with the actual book, you might find that your opinions differ from that of the reviewer, so make sure you have formulated your own opinions of the book, particularly if you intend to cite the work as a reference source for your paper. The following are sources of book reviews.

Book Review Digest. (New York: H.W. Wilson, annual.) A monthly publication, with the exception of February and July, that indexes selected book reviews appearing in approximately 75 English and American periodicals. The orientation is toward popular, rather than scholarly, journals. Approximately 350 book titles with brief descriptions presented each month. Title and subject indexes are provided.

Book Review Index. (Detroit: Gale Research, annual.) A bimonthly publication listing current book reviews in the social sciences, indexed by author.

A Guide to Book Review Citations: A Bibliography of Sources, Richard A. Gray, (Columbus: The Ohio State University Press, 1968.) Provides an annotated list of sources of book review citations.

Index to Book Reviews in the Humanities. (Williamston, Michigan: Phillip Thomson, 1963.) An annual publication that includes book reviews in the social sciences as well as the humanities. Several thousand book titles are indexed in each issue.

Technical Book Review Index. (Pittsburgh: JAAD, 1987.) A monthly publication with the exception of July and August, which indexes reviews appearing in scientific, technical, and trade journals.

MICROFORMS

If it were not for microforms, we would all become buried under the tons of material published every year. Most libraries want to acquire as much of this material as possible in order to maintain an up-to-date, thorough collection of data, but also have limited space that must be utilized as efficiently as possible. Microforms come in a variety of forms: microfilm, microcards, microprint, microfiche, and ultramicrofiche. As an example of the space-saving advantage of microforms, a 4" x 6" microfiche can hold up to 98 book pages. The ultramicrofiche method can contain as many as 1200 pages on a 2" x 2" card.

A point to keep in mind is that some materials available in microform cannot be found in print, such as rare books, periodicals, manuscripts, government documents, and newspapers. But despite these advantages, students sometimes become intimidated by the special readers and the rows of filing cabinets filled with drawer after drawer of cards. And unless you have access to a library that loans microfiche and microfiche readers, you cannot take the material home as you can a book. Nonetheless, microforms are here to stay and will undoubtedly increase in usage during the years ahead.

Books on microform will be listed as such in the card catalog. Government documents, serials, periodicals, and other publications on microform are identified through corresponding indexes. If you are uncertain about which materials are on microform and which are not, check the library's guide to their microform collection. This should be available at the reference desk and the microform service desk.

Still confused about microforms? Don't be intimidated. Ask the reference librarian for assistance.

4

Indexing Services

INDEXES

Indexes are specialized bibliographic tools that delve into a variety of subjects or academic disciplines. They provide a quick method for locating literature on a specified topic in an organized fashion. Library materials covered by indexing services are important contributors to the content of reports, term papers, and other research projects. Journal literature, for example, is current and is reflective of trends in the field. Results of recent research can be found in journal literature and it is also easy to review a variety of points of view on a given topic by referring to various journals. It is difficult to obtain these advantages from books found in the card catalog, and thus it is necessary to utilize sources of information other than those found in the card catalog and *Books in Print*.

Bibliographical information in an index includes the author's name, the title of the publication, the name of the publishing journal or periodical, the date of publication, and the length of publication.

There are several different kinds of indexes, the most common of which are subject and author indexes. All publications dealing with a particular subject area or topic will be categorized and alphabetized. If you are looking for articles on a certain subject, such as racketeering, look in the subject index under racketeering. The index will give you a list of periodicals that have articles on racketeering. Next, go to the library's checklist of periodicals. Look up the titles of the periodicals you need and if the library has them, you are ready to retrieve them.

Following the subject index, most indexes will include an alphabetized author index that provides a listing of publications by author, rather than by subject matter. Other kinds of indexes include geographical indexes, abbreviations indexes, reference indexes, and keyword-title indexes in which the initial work of a heading or subheading is indexed.

Current indexes are generally published on a monthly, bi-weekly, or quarterly basis and include those publications of the preceeding months or weeks. Cumulative indexes are also of great value because they contain listings of publications on a particular subject matter that have been published within the last three months to one year. These indexes are then published quarterly or annually, respectively. There are also retrospective indexes that include articles on a particular subject matter published during previous decades. Most libraries will locate their indexes near the card catalog in the Reference Department.

One of the most popularly used indexes is the *Reader's Guide to Periodical Literature*. This is a cumulative, alphabetized author/subject index to periodicals of general interest published in the United States. *Reader's Guide* covers publications such as *Time*, *U.S. News and World Report*, *Consumer Reports*, and *Newsweek*, among many others. Topic headings relating to criminal justice included in the *Reader's Guide* vary from month to month, depending upon the subjects of the articles cited. Typical citations will probably include the following subject headings:

capital punishment			juvenile delinquency
commercial crimes			narcotics
crime and criminals			prisons
crime prevention			self-defense
detectives				trials
escapes					victims of crime
fugitives				women and crime
gangs

Also, look under specific crimes such as arson, bribery, burglary, fraud, murder, robbery, and so forth.

The majority of students are probably more familiar with this periodical index than with any other. However, its use in college papers, particularly scholarly research papers, is generally restricted. The use of general interest publications as sources for research papers is discouraged by many professors, so it is wise to check for any such restrictions before consulting *Reader's Guide* for information. In addition, all other available avenues of information such as abstracts and indexes of professional journals should first be exhausted. However, if you are familiar with *Reader's Guide* you should have little trouble using the more specialized indexes, as they all list articles by subject.

ABSTRACTING INDEXES

An abstracting index will include all of the bibliographical information presented in a regular index, but it will also include a brief synopsis or summary of the publication. The summary includes the main theme of the article and will generally summarize results of any research conducted. After reading an abstract, the reader should have a better idea of the total content of the original publication so that he or she can judge whether there is a need to consult the entire text.

The effective use of index and abstract services is the key to a thorough review of the literature for any particular subject and for both current and retrospective searches. There exists such a vast amount of literature in any given field of study that even avid readers cannot expect to keep pace with it. Thus, the indexing services first assist the researcher by organizing the printed matter by topic, author, etc. Then, once the researcher has gained an insight into the literature available on his or her topic, he or she can read the condensed summaries of the publications provided by the abstract services to find the articles that will be most applicable to his or her research needs. An example of an abstract is provided below:

Webster, Stephen H., and Kenneth E. Matthews, Jr., ''Survey of Arson and Arson Response Capabilities in Selected Jurisdictions.'' (Washington: United States Department of Justice, Law Enforcement Assistance Administration Item 968H-1, February, 1979, p. 41).

Report on arson incidence and the resources and activities of arson control units in 174 cities with 50,000 or more population. Data are based on 1978 mail survey of fire chiefs and cover fiscal years ending 1977 or 1978.

Contents:

A. Narrative analysis, with text, statistics, four charts, and eleven tables on relationship between total fire and arson rates, and 1970-75 change in city size; arson motives and dollar losses; legal restrictions on sharing information with insurance companies; and arson investigation and prevention activities and equipment (pp. 1-27).

B. Appendices with facsimile questionnaire and one table showing for each survey city 1975 population; fire department budget; number and types of fire; arson investigations, arrests, and fatalities; and arson unit characteristics and training (pp. 18-41).

Source: *American Statistics Index 1979*, Abstracts Volume, Supplement No. 5 (Washington: Congressional Information Service) Page 76.

A student researching financial implications of arson, for example, would probably want to consult the entire text of the article because the abstract specifically indicated that dollar loss due to arson was a part of the subject matter addressed.

There are many specialized abstracts and indexes relating to criminal justice and any library is bound to have some of them. Several of the most pertinent abstracts and indexes to criminal justice are briefly described below, followed by a listing of many others that may also be of service to the criminal justice student.

Abstracts of Supreme Court Decisions Interpreting the Interstate Commerce Act. Association of Transportation Practitioners, 1211 Connecticut Ave. N.W. Ste. 310, Washington DC 20036.

Abstracts on Adult Corrections, 1983-1990. Includes more than 1,600 abstracts on community-based and institutional adult corrections. (Monsey, NY: Criminal Justice Press).

Abstracts on Juvenile Justice and Delinquency, 1983-1990. Includes more than 1,600 abstracts on juvenile justice systems, corrections, courts, policing and delinquency causes, patterns, prevention. (Monsey, NY: Criminal Justice Press).

Abstracts on Police, 1983-1990. Includes more than 1,500 abstracts on police management, community policing, personnel and other topics. (Monsey, NY: Criminal Justice Press).

Applied Science and Technology Index. A cumulative index to English language periodicals. It contains subject and author indexes. Subject fields indexed include aeronautics and space science, chemistry, computer technology and applications, construction industry, energy resources and research, fire and fire prevention, food and food industry, geology, machinery, mathematics, minerology, metallurgy, oceanography, petroleum and gas, physics, plastics, textile industry and fabrics, transportation, engineering, and other industrial and mechanical arts. Of particular interest to criminal justice students would be the topic headings: crime and criminals, criminal investigation, crime prevention, crimes aboard aircraft, criminal statistics, security, burglar alarms, and other specific technological security items. (New York: H.W. Wilson Company).

Criminal Justice Abstracts. (Formerly Crime and Delinquency Literature.) Sponsored by the National Council on Crime and Delinquency, Hackensack, NJ, this source is published quarterly (March, June, September, December) and cumulated annually. It contains in-depth abstracts of current literature, international in scope, on criminal justice policies, theories, programs, and administration. Headings include: Crime and the Offender, Juvenile Delinquency and the Delinquent, Law and the Courts, Law Enforcement and the Police, Corrections, Drug Abuse, and Related Social Issues. Also included are Letters to the Editor and a subject index. Each issue contains approximately 150 abstracts of the latest books, articles, reports, and studies published worldwide.

Criminal Justice Periodical Index. A comprehensive criminal justice periodical reference source published three times annually (May, September, January). The final issue in January is cumulative. The reference source contains thousands of specialized entries, from over 90 significant criminal justice journals. Entries are listed under various subject headings such as family disturbance/intervention, hostages, pre-trial diversion, terrorism, etc. (University Microfilms International.)

Criminology & Penology Abstracts. Indexed: Excerp. Criminol. Former titles: Abstracts on Criminology and Penology; Excerpt Criminologica. (Amsteveen, Netherlands: Kugler Publications, 1961).

Current Law Index. 1980-date. Covers the same subject-matter as the *Index to Legal Periodicals*, but the range of journals indexed is much broader and the indexing more thorough.

Human Resources Abstracts. This complements *Public Administration Abstracts*. It is international in coverage and abstracts material not found elsewhere. Covering such subject areas as public policy and planning, and public health, it is an excellent resource in public administration. (Newbury Park, CA: Sage Publications).

Index to Canadian Legal Periodical Literature. (Text in English and French) q. P.O. Box 386, N.D.G. Station, Montreal, Que. H4A 3P7, Canada (1960).

Index to Chinese Legal Periodicals/Chung Wen Fa Lu Lun Wen So Yin. a. University, Library—Tung Wu Ta Hsueh Tu Shing Kuan, Wai Shuang Hsi, Taipei, Taiwan, Republic of China. (reprint service avail.) Key Title: Zhongwen Falu Lauwen Suoyin. (1970).

Index to Foreign Legal Periodicals. (Subject headings in English with translation into French, German and Spanish included in a. cumulation) 1960. q. (a. cumulations) (American Association of Law Libraries, School of Law Library) Description: Indexes legal and business periodicals from 59 countries. Includes legal essays. (Berkeley, CA: University of California Press, 1960).

Index to Indian Legal Periodicals. (New Delhi, India: Indian Law Institute, 1963).

Index to International Public Opinion. Prepared by Survey Research Consultants International, Inc. Annual. (see Chapter 14, "Sources of International Data" for a complete description).

Index to Legal Books. M.C. Susan DeMaio (ed.). Description: Merges and cites index entries from leading law books, national in scope and importance, and cross-references under major legal subject categories. (New York: R.R. Bowker, Legal Reference Publishing).

Index to Legal Periodicals, published in two series. [1] Vol. 1 (1908)—Vol. 18 (1925) and [2] Vol. 1 (1926)—to date. A subject index without abstracts, covering English language law journals. There is a useful "Table of Cases Referred to in Articles" in each issue starting with 1917.

Index to Periodical Articles Related to Law. Covers law-related articles in general social science periodicals which are not indexed in *Index to Legal Periodicals.* (Dobbs Ferry, NY: Glanville Publishers, Inc., 1974).

International Federation for Documentation. P-Notes. 1931. Federation Internationale d'Information et de Documentation— International Federation for Information and Documentation, Box 90402, 2509 LK The Hague, Netherlands. (Subscr. to: Distribution Centre, Blackhorse Rd., Letchworth, Herts. SG6 1HN, United Kingdom)

Police Science Abstracts. This international abstracting service provides over 1,500 abstracts concerning police science, the forensic sciences, and forensic medicine. *Police Science Abstracts* is published six times a year (January, March, May, July, September, and November) and the last issue includes cumulative subject and author indexes. (Amsterdam, Netherlands: Kugler Publications).

Psychological Abstracts. The leading abstracting index for the field of psychology. It is published monthly and cumulated annually. It provides synopses on an international basis of literature in psychology and related disciplines. Subject and author indexes are provided. Subject headings of related criminal justice articles that have been abstracted include: adjudication, correctional institutions, crime, criminals, conviction, criminal law, criminology, prisons, as well as specific crimes, i.e., homicide, rape, etc. (This is also available as a computerized database—see Chapter 9, "Computerized Literature Searches.") (Arlington, Virginia: Psychological Abstracts Information Service, American Psychological Association.)

Public Affairs Information Service (PAIS). Robert S. Wilson (ed.). This abstracting index is published monthly and cumulated annually. It covers many sources of literature of the social sciences. Broad categories include economics, business, finance, banking, government, public administration, public policy, political science, and statistics. Subject headings relating to criminal justice include black criminals, capital punishment, crime, crime and criminals, computers and crime, correction, crime news, crime prevention, crime records, criminal investigation, criminal jurisdiction, criminal justice, criminal law, criminal liability, criminal procedure, criminal research, criminal syndicalism, criminals-insane, female offenders, juvenile delinquents, parole, political crimes, victims of crime, and white collar crimes, as well as specific crimes. (*PAIS* is also available in a computerized database—see Chapter 9, "Computerized Literature Searches.") (New York: Public Affairs Information Service, Inc.)

Sage Public Administration Abstracts. This is the only indexing service devoted exclusively to public administration. International in coverage, the material abstracted includes books, pamphlets, government publications, speeches, legislative research studies, and ephemera, in addition to journal articles. (Newbury Park, CA: Sage Publications).

Social Science Citation Index. An international index of articles appearing in more than 1,000 social science journals. An index of previously published articles that are being cited in current literature is included. This enables one to follow the development of ideas and hypotheses and reactions to them over a period of time. Keyword-title and author indexes are also included in this annual publication.

Social Sciences Index. A cumulative index to English language periodicals in the fields of anthropology, area studies, economics, environmental sciences, geography, law and criminology, medical sciences, political science, psychology, public administration, and sociology. Access is by author and subject entries. Annual cumulations. (New York: H.W. Wilson Company.)

Social Work Research and Abstracts. Articles and books are abstracted with subject and author access, in addition to an original research paper in each issue.

Sociological Abstracts. Published five times yearly (April, June, August, October and December). These issues are cumulated annually. Subject headings pertaining to criminal justice include crime, criminal, criminality, criminally, criminogenic, criminogenesis, criminology, delinquency, delinquent, and courts, as well as specific crimes. (San Diego: Sociological Abstracts, Inc.) (This is also available in a computerized database—see Chapter 9, "Computerized Literature Searches.")

The following is a list of other pertinent or related abstracts and indexes.

ABC Political Science
Abstracts on Police Science
Advance Bibliography of Law and Related Fields
Alcoholism Digest Annual
Applied Science and Technology Index
Bibliography on Foreign and Comparative Law
Biography Index
Book Review Digest
British Technology Index
Bulletin Signaletique 390: Psychology et Psychopathology, Psychistrig
Bulletin Signaletique 524: Sociology
Business Periodicals Index
Canadian Book Review Annual
Canadian Business Periodicals Index
Computer Abstracts
Crime and Delinquency Literature
Cumulative Book Index
Current Contents, Social and Behavorial Sciences
Current Index to Journals in Education
Current Index to Statistics
Current Publications in Legal and Related Fields
Dissertation Abstracts
Drug Abuse Bibliography
Education Index
Federal Index
Gallup Opinion Index
Government Reports
Highway Safety Literature

Humanities Index
Index Medicus
Index to Book Reviews in the Humanities
Index to Current Urban Documents
Index to Post-1944 Periodical Articles on Political, Economic, and
    Social Problems
Index to U.S. Government Periodicals
International Bibliography of the Social Sciences—Economics
International Bibliography of the Social Sciences—Political
International Bibliography of the Social Sciences—Sociology
International Political Science Abstracts
Key to Economic Science and Managerial Sciences

London Bibliography of the Social Sciences
Magazine Index
The National Newspaper Index
Peace Research Abstracts Journal
Personal Management Abstracts
Population Index
Poverty and Human Resources Abstract
Sage Public Administration Abstracts
Sage Race Relations Abstracts
Sage Urban Studies Abstracts
Ulrich's International Periodicals Directory
Urban Affairs Abstracts

Journals

All too often undergraduate students return from an excursion to the library and tell their professor a sad tale of woe. "I looked in the library and there isn't anything on "Patrol-Based Investigation," or another topic they are researching.

This situation requires some translation and decoding. What usually happens is this: the undergraduate student, new to the major, goes to the library in search of a *book* on the specific topic they are interested in. After going through the library's card catalogs and not finding a *book* on the topic, they conclude that there is "nothing" on the subject.

It is one of the sad facts of academic life that most students are not exposed to the major scholarly journals in their field until they reach the graduate level.

Chapter 5 of this book lists in alphabetical order, and by category, many of the major (and minor) scholarly journals in Criminal Justice.

First, the undergraduate student needs to be aware that refereed journals are the repository of much of the scholarly research that is produced in a scientific field. Second, the undergraduate needs to know that there is a systematic way to research their topic. The major methods are by consulting one of the abstracts or indexes to the journals as spelled out in Chapter 4, or by doing a computer search of the topic by using one of the computerized data bases shown in Chapter 9.

The most important point for the student to understand is that the majority of research and most current information will be found in scholarly journals and not books.

One further distinction needs to be made concerning the difference between a refereed publication and a trade magazine.

Refereed journals usually only accept an article for publication after it has been reviewed by three reviewers (called "referees") and a strong majority feel that the article is methodologically sound and that it contributes knowledge to the field. In the scholarly world, having an article accepted for publication in a major refereed journal is considered meritorious and an honor. Trade publications have their place, but because they do not require the same level of academic rigor and may in fact be selected for publication on the basis of "appeal to the subscriber," an article in a trade magazine is not considered as valid as a refereed academic journal article.

The following is a list of the major refereed journals and trade magazines in the field.

CORRECTIONS

Apalachee Diary, Apalachee Correctional Institution, P.O. Box 699, Seads, FL 32460. [ceased publication]

California Correctional News, 211 Lathrop Way Suite M. Sacramento, CA 95815-4242.

Canadian Journal of Criminology, 55 Parkdale Ave., Ottawa K1Y 1E5, Ontario, Canada.

Contact Newsletter, P.O. Box 81826, Lincoln, NE 68501. [ceased publication]

Correctional Industry Association Newsletter. 706 Middlebrooks Circle, Tallahassee, FL 32312.

Corrrections Compendium, 3900 Industrial Ave. North, 2nd Floor, Box 81826, Lincoln, NE 68501-1826.

Corrections Digest, 3918 Prosperity Ave. Ste. 318 Fairfax, VA 22031-3334.

Corrections Today, American Correctional Association, 8025 Laurel Lakes Ct., Laurel, MD 20707.

Corrective and Social Psychiatry and Journal of Behavioral Technology Methods and Therapy, Martin Psychiatric Research Found., Box 3365, Fairfield, CA 94533-0587.

Federal Probation, Adm. Office of the U.S. Courts Probation Division, Washington, D.C. 20544.

Fortune News, Fortune Society 39 W., 19th St. New York, NY 10011.

Grapevine, Box 49122, Chicago, IL 60649-0122.

Howard Law Journal, Howard University School of Law, 2900 Vanness St. N.W., Washington, DC 20008.

Jail & Prisoner Law Bulletin, Americans for the Effective Law Enforcement Inc., 5519 N. Cumberland Ave., St. 1008, Chicago, IL 60656-1498.

Journal of Correctional Education, Kancz, McGing & Assoc. Inc. Box 75502, St. Paul, MN 55175.

Journal of Offender Counseling Services and Rehab., The Haworth Press, Inc. 12 West 32nd St. New York, N.Y. 10001.

National Prison Project Journal, American Civil Liberties Union Foundation, Inc., National Prison Project, 1616 P St. N.W. Ste. 340 Washington, D.C., 20036.

National Review of Criminal Sciences, Nat. Center for Social & Criminological Research, Zamebek, P.O. Cairo, Egypt.

New England Journal on Prison Law, 154 Stuart Street, Boston, MA 02116-5687.

Prison Action Group Newsletter, 121 N. Fitzhugh Street, Rochester, NY 14614.

The Prison Journal, 311 South Juniper Street, Philadelphia, PA 19107.

Probation Journal, Nat. Assoc. of Probation Officers, 3-4 Chivalry Rd., Battersea, London SW11 1HT England.

Probation and Parole, Box 114, Canal St. Sta., New York, NY 10013.

Probation & Parole in the U.S., U.S. Dept. of Justice, Bureau of Justice Statistics, 633 Indian Ave. N.W., Washington, D.C. 20531.

Question Mark, Norfolk Inmate Council Publishing, Box 43, Norfolk, MA 02056-0043.

Rocketeer Missouri Training Center For Men, Box 7, Moberly, MO 65270.

Southern Coalition Report on Jails and Prisons, Box 120044 Nashville, TN 37212.

COURTS AND THE LAW

American Criminal Law Review, Georgetown Univ. Law Center, 600 New Jersey Ave. NW Washington, D.C. 20001.

American Journal of Comparative Law, American Association for Comparative Study of Law Inc., University of California, Boalt Hall, Berkeley, CA 94720.

American Journal of Criminal Law, University of Texas, Austin School of Law Publ. 727 E. 26th St., Austin, TX 78705-3299.

California Youth Authority Status of Female Employees Report, 4241 Williamsburgh Drive, Sacramento, CA 95823.

Case Western Reserve Law Review, School of Law, 11075 East Blvd., Cleveland, OH 44106.

Chicago Kent Law Review, Chicago Kent College of Law, 77 S. Wacker Dr., Chicago, IL 60606.

Civil Disorder Digest, P.O. Box 185, Harvard Square Station, Cambridge, MA 02138.

Columbia Human Rights Law Review, Columbia University School of Law, 435 West 116th Street, New York, NY 10027.

Columbia Journal of Transnational Law. Columbia University School of Law, 435 West 116th Street, New York, NY 10027.

Cornell International Law Journal, Cornell Law School, Myron Taylor Hall. Ithaca, NY 14853.

Court Review, American Judges Assoc. 300 Newport Ave., Williamsburg, VA 23187-8798.

Criminal Defense, Newsletter State Hpellate Defender, Office Legal Resources Project, 3rd floor North Tower, 1500 6th Ave., Detroit MI 48226.

Criminal Justice, Howard League, 322 Kennington Park Rd., London SE11 4PP, England.

Criminal Law Bulletin, Warren, Gorham, & Lamon Inc. One Penn Plaza, New York, NY 10119.

Criminal Law Quarterly, Canada Law Book Co., Ltd., 240 Edward, Aurora, Ontario L4G 3S9 Canada.

Criminal Law Review, Clark Boardman Co., Ltd., 435 Hudson St., New York, NY 10014.

Denver Univ. Law Review, University of Denver, College of Law, Porter Adm. Bldg. 7039 E. 18th Ave., Denver Co. 80220-1826.

Duke Law Journal, Duke University, School of Law, Durham Room 006 NC 27706.

Emory Law Journal, Emory University, School of Law, Gambrell Hall, Atlanta GA 30322.

Federal Bar News-Journal, Federal Bar Association, 1815 H. St. Ste. 408 N.W. Washington, DC 20006.

Federal Probation, Adm. Office of the U.S. Courts, Probation Division, Washington, D.C. 20544.

Federal Trial News, American Bar Association, National Conference of Fed. Trial Judges, 750 N. Lake Shore Dr. Chicago, IL 60611.

Georgetown Law Journal, Georgetown University Law Center, 600 New Jersey Avenue, N.W., Washington, DC 20001.

Harvard Civil Rights Civil Liberties Law Review, Harvard Law School, Holmes Hall, Rm. 50, Cambridge, MA 02138.

Harvard Law Review, Gannett House, Cambridge, MA 02138.

Hastings Law Journal, Hasting College of the Law, 200 McAllister Street, San Francisco, CA 94102-4978.

Insurance Law Journal, Butterworth's Pty. Ltd. 271-273 Lane Cove Rd. North Ryde N.S.W. 2113, Australia.

International Journal of Offender Therapy and Comparative Criminology, 114 Gaines Hall, 840 S.W. Gaines Road, Portland, OR 97201.

International Review of Criminal Policy. United Nations, Department of Social Affairs, New York, NY 10017.

Journal of Crime and Justice, Anderson Publishing Co., 2035 Reading Rd., Cincinnati OH 45202.

Journal of Criminal Justice, Maxwell House, Fairview Park, Elmsford, NY 10523.

Journal of Criminal Law and Criminology, Northwestern Univ., School of Law, 357E. Chicago Ave., Chicago IL 60611.

Journal of Divorce, The Haworth Press Inc. 12 W. 32nd St., New York, NY 10001.

The Journal of Law & Economics, The Univ. of Chicago Press, Journals Division, P.O. Box 37005, Chicago, IL 60637.

Journal of Legal Education, Assn. of American Law Schools, Univ. of Iowa, College of Law Iowa City, IA 52242.

Journal of Legal Studies, University of Chicago Press, Journals Division. 5720 S. Woodlawn Ave. Chicago, IL 60637.

Journal of Psychiatry and Law, 157 Chambers Street, New York, NY 10007.

Journal of Quantitative Criminology, Plenun Press, 233 Spring Street, New York, NY 10013.

Journal of Research in Crime and Delinquency, Sage Publications, Inc. 2111 W. Hillcrest Dr., Newbury Park CA 91320.

Journal of Security Administration, London House Press, 1550 Northwest Highway, Suite 302, Park Ridge, IL 60068.

Judicature, 25 E. Washington, Suite 1600 Chicago, IL 60602-1805.

Jurimetrics Journal, Amer. Bar Assoc., 750 N. Lake Shore Dr. Chicago, IL 60611.

Law & Social Inquiry, The Univ. of Chicago Press, Journals Division, 750 N. Lake Shore Dr., Chicago, IL 60611.

Law Technology, 1000 Connecticut Ave. Suite 800, Washington, DC 20036.

Law and Contemporary Problems, Duke University School of Law, Room 006 Durham NC 27706.

Law and Human Behavior, Plenum Publishing Corp., 233 Spring St., New York NY 10013.

Law and Society Review, Law & Society Assoc. Hampshire House, Univ. of Massachusetts, Amherst, MA 01003.

Legal Reference Services Quarterly, Haworth Press, 12 W. 32nd St., New York, NY 10001.

The National Bar Bulletin, The National Bar Assoc. 1900 L. St. N.W. Ste. 203, Washington, DC 20036.

National Center for State Courts, Report 300 Newport Ave., Williamsburg, VA 23187.

The National Journal of Criminal Defense, National College of Criminal Defense, Bates College of Law, Houston, TX 77004.

New England Journal on Criminal & Civil Confinement, England School of Law, 154 Stuart St. Boston, MA 02116-5687.

New York University Law Review, 110 W. 3rd St. New York, NY 10012.

Notre Dame Law Review, Box 988 Notre Dame, IN 46556.

Pennsylvania Board of Probation and Parole, Box 1661, Harrisburg, PA 17110.

Probation and Parole, Box 114, Canal St. Sta., New York, NY 10013.

Probation and Parole Law Reports, Box 88, Warrensburg, MO 64093.

The Prosecutor, 1033 N. Fairfax St., Ste. 200, Alexandria, VA 22314.

Rutgers Computer and Technology Law Journal, Rutgers University, School of Law, 15 Washington St., Newark, NJ 07102.

Search and Seizure Law Report, 435 Hudson Street, New York, NY 10014.

Searchlight, Rt. 8 Cormel, NY 10512.

Soviet Law and Government, 80 Business Park Dr., Armonk, NY 10504.

Soviet Statutes and Decisions, 80 Business Park Armonk, NY 10504.

Stanford Law Review, School of Law, Crown Quadrangle, Stanford University, Stanford CA 94305-8610.

Temple Law Review, Temple Univ. School of Law, Philadelphia, PA 19122.

Trial, Association of Trial Lawyers, 1050 31st St., N.W. Washington, DC 20007.

Uniform Commercial Code Law Journal, One Penn Plaza, New York, NY 10119.

University of Illinois Law Review, College of Law, 504 E. Pennsylvania Ave., Champaign, IL 61820.

Wisconsin Law Review, Law School of the University of Wisconsin, Law Building 975 Bascom Hall, Madison WI 53706.

The Yale Law Journal, 401A Yale Station, New Haven, CT 06520.

CRIMINOLOGY AND CRIMINAL JUSTICE

ACJS Today Newsletter, Academy of Criminal Justice Sciences, Northern Kentucky Univ., 402 Nunn Hall, Highland Heights, KY 41076.

American Journal of Criminal Justice, The Southern Criminal Justice Assoc., School of Justice Administration, College of Urban & Public Affairs, Univ. of Louisville, Louisville, KY 40292.

Australian and New Zealand Journal of Criminology, 271 273 Lane Cove Rd. North Ryde, N.S.W. 2113, Australia.

British Journal of Criminology, Oxford Univ. Press Oxford Journals, Walton St., Oxford OX2 60P England.

Canadian Journal of Criminology, Canadian Association for the Prevention of Crime. 55 Parkdale Avenue, Ottawa, Ont. K1Y 1E5, Canada.

Cjain, Criminal Justice Archive & Information Network, The Univ. of Michigan, P.O. Box 1248, Ann Arbor, Michigan 48106.

CJ International & CJ The Americas, CJ International, 1333 S. Wabash Bar 53, Chicago IL 60605.

Contemporary Crises, Kluwer Academic Publ., P.O. Box 17, 3300 AA Dordrecht, Amsterdam Netherlands.

Crime and Delinquency, Sage Publications, Inc., 2455 Teller Rd., Newbury Park, CA.

Crime & Justice, The Univ. of Chicago Press, 5720 S. Woodlawn Ave., Chicago, IL 60637.

Crime, Law & Social Change, Kluiver Academic Publishers, Journal Dept., P.O. Box 358 Accord Station, Hingham MA 02018-0358.

Crime and Social Justice, P.O. Box 40601, San Francisco, CA 94140.

Criminal Justice and Behavior, Sage Publications Inc. 2111 W. Hillcrest Dr., Newbury Park, CA 91320.

Criminal Justice Ethics, Institute for Criminal Justice Ethics, John Jay College of Criminal Justice, 444 W. 56th St., New York, NY 10019.

Criminal Justice Newsletter, Pace Pub. Inc. 443 Park Ave. S. New York, NY 10016.

Criminal Justice Policy Review, Center for Criminal Justice, Univ. of Massachusetts Boston, Boston MA 02125-3393.

Criminal Justice Review, University Plaza, Atlanta, GA 30303-3091.

Criminologist, Countrywise Press Ltd. Little London, Chichester West Sussex, P.O. 19 IPG England.

The Criminologist, American Society of Criminology, 1314 Kinnear Rd. Ste. 212, Columbus, OH 43212.

Criminology, American Society of Criminology ASC 1314 Kinnear Rd., Columbus, OH 43212.

Criminology: An Interdisciplinary Journal, The American Society of Criminology, 1314 Kinnear Rd., Columbus OH 43212.

The International Criminal Justice Review, College of Public & Urban Affairs, Georgia State Univ. University Plaza, Atlanta, GA 30303-3091.

International Journal of the Sociology of Law, Academic Press Ltd., 2428 Oval Rd., London NW1-7DX England.

International Journal of Comparative and Applied Criminal Justice, Dept. of Adm. of Justice, Box 95, Wichita, KS 67208.

International Journal of Offender Therapy and Comparative Criminology, Oregon Health Sciences University, Dept. of Psychiatry 114 Gaines Hall, Portland, OR 97201.

International Review of Criminal Policy, United Nations, Department of Social Affairs, U.N. Publications Rm. DC 2853, New York, NY 10017.

Journal of Contemporary Criminal Justice, School of Applied Arts & Sciences, Dept. of Criminal Justice California State Univ. Long Beach. 1250 Bellflower Blvd. Long Beach, CA 90840.

Journal of Crime and Justice, Midwestern Criminal Justice Assoc. Anderson Pub. Co. 2035 Reading Rd., Cincinnati, OH 45202.

Journal of Criminal Justice, Pergarmon & Maxwell House, Fairview Park, Elmsford, NY 10523.

Journal of Criminal Justice Education, Academy of Criminal Justice Sciences School of Criminal Justice, State Univ. of New York at Albany, Albany, NY 12222.

Journal of Criminal Law and Criminology, North Western Univ., School of Law. 357 E. Chicago Ave. Chicago IL 60611.

Journal of Interpersonal Violence, Sage Publications, Inc. 2111 Hillcrest Dr., Newbury Park, CA 91320.

Journal of Research in Crime and Delinquency, Sage Publications, Inc. 2111 Hillcrest Dr., Newbury Park, CA 91320.

Judicature: The Journal of the American Judicature Society, AJS, 25 East, Washington St., Chicago IL 60602.

The Justice Professional, Criminal Justice Institute, Long Island Univ. C.W. Post Campus, Roth Hall, Brookville NY 11548.

The Justice Professional Dept. of Sociology & Social Work, Pembroke State Univ., Pembroke, NE 28372.

Justice Quarterly, Academy of Criminal Justice Sciences, 402 Nunn Hall, Northern Kentucky Univ., Highland Heights KY 41076-1448.

Sociology & Social Research Journal, Dept. of Sociology Univ. of Southern California, Univ. Park, Los Angeles, CA 90089-0032.

Victimology: An International Journal, Victimology Inc. 2333 N. Vernon St. Arlington VA 22207.

Women in Criminal Justice, 10 Alice St. Binghamton, NY 13904-1580.

FORENSICS

American Journal of Forensic Medicine and Pathology, Raven Press 1185 Ave. of the Americas, New York, NY 10036.

American Journal of Law and Medicine, American Society of Law & Medicine, 765 Common Wealth Ave. Ste. 1634 Boston MA 02215.

The Expert and the Law, National Forensic Center. P.O. Box 3161, Princeton, NJ 08543.

Forensic Accounting Review, Computer Protection Systems, Inc. 150 N. Main St., Plymouth, MI 48170.

Forensic Science Gazette, Box 35728, Dallas TX 75235.

Identification News, International Assoc. for Identification Box 3054 Kinston, NC 28501.

Inform Quarterly Newsletter, Int. Reference Org. in Forensic Medicine & Sciences, Clo Dr. William G. Eckert Ed. Box 8282, Wichita KS 67208.

Journal of Forensic Sciences, 1916 Race Street, Philadelphia, PA 19103.

Medico Legal Bulletin, Department of Health, Medical Examiner Division, 9 North 14th Street, Richmond, VA 23219.

News & Views in Forensic Pathology, Amer. Academy of Forensic Sciences & The Forensic Sciences Foundation Inc. 11400 Rockville Pike, Ste. 515, Rockville MD 20852.

News & Views in Forensic Toxicology, Amer. Academy of Forensic Sciences. The Forensic Sciences Foundation, Inc. 11400 Rockville Pike Ste. 515, Rockville MD 20852.

JUVENILE DELINQUENCY

Juvenile and Family Court Journal, Natl. Council of Juvenile and Family Court Judges, University of Nevada/Reno P.O. Box 8970, Reno NV 89507.

Juvenile Justice, National Council of Juvenile Court Judges. Judicial College Bld. Univ. of Nevada, Reno, NV 89507.

Juvenile Justice Digest, Washington Crime News Services, 3918 Prosperity Ave. Ste. 318, Fairfax, VA 22031-3334.

Juvenile Law Digest, National Council of Juvenile & Family Court Judges, University of Nevada, P.O. Box 8978, Reno NV 89507.

NARCOTICS AND DRUG ABUSE

Advance in Alcohol and Substance Abuse, The Haworth Press, Inc. 12 W. 32nd St., New York, NY 10001.

Alcoholism Treatment Quarterly, The Haworth Press, Inc. 12 W. 32nd St., New York, NY 10001.

Bulletin on Narcotics, United Nations Publications, Room DC 2-853 New York, NY 10017.

Contemporary Drug Problems, Federal Legal Publications, Inc., 157 Chambers St., New York, NY 10002.

Drug Abuse & Alcoholism Newsletter, Vista Hill Foundation 3420 Camino del Rio North Ste. 100, San Diego, CA 92108.

Drug Enforcement, (BNDD Bulletin) Drug Enforcement Administration/U.S. Dept. Justice, 1405 I St., N.W., Washington, DC 20537.

Drugs and Society, The Haworth Press, Inc. 12 W. 32nd St., New York, NY 10001.

Drugs in the Work Place, Business Research Publications, Inc. 817 Broadway, New York NY 10003.

International Drug Report, International Narcotic Enforcement Officers Association, 112 State St., Ste. 1200, Albany, NY 12207.

Journal of Adolescent Chemical Dependency, The Haworth Press, Inc. 12 W. 32nd St., New York, NY 10001.

Journal of Chemical Dependency Treatment, The Haworth Press, Inc. 12 W. 32nd St., New York, NY 10001.

Journal of Drug Issues, Box 4201, Tallahassee, FL 32303.

Narcotics Control Digest, Washington Crime News Services, 3918 Prosperity Ave. Ste. 318, Fairfax, VA 22031.

Substance Abuse Issues, Movish & McLennan Comp., 1166 Avenue of the Americas, New York, NY 10036.

Washington Drug Letter, Washington Bus. Information Inc. c/o Karen Harrington 1117 N. 19th St., Arlington, VA 22209.

POLICE

Accident Analysis and Prevention, Maxwell House, Fairview Park, Elmsford, NY 10523.

American Journal of Police, Anderson Publishing Co., 2035 Reading Rd., Cincinnati, OH 45202.

Australian Police Journal, New S. Wales Police Dept., Co. G.P.O. Box 45 Sydney N.S.W. 2001, Australia.

California Highway Patrolman, Box 161209, Sacramento, CA 95816.

Campus Law Enforcement Journal, Int. Assoc. of Campus Law Enforcement Administration. 638 Prospect Ave., Hartford, CT 06105.

Canadian Police Chief, 112 Kent St. Ste. 1908 Place de Ville Tower ''B,'' Ottawa, Ontario, K1P 5P2 Canada.

Canadian Police College Journal, P.O. Box 8900 Ottawa, Ontario K1G 3J2, Canada.

Enforcement Journal, National Police Assoc., 1316 Gardner Ln., Louisville, KY 40213.

FBI Law Enforcement Bulletin, U.S. Federal Bureau of Investigation 9th St. & Pennsylvania Ave. N.W., Washington DC 20535.

From the State Capitals, Public Safety, 300 N. Washington St., Alexandria VA 22314.

Georgia FOP News, 2684 Industrial Row Troy, MI 40804.

Illinois Police Association Official Journal, Illinois Police Assoc. 6857 Oxford St., Minneapolis, MN 55426.

Illinois Sheriff's News, 413 West Monroe, Springfield, IL 62705.

International Criminal Police Review, Senor Director General de Seguridad, Oficillia Mayor Puerta de Sol, Madrid, Spain.

International Drug Report, Suite 1200, 112 State Street, Albany, NY 12207.

Iowa Police Journal, Iowa State Policeman's Assoc., Box 1768 Fort Dodge, IA 50501.

Journal of Drug Education, Baywood Publ. Co. 26 Austin Ave. Box 337, Amityville, NY 11701.

Journal of Police Science and Administration, International Assoc. of Chiefs of Police, Inc. Ste. 200 1110 N. Glebe Rd., Arlington, VA 22201.

The Justice System Journal, Institute for Court Management, Denver, CO 80202.

Kansas Peace Officer, Box 2592, Wichita, Kansas 67201.

Law Enforcement Journal, Box 21, Bethel Island, CA 94511.

Law Enforcement News, John Jay College of Criminal Justice Criminal Justice Center 444 W. 56th St., New York, NY 10019.

Law Enforcement Technology, 210 Crossways Park Dr., Woodbury, NY 11797.

The Law Officer's Bulletin, The Bureau of Nat. Affairs, Inc. 1231 25th St. N.W., Washington, DC 20037.

Law and Order, Hendon Inc., 1000 Skokie Blvd., Wilmette, IL 60091.

Long Island Police News, Box 36, Copiague, NY 11726.

Maryland Crime Control Directory, Box 3208, Baltimore, Maryland 21228.

Michigan Peace Officer, State Lodge of Michigan, G 3094 Bertha, Flint, Michigan 48504.

Michigan Police Chief's Newsletter, 2248 E. Mt. Hope Ste. H., Okemos, MI 48864.

Military Police, U.S. Army M.P. School, Ft. McClellan, Alabama 36205.

Minnesota Police Journal, Minnesota Police and Peace Officers Assoc. 525 Park St., St. Paul, MN 55103.

Minnesota Sheriff, 287 E. Sixth Street, St. Paul, MN 55101.

Missouri Police Chiefs Journal, Central Missouri State University, Suite 400 A. Hunphrey's Blds, Warrensburg, MO 64093.

Narcotics Control Digest, Washington Crime News Services, 3918 Prosperity Ave. Ste. 318, Fairfax, VA 22031-3334.

National Sheriff, Nat. Sheriff's Assoc. 1450 Duke St., Alexandria, VA 22314— 3403.

Newsletter for Dispatchers, PSCS Ltd., 1807 co. 24th Ave. Longmont, CO 80501.

Oklahoma Law Enforcement Bulletin, State Bureau of Investigation, 2132 N.E. 36th Oklahoma City, OK 73107.

On The Beat, 299 Broadway, New York, NY 10007.

Kansas Peace Officer, Box 2592, Wichita, KS 67201.

Pennsylvania Chiefs of Police Association Bulletin, 2941 N. Front St., Harrisburg, PA 17110.

Pennsylvania Police Criminal Law Bulletin, 2579 Warren Rd., Indiana, PA 15701.

Police, Police Federation, 15 17 Langley Rd., Surbiton, Surrey, KT6 6LP England.

Police and Law Enforcement, 56 E. 13th Street, New York, NY 10003.

Police Chief, International Assoc. of Chiefs of Police Inc. Ste. 200 1110 N. Glebe Rd. Arlington, VA 22201.

Police Journal, E. Row Little London, Chichester, Sussex P019 IPG England.

Police Law Journal, Appalachian State University, Boone, NC 28608.

Police: The Law Officer Magazine, Hare Publications 6200 Yarrow Dr., Carlsbad, CA 92008.

Police Management Review, Planning Bureau, Police Dept. City of New York, NY 10038.

The Police Plaintiff, North Publishing Box 3132 Glen Ellyn, IL 60138-3132.

Police Product News, 6200 Yarrow Dr., Carlsbad, CA 92008.

Police Review, 14th Street Cross Street London, EC1N 8FE England.

Police Studies, Anderson Pub. Company, 2035 Reading Rd., Cincinnati, OH 45202.

Police Times, American Federation of Police 1000 Connecticut Ave. N.W. Ste. 9, Washington, Dr. 20036.

Policing & Society: An International Journal of Research & Policy, STBS Marketing Department P.O. Box 786, Cooper Station, New York, NY 10276.

Royal Canadian Mounted Police Quarterly, Royal Canadian Mounted Police, Ottawa, Ont. K1A OR2 Canada.

Sheriff and Police Reporter, 848 N.W. 97th St. Seattle, WA 98117-2211.

SECURITY AND CRIME PREVENTION

Access Control, Communications Channels, Inc. 6255 Barfield Rd., Atlanta, GA 30328.

Alert Bulletin, Aviation Crime Prevention Instit. P.O. Box 3443, Fredrick, MD 21701.

Assets Protection, Assets Protections Pub. P.O. Box 5323, Madison, WI 53705.

Bank Fraud, Bank Administration Inst. 60 Gould Center, Rolling Meadows, IL 60008.

Burning Issues, ANSUL Fire Protection 1 Stanton St. Marinette, WI 54143-2542.

Canadian Security, Security Publishing Ltd., Box 854, McLean, VA 22101.

Cerebus Security, Cerberus Ltd. Maennedorf, Switzerland, C 4 8798.

College Security Report, Rusting Pub. 403 Main St., P.O. Box 190 Fort Washington, NY 11050.

Computer Security, Computer Security Institute, 360 Church St., Northborough, MA 01532.

Computer Security Digest, Computer Protection Systems, Inc. 150 N. Main St., Plymouth, MI 48170, 313-459-8787.

Corporate Security Digest, Washington Crime News Services 3918 Prosperity Ave., Ste. 318, Fairfax, VA 22031-3334.

Corporate Security International, Lloyd's of London Press 611 Broadway, New York, NY 10003.

Counter-Terrorism & Security Intelligence, Interests, Ltd. 8512 Cedar St. Silver Spring, MD 20910-4322.

Crime Control Digest, Washington Crime News Services, 3918 Prosperity Ave. Ste. 318, Fairfax, VA 22031-3334.

Crime Prevention Review, Attorney General's Office Crime Prevention Unit. 3580 Wilshire Blvd. Suite 938, Los Angeles, CA 90010.

Cryptologia, Rose-Hulman Institute of Technology, Terre Haute IN 47803.

Data Processing & Communications Security, Assets Protection Pub. P.O. Box 5323, Madison, WI 53705.

EDPACS, The EDP Audit Control and Security Newsletter, P.O. Box 129, Hillsboro, TN 37342.

Employment Screening & Testing Report, Strafford Pub., Inc. 1375 Peachtree St. NE, Ste. 235, Atlanta, GA 30367.

The Expert Witness Journal, Expertise Institute, Inc., Box 38-1494, Miami, FL 33138.

Fraud & Theft Newsletter, Fraud & Theft Information Bureau 217 N. Seacrest Blvd., P.O. Box 400, Boynton Beach, FL 33425.

Hospital Security & Safety Management, Rusting Publications P.O. Box 1032, Port Washington, NY 11050.

The Investigative Journal, PI Pub. Inc., P.O. Box 11628, Jacksonville, FL 32239-1628.

Investigative News, Marathon Press 13575 Martinique Dr., Chino Hills, CA 91709.

The Investigator, John E. Reid & Associates, Inc. 250 S. Wacker Dr. Ste. 1100, Chicago, IL 60606.

The Journal of Polygraph Science, National Training Center of Lie Detection, Inc. 200 W. 57th St. Ste., 1400, New York, NY 10019.

Library Security Newsletter, Haworth Press, Libr. and Archival Security, 149 5th Ave., New York, NY 10010.

The Lipman Report, Gaurusmark, Inc. P.O. Box 444, Memphis, TN 38101.

Military Police Journal, U.S. Army MP School Ft. McClellan, AL 36205-5030.

On The Line Newsletter, American Correctional Assn. 4321 Hartwick Rd. Ste. L-208, College Park, MD 20740.

Parking Security Report, Rusting Pub. P.O. Box 190, Port Washington, NY 11050.

Police & Security Bulletin, Lomond Pub. P.O. Box 88, Mt. Airy, MD 21771.

Police & Security News, Days Communications, Inc. 1690 Quarry Rd. Kulpsville, PA 19443.

Privacy Journal, P.O. Box 15300 Washington, DC 20003.

Private Security Case Law Reporter, Strafford Pub. Inc. 1375 Peachtree St. NE Ste. 235, Atlanta, GA 30367.

Protection of Assets Bulletin, The Merritt Company 1661 9th St., Santa Monica, CA 90404.

Protection Officer, P.O. Box 428, Cochrane, Alta. T0L 0W0 Canada.

Risk Assessment, Business Risks Int. 3100 West End Ave. Ste. 550, Nashville, TN 37203.

The Risk Report, Int. Risk Management Inst., Inc. 12222 Merit Dr. Ste. 1660, Dallas, TX 37203.

The Risk Retention Reporter, P.O. Box 50147, Pasadena, CA 91115-0147.

Security, Cahners Plz., 1350 E. Touhy Ave. Box 5080, Des Plaines, IL 60018.

Security Distribution and Marketing, 1350 E. Touhy Ave. Box 5080 Des Plaines IL 60018.

Security Gazette, AGB Business Publications, Ltd. Audit House Field End Rd. Rouslip Middx HA4 9LT, England.

Security Journal, Sponsored by the ASIS Foundation Published by Butterworths 80 Montvale Ave., Stoneham, MA 02180.

Security Law Newsletter, 1330 New Hampshire Ave. N.W., Ste. 1014, Washington, DC 20036.

Security Letter, 166 E. 96th St., New York, NY 10128.

Security Management, ASIS, 1655 North Fort Myer Dr. Ste. 1200, Arlington, VA 22209.

Security Management, Bureau of Business, Practice, 24 Rope Ferry Rd., Waterford, CT 06386.

Security Personnel Newsletter, Security Seminars Press, P.O. Box 70162, Ocala, FL 32670.

Security Police Digest, U.S. Air Force Chief of Security Police, Washington, DC 20314.

Signal, Suite 1150 170, Pennsylvania Blvd., N.W., Washington, DC 20004.

Social Defense, Department of Social Welfare, Block 1 Wing 7, Ramakrishna-puram, New Delhi 22, India.

The Stolen Art Alert, Intl. Foundation for Art Research Inc. 46 E. 70th St., New York, NY 10021.

Terrorism, J.L. Scherer, 4900 18th Ave., South Minneapolis, MN 55417.

TVI Report (Terrorism, Violence, Insurgency Journal), TVI Inc. Box 1055, Beverly Hills, CA 90210.

Wrongful Termination Litigation Reporter, Andrews Publication, Inc., P.O. Box 200, Edgemont, PA 19028.

SELECTED POLITICAL SCIENCE JOURNALS

American Journal of Political Science, University of Texas Press, Journals Dept., AJPS, Box 7819, Austin, TX 78713.

American Political Science Review, 1527 New Hampshire Ave., N.W. Washington, DC 20036.

American Politics Quarterly, Sage Publications, 2111 W. Hillcrest Dr., Newbury Park, CA 91320.

Journal of Politics, Southern Political Sciences Association, Univ. of Texas Press, Box 7819, Austin, TX 78713.

New American, 395 Concord Ave., Belmont, MA 02178.

Policy Review, The Heritage Foundation, 214 Massachussetts Ave. N.E., Washington, DC 20002.

Political Science Quarterly, The Academy of Political Science, 2852 Broadway, New York, NY 10025-7885.

Western Political Quarterly, University of Utah, Salt Lake City, UT 84112.

SELECTED PSYCHOLOGY JOURNALS

American Academy of Psychiatry and the Law Bulletin, 1211 Cathedral St., Baltimore, MD 21201.

Archives of General Psychiatry, Amer. Medical Assn., 525 N. Dearborn St., Chicago, IL 60610.

Criminal Justice and Behavior, Sage Publications, Inc. 2455 Teller Rd., Newbury Park, CA 91320.

Journal of the American Psychoanalytic Association, International Univ. Press 59 Boston Post Rd., Madison, CT 06443.

Journal of Applied Behavior Analysis, c/o University of Kansas, Human Development Lawrence, KS 66045.

Journal of Applied Social Psychology, 7961 Eastern Ave., Silver Springs, MD 20910.

Journal of Personality, Box 6697, College Station, Durham, NC 27708.

Journal of Psychiatry & Law, Federal Legal Publications, Inc. 157 Chambers St., New York, NY 10007.

Journal of Research in Personality, Academic Press Inc. 1250 6th Ave., San Diego, CA 92101.

Journal of Social Psychology, Heldref Pub. 4000 Albermarle St., N.W., Washington DC 20016.

Law and Human Behavior, Plenum Publishing Corp. 233 Spring St., New York, NY 10013.

The following journals are published by the American Psychological Association, 1200 17th St. N.W., Washington, DC 20036.

Contemporary Psychology; Journal of Abnormal Psychology; Journal of Applied Psychology; Behavioral Neuroscience; Clinician's Research Digest; Journal of Comparative Psychology; Journal of Consulting and Clinical Psychologist; Psychological Assessment: A Journal of Cons and Clinical Psychology; Journal of Education Psychology: Psychological Bulletin; Journal of Counseling Research and Practice; Journal of Experimental Psychology: General; Journal of Experimental Psychology: Learning; Memory and Cognition; Journal of Experimental Psychology: Human Perception and Performance Psychological Review; Journal of Personalities and Social Psychology; Development Psychology; Journal of Experimental Psychology Animal Behavior Processes; Psychology and Psychological Abstracts.

Also Consult the Following:

Journals in Psychology: A Resource Listing Authors, 1990 Edition.

Journals in Psychology is a reference source and can answer many of your questions about where to submit your papers for publication. *Journals in Psychology*, APA's directory written exclusively for Psychology authors, gives you complete information on over 280 U.S. periodicals in the behavioral and social sciences. All this information in one handy guidebook helps save time, money, and effort. It contains editor's name/address, editorial policy, circulation, index terms, publisher, select notes on submissions, and more.

SELECTED SOCIOLOGY JOURNALS

Adolescence, Libra Pub. 3089 C Clairmont Dr. Ste. 383, San Diego, CA 92117.

American Behavioral Scientist, Sage Pub. 2455 Teller Rd., Newbury Park, CA 91320.

American Journal of Sociology, Univ. of Chicago Press, 5801 Ellis Ave., 4th Flr., Chicago, IL 60637.

American Sociological Review, 1722 N. Street, N.W. Washington, DC 20036.

Child Welfare, 440 First St., N.W., Ste. 310, Washington, DC 20001.

Environment and Behavior, Sage Pub. 2455 Teller Rd., Newbury Park, CA 91320.

Family Process, 149 E. 78th St. New York, NY 10021.

Journal of Applied Behavorial Science, 55 Old Post Rd. No. 2 Box 1678, Greenwich, CT 06836-1678.

Social Justice Review, 3835 Westminster Place, St. Louis, MO 63108.

MISCELLANEOUS

American Journal of Orthopsychiatry, 19 W. 44th St., New York, NY 40036.

American Polygraph Association Newsletter, Box 1061, Severna Park, MD 21146.

California Office of Criminal Justice Planning Bulletin, 3149 Clairidge Way, Sacramento, CA 95823.

Community Home Schools Gazette, 85 Exeter Road Dawlish EX7 OA6 England.

Economic Crime Digest, National District Attorneys Association, 1033 N. Fairfax St. Ste. 200, Alexandria, VA 22314-1503.

Family and Conciliation Courts Review, Sage Publications, Inc., 2455 Teller Rd., Newbury Park, CA.

Fire and Arson Investigator, Int. Assn. of Arson Investigators, Box 91119, Louisville, KY 40211.

Full Disclosure, Box 903 Libertyville, Illinois, 60048.

IACP News, IACP Publications Dept. 1110 N. Glebe Rd. Ste. 200, Arlington, VA 22201.

Insurance Industry Newsletter, Box 18630, 4325 Old Shepherdsville Rd., Louisville, KY 40218.

Interface, Search Group. Inc. 7311 Green haven Dr. Ste. 145, Sacramento, CA 31036.

International Journal of Comparative and Applied Criminal Justice, Department of Administration of Justice Box 95 Wichita State University, Wichita, KA 67208.

International Risk Management, Inst. Inc. 12222 Ment Dr. Ste. 1660 Dallas, TX 75251-2217.

Journal of Family Violence, Sage Publications, Inc., 2455 Teller Rd., Newbury Park, CA.

The Journal of Polygraph Science, The Nat. Training Center of Lie Detection, Inc. 200 W. 57th St. Ste. 1400, New York, NY 10019.

Organized Crime Digest, Washington Crime News Services, 3918 Prosperity Ave. Ste. 318, Fairfax, VA 22031-3334.

Polygraph, APA, P.O. Box 1060, Severna Park, MD 21146.

RAND Checklist, Published Monthly, The RAND Corporation, 1700 Main St. P.O. Box 2138, Santa Monica, CA 90406-2138.

The Sentinel Industrial Risk Insurers, 85 Woodlands St., Hartford, CT 06120.

Victimology, An International Journal Victimology, Inc. 2333 N. Vernon St., Arlington, VA 22207.

Violence & Victims, Springer Publ. Company, 536 Broadway, New York, NY 10012.

Violence Update, Sage Publications, Inc., 2455 Teller Rd., Newbury Park, CA.

Works Consulted

The Serials Directory, An Inter. Reference Book EBSCO Publishing Division of EBSCO Industries, Inc. P.O. Box 1943 Birmingham, AL 35201-1943.

The Standard Periodical Directory, 14th ed. Oxbridge Community, Inc. 1991.

Ulrich's International Periodicals Directory, 1990-91 Including Irregular Serials & Annuals 29th ed. R.R. Bowker, Division of Reed Pub. (USA) Inc. New York.

6

General Reference Sources

This chapter will introduce the student to many of the reference sources that are published. Your reference librarian will be familiar with most of these sources and will be able to help you locate the specific information you are looking for. Of course, the larger the holdings of a particular library, the more of these reference sources you will be able to locate.

Among the major reference sources listed in this section are:

Biographies: Written histories of an individual's life which gives an account of their achievements.

Dictionaries: Reference books that list alphabetically names or terms that are of importance to the discipline.

Encyclopedias: Collections of general information and knowledge that give a comprehensive treatment to the particular subject arranged in alphabetical order.

Almanacs: Publications usually published annually that contain information in statistical or tabular form.

Newspapers: One of the fastest sources of information available to the general public. Although they may not be the most accurate, most major newspapers are archived on microfilm and provide a source for the retrieval of contemporary journalism.

Annuals and Yearbooks: Annuals are publications most often on subjects that are published each year. Yearbooks are compilations of statistics or facts.

Information Guides: Collections and classifications concerning the storage and retrieval of recorded knowledge.

Reference materials are guides to information about particular subjects. They may be general, such as a general encyclopedia, which encompasses a wide variety of subjects, or they may be more specific, such as a dictionary of legal terms. Students new to the research process may be overwhelmed by the number of reference sources to be found in most libraries, and generally there is some overlapping and repetition among them, so specific information can sometimes be found in several sources. Generally, however, reference materials are designed to fill a specific need, and each will have some new information to contribute to the field.

Reference tools vary with regard to the information they contain. Some provide very detailed information while others may offer only brief coverage, and still others will contain very diverse collections of facts. Dictionaries, encyclopedias, bibliographies, biographical indexes, directories, almanacs, and atlases are all examples of reference materials. As a rule, they are not designed to be read cover to cover, but to be consulted for specific information. Therefore, these references are generally not circulated outside the library but can be checked out for use within the library, usually for a set period of time.

THE FLOOD OF INFORMATION

As can be seen by the vast number of listings in this book, the student/scholar is faced with a tremendous amount of information. There are several types of information sources. You should be aware of the distinctions between them.

Primary Source: The the original data or information.

Secondary Source: Information of data that has been edited, analyzed, evaluated, or manipulated. Secondary sources are usually books or articles.

Scholarly Literature: Journals such as *Criminology* or *Justice Quarterly* are written by scholars for other scholars.

Professional Literature: Magazines such as *Police Chief* that are written for the practitioner in the field.

Popular Literature: Magazines that are indexed in the *Reader's Guide to Periodical Literature*. This would include magazines such as *Time, Newsweek,* and *U.S. News and World Report.*

The "Granddaddy" of all guides to reference books is published by the American Library Association and titled *Guide to Reference Books,* Tenth edition. This is the most massive work available on reference sources. Unfortunately, at the time of this writing the most recent edition was the tenth edition in 1986. The next edition is scheduled for 1992. Of special interest to the Criminal Justice researcher is the section on Social and Behavioral Sciences which is over 300 pages long. Eugene P. Sheelty (ed.) (Chicago, IL: American Library Association, Chicago, 1986).

American Reference Books Annual. Wynar, Bohdan S. (ed.) Annual. Comprehensive listing of reference books published in United States during preceding year with brief descriptive reviews. Arranged by subject, then by type of reference work. Index. (Littleton, CO: Libraries Unlimited, 1970 to date).

Editorial Research Reports. An excellent source for an overview of your topic. Long articles are presented on newsworthy topics, such as "Capital Punishment" (Jan. 18, 1985), "Teenage Drinking" (May 15, 1981), "Violent Crime" (March 13, 1981), "Drug Smuggling" (Feb. 8, 1985), "Prison Overcrowding" (August 1987), and "Gun Control" (Nov. 1987). Bibliographies at the end of each chapter lead to further materials. Weekly updates. (Washington, DC: Congressional Quarterly Inc., 1962-87).

How and Where to Find the Facts: Researching Criminology. Jack E. Whitehorse. (Saratoga, CA: R & E Publishers, 1983).

How and Where to Find the Facts: Researching Corrections Including Probation and Pardon. (Saratoga, CA: R & E Publishers, 1983).

Biography

Webster's Biographical Dictionary. The purpose of this Merriam-Webster Dictionary is to provide in a single volume a work of biographical reference not restricted in its selection of names by considerations of historical period, nationality, race, religion, or occupation, and to supply the reader with full information on the syllabic division and the pronunciation of the names included. Since the Dictionary is intended primarily for English-speaking users, American and British names have been included on a generous scale and often accorded fuller treatment.

The number of names included (upwards of 40,000) will be found adequate for the usual purposes of most consultants. Only in certain classes of contemporaries may some consultants feel an inadequacy. The names of persons prominent (sometimes only briefly) in sports, in motion pictures, in the contemporary theater, and in radio are so numerous that the editors were compelled, however reluctantly, to curtail their representation to the minimum, relying on the many specialized works of reference and the great volume of current periodical literature in these fields to supply the wants of consultants particularly interested in such names. As for the treatment given each entry, every effort has been made to provide information most likely to be sought by the consultants of this Dictionary. Names of persons included because of a single incident, a single writing, a single discovery, are accorded the briefest treatment, with emphasis duly laid on this single item. In this way, additional space has been obtained to provide longer entries for persons whose lives or works contain many details likely to be sought by the consultant.

Reference Books

Guide to Microforms in Print. James A. Dias (ed.) An annual, cumulative, alphabetized guide to books, journals, and other materials with the exception of theses and dissertations that are available in microform from United States publishers. (Washington, DC: Microcard Editions, 1990).

Introduction to Reference Work, Volume I: Basic Information Sources. Volume II: Reference Services and Reference Processes. The first volume concerns basic reference sources: bibliographies, abstracts, indexes, etc. The second volume explores channels of communication, reference searches, automation, and other reference services and processes. (New York: McGraw-Hill, 1987).

National Directory of Addresses and Telephone Numbers. This directory has information for over 75,000 corporations, all SEC registered companies, major law and accounting firms, banks and financial institutions, Zip and Area Code Guide, Toll Free Numbers, hotels and vacation resorts, consumer/government information, airlines and car rental agencies. Federal government, executive, legislative and judicial branches, independent agencies, federal information centers, embassies, county and state government offices, colleges and universities, 2- and 4-year colleges, graduate schools and programs. Associations and organizations, national associations, foundations, political parties, unions, UN agencies and missions, computer hardware/software services, hospitals, media and information sources, newspapers, magazines, radio, TV stations and cable, business newsletters, research services, business service firms, advertising agencies, brokerage firms, messengers and couriers, business finance sources, venture capital firms, SBA offices, state and local lending institutions. (Hillside, IL: Concord Reference Books).

The Reference Shelf. For sixty years The Reference Shelf has been a dependable source of objective and thorough coverage of vital and often controversial social issues and trends, providing timely information for research papers and oral reports, classroom discussion and debate, and independent study. Consisting of excerpts from a wide range of influential publications, each of the six Reference Shelf compilations published each year is devoted to a single issue of contemporary concern, and covers historical background, current concerns, and future implications. The 1985 volume of The Reference Shelf will give the same balanced coverage to these important topics: immigration, the federal deficit, sports in America, drugs and alcohol, capital punishment, representative American speeches, 1984-1985. (Bronx, NY: H.W. Wilson Co., 1990).

A Research Guide for Law Enforcement and the Criminal Justice System. Jack E. Whitehouse. This publication is a comprehensive bibliography of bibliographies, journals, research and reference materials published prior to 1983. This 162 page (in very small print) source book lists references for a full range of criminal justice topics including research methodology, general reference, demography and social indicators, field operations, investigations, police methods and tactics, auxiliary and staff functions, police community relations, comparative police administration, forensic sciences, industrial security, police management, police personnel administration, courts, corrections, probation and parole, crime and criminology, specific crimes (i.e., arson, burglary, kidnapping, etc.), juvenile delinquency, crime prevention, terrorism, extremist groups, violence, civil disorder, criminal law, social problems and criminal justice related journals. This is an excellent bibliography although some of the material is somewhat dated. (Saratoga, CA: R & E Publishers, 1983).

State Court Organization, 1987. Presents an overview of the structure, administration, and jurisdiction of court systems in all 50 states and United States territories. Information regarding aspects of the states' judicial systems, and comparisons of the existing court system and the American Bar Association Standards relating to court organization is included. (Williamsburg, VA: American Bar Association Committee on Implementation of Judicial Administration, National Center for State Courts Publications Department, 1987).

Use of Criminology Literature. Martin Wright (ed.) Provides a guide to major literature sources and reference tools through the collection of short chapters on specific topics relating to criminology. A variety of topics is included. (Hamden, CT: Archon Books, 1974).

Reference materials that may also provide assistance to the criminal justice student include those concerned with political and social science, as well as psychology. Selected references in these areas are described below.

Political Science

The Book of States. A biennial publication which presents information on the structure, operations, financial and functional activities of state governments, and provides a complete listing of elected state officials and members of the legislature. Up-to-date supplements are provided. (Lexington, KY: Council of State Governments).

General References

American Reformers. Alden Whitman (ed.) Offering concise biographies of 508 men and women who were the principal architects of reform in America from the seventeenth century to modern times, this authoritative reference work is designed for students and the general reader. The book considers a broad range of reformers from all political and ideological persuasions, including the movements for religious tolerance, abolition, freedom of speech, Native American rights, racial and sexual equality, universal suffrage, labor rights, prison reform, and temperance. The list of subjects includes such well known reformers as Anne Hutchinson, Thomas Paine, Henry David Thoreau, Harriet Tubman, Harriet Beecher Stowe, "Mother" Bloor, Eugene V. Debs, Herbert Croly, Margaret Sanger, Clarence Darrow, Louis Brandois, and Malcolm X. However, *American Reformers* is especially notable for its coverage of those men and women active in numerous causes who are not so widely known or written about. (Bronx, NY: H.W. Wilson Co., 1985).

The Standard Periodical Directory. Includes information on approximately 20,000 periodicals published in the United States and Canada. (New York: Oxbridge Communications, 1992).

Subject Directory of Special Libraries and Information Centers. Margaret Young, et al. (eds.) An excellent source containing names and addresses of law and other special libraries. (Detroit, MI: Gale Research Company, 1990).

Ulrich's International Periodicals Directory. Lists by subject approximately 28,000 periodicals published in over 100 countries, and provides information on frequency of publication, subscription price, address of publisher, and which, if any, periodical indexes cover the journal. (New York: R.R. Bowker, 1990-1991).

Dictionaries

As with encyclopedias, there are many specialized dictionaries and those pertaining to criminal justice may prove to be a valuable source for bits and pieces of information. Several pertinent dictionaries are listed below.

The Alcohol/Drug Abuse Dictionary and Encyclopedia. John J. Fay. Professionals and lay persons alike will find this extensive dictionary and encyclopedia essential to the understanding of the basic terms and concepts of alcohol and drug abuse. More than 1400 entries are defined and cross-referenced, from the street jargon of the illicit drug subculture to the complex dialect of pharmacology.

Insights into the special worlds of addicts, traffickers, police officers, jurists, and others are also examined. (1988).

The American Political Dictionary, Eighth edition. Jack C. Plano. (New York: Holt, Rinehart & Winston, 1989).

Ballentine's Law Dictionary. James A. Ballentine. Defines English and Latin legal terms and phrases and lists abbreviations of legal literature. (Rochester, NY: Lawyers Co-operative Publishing Company, 1969).

Black's Law Dictionary, Sixth edition. Henry C. Black. No doubt the best known and widely used legal dictionary. Defines words, terms, phrases, ranging from early to modern usage and covers all forms of law. A table of abbreviations is included.(St. Paul, MN: West Publishing, 1990).

Butterworth's Security Dictionary: Terms and Concepts. John Fay. More than a listing of definitions, *Butterworth's Security Dictionary* explains and describes the context for terms and concepts that have become a part of the multidisciplinary world of today's security profession. Containing over 5,000 definitions and abbreviations, it also gives ready access to the basic principles behind procedures in security as well as legal and organizational concepts. (Stoneham, MA: Butterworth, 1987).

Crime Dictionary. Ralph De Sola. This dictionary combines the terms used by both criminals and law enforcement professionals. In preparation for 12 years, it is an exhaustive compilation containing definitions of over 10,000 terms relating to every aspect of law and law enforcement. From types of weapons, nicknames of prisons, names of terrorist groups, medical and psychiatric terms relating to criminals, to the definitions of slang used by criminals, its scope is immense. Appendices. Bibliography. (New York: Facts on File, 1981).

The Criminal Justice Dictionary, Second edition. Erik Beckman. (Ann Arbor, MI: Pierian, 1983).

Dictionary of American Penology. Vergil L. Williams (ed.) Covers a broad range of topics dealing with prisons and prisoners today. Each topic covered includes a bibliography of sources. Includes overall coverage of correctional systems of each state in the U.S. (Westport, CT: Greenwood Press, 1979).

Dictionary of Behavior Science, Second edition. Benjamin B. Wolman. (San Diego: Academic Press, 1989).

A Dictionary of Concepts on American Politics. James B. Whisker (New York: John Wiley, 1980).

The Dictionary of Criminal Justice, Third edition. Dr. George R. Rush (ed.) An alphabetical compilation of over 4,000 definitions of terms important to the study of criminal justice. The addition of over 700 Supreme Court case summaries provides a valuable new dimension to the volume's utility. (Guilford, CT: Dushkin Publishing Group, 1991).

The Dictionary of Criminal Justice Data Terminology. This dictionary defines criminal justice terms used in statistical reports issued by the Federal Government. It also proposes model definitions so that criminal justice experts can use the terms more consistently. (Rockville, MD: National Criminal Justice Reference Service, 1981).

A Dictionary of Criminology. Dermot Walsh and Adrian Poole. (London and Boston: Routledge & Kegan Paul, 1983.)

The Dictionary of English Law, Second edition. John Burke. Changes in this edition reflect the exclusion of Scottish legal terms, reorganization of the court system, remodelling of local and central government, etc. A first supplement was published in 1981. (London, UK: Sweet & Maxwell, 1977).

A Dictionary of International Law and Diplomacy. Melquiades J. Gamboa. (Quezon City, Philippines: Central Lawbook Publishing Company, 1974).

The Dictionary of Political Analysis, Second edition. Jack C. Plano. (Santa Barbara, CA: ABC-Clio, 1982).

A Dictionary of Politics. Walter Laquer (ed.) (New York: Free Press, 1974).

Dictionary of Street Alcohol and Drug Terms. Dr. Peter Johnson (ed.) Catalogs and defines over 3500 words, names and expressions. Includes more than 750 Hispanic terms, fast becoming the dominant lingo across North, South and Central America. Marijuana, for example, has more than 700 other names. Also explained is drug and alcohol sign language. (Upland, PA: DIANE Publishing Co., 1988).

Elsevier's Dictionary of Criminal Science. Johann A. Adler. (Amsterdam: Elsevier, 1960).

Encyclopedic Dictionary of American Government, Fourth edition. (Guilford, CT: Dushkin Publishing Group, 1991).

Encyclopedic Dictionary of American History, Fourth edition. (Guilford, CT: Dushkin Publishing Group, 1991).

Kelley's Security Thesaurusory. Woody A. Kelley. (Gurley, AL: Concept VIII, 1977).

Law Dictionary, Second edition. Steven H. Gifis. Intended as a ready reference source in paperback for the student. More than 3,000 terms are defined, many with relevant legal citations. Pronunciation indicated for Latin and French terms. Appendixes provide American Bar Association Code (1969) and Rules (1983). (Woodbury, NY: Barron's, 1984).

Law Dictionary for Non-Lawyers. Daniel Oran. (St. Paul, MN: West, 1975).

Legal Terms and Concepts in Criminal Justice. Michael M. D'Auria, Gary D. Helfand, and Herbert F. Ryan. Divided into three parts, this book both defines and explains the most important and widely used words and concepts in the American system of law. Part I focuses in on the words, terms, and phrases directly related to criminal justice. Part II is a comprehensive listing of criminal justice abbreviations and acronyms. The last section defines the latest and most common drug terms related to substance abuse. (Wayne, NJ: Avery Publishing Group Inc., 1983).

Modern Legal Glossary. Kenneth R. Redden and Enid L. Veron. A dictionary "devoted exclusively to a definition of legal terms and related concepts, both old and new" (Pref.), as well as professional associations, government agencies, international organizations, foreign expressions, popular names of cases and statutes, trials, ancient codes, and biographies. (Charlottesville, VA: Michie Co., 1980).

The New Dictionary of Statistics: A Complement to the Fourth Edition of Mulhall's "Dictionary of Statistics." August D. Webb. (London, UK: George Routledge and Sons, Ltd., 1974).

Oran's Dictionary of the Law. Daniel Oran. A basic dictionary, with standard pronunciation indicated for foreign terms. Appendix provides a brief guide to legal research. (St. Paul, MN: West Publishing, 1983).

The Police Dictionary and Encyclopedia. John J. Fay. More than 4900 law enforcement terms and phrases are defined and explained in this comprehensive work. Examples are provided where necessary and applications of important practices have been delineated. The entry-level officer, as well as the seasoned veteran, will find the text to be a valuable guide in updating his or her working vocabulary. (Springfield, IL: Charles C Thomas, 1988).

Public Administration Dictionary, Second edition. Ralph C. Chandler and Jack C. Plano. (Santa Barbara, CA: ABC-Clio, 1982).

Security Dictionary. Richard Hofmeister. (Indianapolis: Howard W. Sams & Co., 1983).

Thesaurus of Psychological Index Terms, Sixth edition. This vital reference took is available in its 6th edition—revised, updated, and expanded. The Thesaurus contains all the terms used to index the PsycINFO database. PsycLIT on CD-ROM, PsycBOOKS, and Psychological Abstracts. In this new edition, over 230 new terms have been added and integrated. Additional cross references and scope notes help the user locate the right terms, and all terms have been updated to indicate the current number of postings. A "down arrow" feature has been included in this new edition as well. (Arlington, VA: American Psychological Association, 1990).

Words and Phrases 1958 to Date: All Judicial Constructions and Definitions of Words and Phrases by the State and Federal Courts from the Earliest Times. A comprehensive dictionary with frequently revised editions. (St. Paul, MN: West Publishing).

Dictionaries of Slang Terms

American Thesaurus of Slang. L.V. Berrey and Melvin Van den Bark. (New York: Crowell, 1953).

Dictionary of American Slang. Harold Wentworth and S.B. Flexner. (New York: Crowell, 1967).

Slang Today and Yesterday. Eric Partridge. (London, UK: Routledge, 1970).

Encyclopedias

There are many different specialized encyclopedias, but few pertain specifically to criminal justice, and some of these are quite dated. Nevertheless, a brief listing of encyclopedias oriented toward criminal justice and related subjects is given below. Many of these provide good references for terminology and concepts for fundamental course work and review material for senior and graduate students.

American Jurisprudence, 2d. Updated with pocket parts and replacement volumes. (Rochester, NY: Lawyer's Co-operative Publishing Co .).

Best Encyclopedias: A Guide to General and Specialized Encyclopedias. Kenneth K. Kister. The reference lists and describes all major encyclopedias published around the world. (Phoenix, AZ: ORYX Press, 1986).

The Concise Encyclopedia of Crime and Criminals. Harold Scott. A useful volume despite its age and lack of index. Some articles are quite extensive; most important movements and ideas are covered. The large number of biographies, unusual for their inclusion of lawyers, judges, and detectives, as well as criminals and criminologists, are particularly helpful. (New York: Hawthorn Books, 1961).

Corpus Juris Secundum. Updated with pocket parts and replacement volumes. This can be used to provide a broad overview of a topic. Articles also cite cases illustrating the points under discussion. In addition to subject indexes, this encyclopedia includes detailed analytical tables of contents for each article. (St. Paul, MN: West Publishing Co.).

Encyclopedia of Business Information Sources. Paul Lasserman, Managing Editor. Not intended to provide answers to particular questions, but rather to list sources which are likely to be the "right place to begin" in seeking those answers.

The subject headings used in EBIS are primarily of three types:
  1) Line-of-business designations
  2) Product and process designations
  3) Function and service designations

Subject headings are arranged alphabetically.

Under each subject will be found citations of sources of all kinds which the editors believe would be helpful to a user needing information on that particular subject. The sources gathered together in EBIS subject entries include the following types, each represented by a subheading within the entry (although not all types of sources are found in all entries), arranged in this sequence:

Encyclopedia and Dictionaries
Handbooks and Manuals
Bibliographies
Abstract Services and Indexes
Trade Associations and Professional Societies
Periodicals
Directories
Biographical Sources
Statistics Sources
Price Sources
Almanacs and Yearbooks
Financial Ratios
Other Sources
General Works
Research Centers and Institutes
On-Line Data Bases

For the researcher interested in white-collar crime, this source may prove valuable. (Detroit, MI: Gale Researchers, 1983).

✓ *The Encyclopedia of American Crime.* Carl Sifakis. With over 1500 readable entries, this thoroughly illustrated volume describes the lives and deeds of 700 of the most villainous characters in our history. (New York: Facts on File, 1982).

The Encyclopedia of American Government. Contains up-to-date information about every major area of American government and politics: the presidency, congress, the supreme court, lobbies and lobbyists, the federal bureaucracy, state and local government, citizenship and civil rights, the constitution, political parties, the electoral process, public opinion and pressure groups, domestic policy, national defense, government regulation, the federal court system, the administration of justice, state court system, the federal budget and taxation, foreign policy, and much more. (Guilford, CT: DPG Reference Publishing Inc.).

Encyclopedia of American Scandal. George Kohn. (New York: Facts on File, 1990).

✓ *Encyclopedia of Associations,* Fourteenth edition. A guide to national and international non-profit organizations in all fields. Includes description of programs, addresses, phone numbers, and names of chief officials. (Detroit, MI: Gale Research Co., 1980).

✓ *Encyclopedia of Bioethics.* (New York: The Free Press, 1978).

✓ *Encyclopedia of Clinical Assessment.* (New York: The Free Press, 1980).

✓ *Encyclopedia of Crime and Justice.* Sanford H. Kadish (ed.) An excellent source for background information on a variety of topics dealing with the study of crime and criminal justice. Provides long articles on topics such as "Alcohol and Crime," "Aged and Crime," "Capital Punishment," "Drinking and Driving," etc. Articles are accompanied by bibliographies of books, journal articles, and other materials useful for further research. (New York: Macmillan, 1983).

✓ *The Encyclopedia of Drug Abuse.* Robert O'Brien and Sidney Cohen, M.D. (New York: Facts on File, 1984).

Encyclopedia of Espionage: From the Age of Jericho to the Age of James Bond. Ronald Seth. Text with bibliography. (Garden City, NY: Doubleday, 1974).

Encyclopedia of Governmental Advisory Organizations. Basic information on presidential and public advisory committees, boards, panels, task forces and commissions serving in a consultative or investigative capacity. (Detroit, MI: Gale Research, 1981).

✓ *The Encyclopedia of Management,* Third edition. Concise articles on a wide variety of topics, with bibliographies and suggestions for additional relevant topics to check. (New York: Carl Heyel, 1982).

Encyclopedia of Murder. Colin Wilson and Patricia Pitman. Text with bibliography. (New York: Putnam, 1962).

The Encyclopedia of Police Science. William G. Bailey (ed.) (New York: Garland, 1989).

Civil Rights for State & Federal Prisoners, Vol. III. Jack L. Kunsman. (Encyclopedia of Prisoners' Rights Ser., 1982).

Drugs & Crime. Dorothy Hoobler and Thomas Hoobler. Encyclopedia of Psychoactive Drugs Series: No. 2. (New York: Chelsea House, 1988).

The Encyclopedia of Words and Phrases, Legal Maxims (Canada 1825 to 1978), Third edition. Gerald D. Sanagan. A dictionary which attempts "to extract from Canadian judicial decisions . . . all materials shedding light on the meaning of words and phrases, both legal and otherwise." References to cases and decisions are provided, with notation indicating national or provincial courts. (Toronto: R. De Boo, 1979).

Open Files: A Narrative Encyclopedia of the World's Greatest Unsolved Crimes. Jay Robert Nash. (New York: McGraw-Hill, 1983).

Spy/Counterspy: An Encyclopedia of Espionage. Vincent Buranelli and Nan Buranelli. The 400 articles in the encyclopedia cover the highlights of espionage, the people, events, organizations, and techniques in its history. The emphasis is on America and Europe. Included are historical figures, the CIA, KGB, M15, SMERSH, MOSSAD, and their historical counterparts. Primary and secondary sources are used. (New York: McGraw-Hill, 1982).

✓ *World Encyclopedia of Police Forces and Penal Systems.* George Thomas Kurian. (New York: Facts on File, 1989).

Encyclopedias of education which may also serve as useful sources of information include:

American Peoples Encyclopedia. (New York: Grolier, annual).

Collier's Encyclopedia. (New York: Collier, annual).

Columbia Encyclopedia. (New York: Columbia University Press, 1963).

✓*Encyclopedia Americana.* (New York: Americana Corporation, annual).

✓*Encyclopedia Britannica.* (Chicago: Encyclopedia Britannica, 1974).

✓*Encyclopedia of Educational Research.* Robert L. Ebel. (New York: Macmillan, 1969).

✓*The Encyclopedia of Education.* (New York: Macmillan Publishing Company and the Free Press, 1971).

Encyclopedia International. (New York: Grolier, annual).

Popular Crime Encyclopedias

✓*Almanac of World Crime.* Jay Robert Nash. Narrative descriptions of some of the world's most famous or bizarre crimes and criminals. (Garden City, NY: Anchor Press/Doubleday, 1981).

✓*Bloodletters and Badmen:* A Narrative Encyclopedia of American Criminals from the Pilgrims to the Present. Jay Robert Nash. (New York: M. Evans, 1973).

Look for the Woman: A Narrative Encyclopedia of Female Poisoners, Swindlers, and Spies from Elizabethan Times to the Present. Jay Robert Nash. (New York: M. Evans, 1981).

The Murderers' Who's Who: Outstanding International Cases from the Literature of Murder in the Last 150 Years. J.H.H. Gaute and Robin Odel. Gives a brief account of almost every famous murder case for the period covered. Includes bibliographies for each case. The classified index includes type of weapon, type of crime, and a list of unsolved crimes. (New York: Methuen, 1979).

Fact Books and Almanacs

✓*The World Factbook.* Produced annually by the Central Intelligence Agency for the use of United States Government officials, and the style, format, coverage, and content are designed to meet their specific requirements. Comments and queries are welcome.

This book of world facts, leaders and governments is an outstanding publication produced by the CIA and is available to the general public and is carried in many libraries.

There have been some significant changes in this edition. In the Government section the former Branches entry has been replaced by three entries—Executive branch, Legislative branch, and Judicial branch. The Leaders entry now has subentries for Chief of State, Head of Government, and their deputies. The Elections entry has been completely redone with information for each branch of the national government, including the date for the last election, the date for the next election, results (percent of vote by candidate or party), and current distribution of seats by party. In the Economy section there is a new entry on Illicit Drugs.

In the section on illicit drugs, a vast amount of information is given. (Washington, DC: Central Intelligence Agency, Public Affairs Division).

Whitaker's Almanack. Established in 1868, this annual British publication is very interesting and gives information on a vast amount of information with nearly 10,000 references. Among the major subject headings are: Government and Public Offices, Law Courts and Offices (England and Wales, Scotland, Northern Ireland), Tribunals, Police Forces, The Armed Forces (The Royal Navy, The Army, The Royal Air Force). (London, UK: J. Whitaker & Sons).

✓ *The World Almanac and Book of Facts* has been published annually since 1868. It contains many topics of interest to criminologists. (Washington, DC: Scripps-Howard).

Handbooks and Manuals

Drug Testing Legal Manual. Kevin B. Zeese. Updated annually. The Manual examines the three primary areas of testing: private employment, government employment, and pre-employment testing. Expert analysis of the applicable statutory and common law issues, with particular attention to matters concerning wrongful discharge . . . privacy and defamation actions . . . negligence claims . . . and Fourth Amendment issues. In addition, the volume covers questions of consent, probable cause, and employer searches. The Manual contains coverage and analysis of recent major Supreme Court decisions. (New York: Clark Boardman Company, Ltd.).

Fraud Examiners Manual. This manual is a complete course for fraud examiners. After passage of the national examination, successful candidates are certified as fraud examiners. (Austin, TX: National Association of Certified Fraud Examiners, 1989).

The Guide to Background Investigations, Fourth Edition. In its 696 pages, The Guide shows large and small companies how to use public records to aid their background checks. Included are over 7500 sources for public records. Easy-to-read entries detail the procedures each office follows in releasing its records.

The Guide enables the user to verify or discover criminal conviction data, college attendance and degrees, worker's compensation claims, driving records, medical licenses and more by phone, mail or fax. Major sections include: criminal records, workers compensation records, driving records, educational records, federal court records, departments of education, medical licensing boards, and corporations. (Tulsa, OK: National Employment Screening Services, 1991).

Handbook of Loss Prevention and Crime Prevention, Second edition. Lawrence J. Fennelly. A one-volume encyclopedia on the entire security field. The *Handbook of Loss Prevention and Crime Prevention* brings together the expertise of over 40 security and crime prevention professionals on the latest technology and trends. Topics include legal aspects of security, executive protection, access controls, internal theft, applicant screening, investigations, and much, much more.

The text is divided into four major parts. "Methods" includes environmental design, security surveys, fire and safety protection, and emergency planning. "Operations and Equipment" deals with locks, lighting, alarms, CCTV, guard forces and physical barriers. "Applications" zeroes in on security in modern society. "Management" analyzes such important functions as planning, data analysis, budgeting, and public relations. (Stoneham, MA: Butterworth Publishers, 1989).

Handbook of State Police, Highway Patrols, and Investigative Agencies. Donald A. Torres. (Westport, CT: Greenwood Press, 1987).

✓ *International Handbook of Contemporary Developments in Criminology.* Elmer H. Johnson (ed.). Contents: v.1, General issues and the Americas; v.2, Europe, Africa, the Middle East, and Asia. Presents state-of-the-art reviews of criminology in specific countries; surveys are written by specialists. Bibliographic references and bibliographies; indexed. (Westport, CT: Greenwood Press, 1983).

Practical Risk Management. This handbook covers all aspects of risk management and insurance related problems. Format and contents: Two loose-leaf binders containing in-depth information on: Administration, Risk Financing and Self-insurance, Insurers, Loss Control/ Claims Management, Legal and Political Aspects, Property Risk and Insurance, Liability Risk and Insurance, Risk Managers Resources, Special Industry Index and Glossary. Annual. (San Francisco, CA: Warren, McVeigh & Griffin).

Pre-Law Handbook. The official guide of ABA-approved law schools. Includes LSAT profiles of recently admitted classes and up-to-date admission standards. (Washington, DC: Association of American Law Schools, 1983).

Protection of Assets Manual. In five loose-leaf volumes and updated continually, this work provides complete coverage of all major loss prevention and private security topics. Annual. (Santa Monica, CA: The Merritt Company).

Risk Management and Insurance Audit Techniques. Dwight E. Levick. In the field of private security and loss prevention one of the higher paying positions and the least understood by persons working in criminal justice is risk management. This reference work has semi-annual updates and will keep the book current on a broad spectrum of topics including updated coverage information, new risk management strategies, the latest developments in self-insurance, plus discussions of risk management techniques and coverages for "special situations"—banks, hospitals, municipalities, construction industries, and many more. Key chapters give a thorough practical discussion on the value of periodic audits, their objectives, how to choose an auditor, and the important role top management plays in the audit process. An in-depth discussion of the administrative responsibilities of managing the insurance program provides a good review for all insurance and risk management professionals.

The basic principles of risk management, plus insights on the major concerns of risk management professionals and their consultants. A sample audit report spells out the general approach commonly taken by the author in conducting an audit and writing a report. You'll learn what you can expect and ask for in your own audits.

Finally, you'll get a set of practical, ready-to-use specimen forms and checklists specially designed as tools for conducting a risk management and insurance audit. Most of these forms are also useful in your day-to-day risk management activities. Annual. (Boston, MA: The John Liner Organization).

SCSC Security Controls and Systems Catalog. Published annually, Security Controls and Systems Catalog is a reference work for specifiers and buyers of security/facility controls and systems. Contents include manufacturers listing, product index of manufacturers literature, industry-wide manufacturers address listing, industry-wide product directory, local sales and service offices. (Indianapolis, IN: MBC Data Distribution Publications).

Security Industry Buyer Guide. A 900-page directory, updated annually, that lists publishers, manufacturers and distributors of security-related products. (Bethesda, MD: C & P Telephone of Virginia).

Security Letter Source Book 1990-1991. Robert D. McCrie (ed.) This established guide to the industry's leading services, suppliers, and manufacturers provides a gold mine of data on the whos, whats, and wheres in the security field. 100% revised and updated, the new edition gives instant access to sources ranging from alarm, guard, patrol, and screening services to specialized products, individual consultants, and investigators. (Stoneham, MA: Butterworth Publishers, 1990).

Security Managers Desk Reference. Richard S. Post and David A. Schachtsiek. A mini-encyclopedia, this quick-access reference provides reliable, up-to-date data on an extremely broad range of security and safety issues. Managers consult it time and again whenever they need information quickly on any security topic, from general management principles and basic security philosophy to specifics such as bomb threats, personnel selection, and CCTV camera placement. (Stoneham, MA: Butterworth Publishers, 1986).

A Sourcebook on Child Sexual Abuse. David Finkelhor et al. (Beverly Hills, CA: Sage Publications, 1986).

U.S. Identification Manual. 700 pages of information with 200 identification formats and continuous updating. Arranged in five sections to verify the identification of documents. Every document is shown in full size and full color where appropriate.

SECTION I
State Identification
The most comprehensive coverage of state identification documents—shown in full color and actual size for fast visual matchup: Every adult, regular driver's license from the U.S. and Canada. Complete details on commercial/chauffeur's cards, cycle and moped permits, minor's licenses; and State ID cards for non-drivers' liquor control cards. Supporting information on military extensions, restricted driver's coding, duplicate licenses, laminations permitted.

SECTION II
Vehicle Registration
All U.S. and Canadian license plates shown in large color reproduction for easy validation. Passenger cars, trucks of all kinds, trailers and motorcycle license plates. Term and expiration for all license plates. All registration stickers in color with detailed explanation. Special registration information section covering—for each U.S. state and Canadian province—alpha-numeric licensing system for all types of vehicles, validation requirements, personalized plate policies.

SECTION III
Federal Identification
A complete reference for dependable verification of U.S. military, immigration and federal employee documents. Color reproductions of all ID cards issued by the various armed forces, including active personnel, reservists, retirees and dependents. Telephone numbers to confirm the validity of federal credentials. Immigration and alien identity documents including immigration and alien registration cards and

permits, arrival-departure records and crewman's landing permit. Social security card coding chart.

SECTION IV
Commercial Documents
An accurate reference for credit cards, including information for immediate verification at any time. Bank cards, travel and entertainment cards shown in full color. Detailed backup on travel and entertainment cards, bank cards, airline, auto rental, gasoline, department stores, hotels, and more. 24-hour telephone numbers and security contacts for emergency assistance and verification. Explanation of numbering system for each card listed

SECTION V
Directory
A specialized directory of federal and state agencies and departments most often contacted in matters of identification and law enforcement. National, regional and local offices with addresses and telephone numbers. Names of persons in charge at offices listed for most effective contact. Arranged alphabetically by agency or department for fast, efficient use. Annual. (Redwood City, CA: U. S. Identification Manual).

Newspapers

Collections of newspapers are a very valuable source of information because they report conditions and events taking place worldwide. Newspapers also report facts that cannot be found in textbooks or other publications. Therefore, the importance of newspapers as a source of information should not be underestimated.

When using newspapers, however, be aware that facts are often intertwined with opinion. Critique the paper for objectivity and compare coverage of an article with that of other newspapers. To help yourself distinguish fact from opinion, learn to recognize the properties of a fact. First, a fact is something such as a person, place, thing, or situation that is experienced through the senses and therefore is known to exist. A fact can be verified by other people through the stimulation of their senses. A fact can also be something which has not been experienced by the senses but is thought to have existed if it is believed that evidence of the fact could be found if we looked for it. A good clue for distinguishing fact from opinion is to learn to identify the "whos, whats, wheres, hows, and whys" (if they exist) of an article. This information will usually provide you with clearly stated facts, although "why" statements often border on being opinions.

The majority of newspaper literature is stored as microform, and the assistance of the librarian may be required in order to view this material. However, it can be set up in a matter of minutes so don't shy away from newspapers or other materials simply because they are not in paper form. Several sources of newspaper information are described below:

Newsbank is an index to news articles in 190 newspapers from 103 cities, representing all 50 states. Printed subject indexes are issued quarterly and cumulated annually, providing subject access to newspaper articles on microfiche. The indexes are divided into twelve categories: Business and Economic Development, Consumer Affairs, Education, Employment, Environment, Government Structure, Housing and Urban Renewal, Law and Order, Political Development, Social Relations, Transportation, and Welfare and Poverty. Business and industrial crime listings are cataloged in the "Business and Economic Development Index."

In addition to Newsbank, there are other sources contained in most libraries that provide access to newspaper articles related to criminal justice. Some of these sources are listed below:

Alternative Press Index
N.W. Ayer and Sons Directory of Newspapers and Periodicals
Chicago Tribune Index
Index to the Christian Science Monitor
London Times Index
Los Angeles Times Index
National Observer Index

New Orleans Times-Picayune Index
Newspaper Index (Covers the Chicago Tribune, Los Angeles Times, New Orleans Times-Picayune,
    and Washington Post)
Newspaper Press Directory
New York Times Index
Wall Street Journal Index
Washington Post Index

These are among the major newspaper indexes. Your library may have additional ones to local newspapers which may also be helpful. By noting the date an event was reported in one of the above indexes, such as the New York Times Index, you can locate similar articles in other newspapers which may be more accessible. (See also Chapter 9, "Computerized Literature Searches," for several computerized newspaper databases, and Chapter 15, "Historical Research Sources," for access to early newspapers.)

Related Sources

Basic Books in the Mass Media: An Annotated Selected Booklist Covering General Communications, Book Publishing, Broadcasting, Film, Magazines, Newspapers, Advertising, Indexes, and Scholarly and Professional Periodicals. Eleanor Blum. The title is self-explanatory and would be helpful in locating a variety of information sources due to its broad scope. (Urbana, IL: University of Illinois Press, 1972).

Crime: As Reported by the New York Times. Arleen Keylin and Arto Di-Mirjian, Jr. A specialized collection of citations pertaining to crime appearing in the New York Times. (New York: Arno Press, 1976).

Editor and Publisher International Yearbook. Contains data on United States, Canadian, and other foreign newspapers covering several aspects of journalism. Annual. (New York: Editor and Publisher, 1920-date).

Editorial Research Reports. Hoyt Gimlin (ed.) Consists of weekly pamphlets containing written editorials on issues of current interest to the American public. Outstanding publications on the topic being discussed are cited. Topics on the administration of justice are frequently discussed. A good source for views on the pros and cons of an issue, which are useful when preparing for debates and class discussions. Subject and title indexes to editorials issued during the previous eighteen years are provided in the semiannual cumulated issues. (Washington, DC: Congressional Quarterly, Inc., 1979).

Editorials on File. A twice monthly selection of editorials from a representative sample of American and Canadian newspapers, with a cumulative subject index. (New York: Facts on File, Inc., 1970-date).

Facts on File, Weekly World News Digest with Cumulative Index. A weekly publication with quarterly cumulated indexes which are rearranged as an annual index at the end of the year. Contains summaries of news printed by various large city newspapers, arranged by subject. (New York: Facts on File, Inc., 1900-date).

Facts on File 5-Year Index. The Facts on File 5-Year Index was developed to meet librarians' and news researchers' requirements. It is based on their suggestions for a fast-working method of multi-annual news indexing. The set of seven 5-Year Indexes gives quick access to the facts of 35 years of national and foreign affairs. The seven 5-Year Indexes now available: 1976-80, 1971-75, 1966-70, 1961-65, 1956-60, 1951-55, and 1946-50. (New York: Facts on File).

Newspaper Indexes: A Location and Subject Guide for Researchers. Anita C. Milner. (Metuchen, NJ: Scarecrow Press, 1977).

Newspapers on Microfilm. Lists thousands of American and foreign newspapers available on microfilm and specifies in which libraries they are available. (Washington, DC: Library of Congress, 1967).

News Broadcasts

Much news is communicated by broadcast media rather than newsprint. Thus, the sources below are of interest.

CBS News Television News Broadcasts. Microfiche. (Glen Rock, NJ: Microfilming Corporation of America, 1975-date).

CBS News Index: Key to the Television Broadcasts. (Ann Arbor, MI: Microfilming Corporation of America, 1975-date). This is a set consisting of microfiche copies of television scripts and printed subject indexes to the microfiche.

Public affairs programs and hard news articles are put on fiche and indexed.

This proves a very rich source of information about current topics in criminal justice. You will have to search a bit to locate stories on specific topics because indexing is broad.

Television News Index and Abstracts. A Guide to the Videotape Collection of the Network Evening News Programs in the Vanderbilt Television News Archive. The above is a special source. The abstracts are very detailed, specifying what was shown as well as what was said, including the names and people who can be heard and seen.

The Television News Index and Abstracts is issued monthly with no cumulations. (Nashville, TN: Vanderbilt University Library, 1968-date).

Annuals and Yearbooks

The Aldine Crime and Justice Annual. Emphasizes developments relating to the criminal justice system. All articles included have been published in other sources during the preceding year. Annual. (Chicago: Aldine, 1973-date).

The Annals of The American Academy of Political and Social Science. Founded in 1891, this academic society publishes annuals that often deal with criminal justice issues, including:

The American Judiciary: Critical Issues. A. Leo Levin and Russell R. Wheeler (eds.). Addressing broad questions of the role and responsibilities of courts in American government and society, eleven articles discuss what courts should do, how they should do their work, and the parts played by other branches. (Newbury Park, CA: Sage Publications, 1982).

Crime and Justice: A Review of Research. Michael Tonry and Norval Morris (eds.) An interdisciplinary forum on criminology, the Crime and Justice series exposes professionals and scholars to the full scope of issues concerning crime, its causes, and its prevention. The criminal lawyer, the sociologist, the psychologist, the political scientist—are all among the professionals who contribute to and benefit from *Crime and Justice's* vital forum.

Crime and Justice is supported by the National Institute of Justice. Points of view or opinions expressed in this series are those of the editors or authors and do not necessarily represent the official position of policies of the U.S. Department of Justice. (Chicago: University of Chicago Press, Journals Division, 1982).

Volume 1
Topics include race relations and the prisoner subculture; ecological and areal studies; American youth violence; police function, structure, and control; deinstitutionalization and diversion of juvenile offenders; crime-causation theory; longitudinal research on crime.

Volume 2
Topics include urban police and crime in 19th-century America; crime and justice in 18th- and 19th-century England; biology and crime; prisoners' rights.

Volume 3
Topics include surveys of victimization; use of hypnosis in court; eyewitness testimony; modern private security; historical trends in violent crimes; rights, utility, and crime.

Volume 4
Topics include violence in school; gun availability and violent crime; gender and crime; crime and mental disorder; situational crime prevention.

Volume 5
Topics include incapacitation; prison labor and industries; prisons for women; sex offenses and offending; plus a special section on criminological research in five nations.

Volume 6
Topics include predictions of dangerousness; community service orders; prison overcrowding; modeling offenders' decisions; delinquency careers; the turnabout in the insanity defense; criminological research in Scandinavia.

Volume 7
Topics include family factors and juvenile delinquency; age and crime; victimization surveys; differences in criminal behavior and court responses among young defendants.

Volume 8
The first thematic volume in the series examines the impact of environmental design on crime; the effects of crime on a community's schools; gentrification and crime rates; and the influence of community context on the recidivism of released offenders. Contributors include Robert J. Bursik, Jr., Leo Schuerman, Soloman Kobrin, Anthony E. Bottoms, Paul Wiles, Scott C.

McDonald, Wesley Skogan, Richard M. McGahey, Robert J. Sampson, Douglas Smith, Lawrence W. Sherman, Ralph Taylor, and Stephen Gottfredson.

Volume 9
Eleven essays discuss the methodology of prediction and classification; the role of these methods in program evaluation research and in application to guidelines for bail, sentencing, and parole; and the legal and ethical considerations that surround the use of these methods. Contributors include Stephen Gottfredson, David Farrington, John Goldkamp, Joan Petersilia, Susan Turner, Richard Berk, Tim Brennan, Daniel Glaser, and Lee Sechrest.

Volume 10
Topics include community policing, co-offending and criminal careers, drunk driving, prison populations, and sentencing reform.

Volume 11
Twelve essays in this multidisciplinary collection review current research on the legal, social, and criminological issues surrounding family violence. Contributors include Elizabeth Pleck, Robert L. Burgess and Patricia Draper, Joseph G. Weis, Irene Hanson Frieze and Angela Browne, James Garbarino, Mildred Daley Pagelow, Gerald T. Hotaling, Murray A. Straus, Alan J. Lincoln, Jeffrey Fagan, Delbert S. Elliott, Daniel G. Saunders, Sandra T. Azar, and Franklin E. Zimring.

Volume 12
Topics include parole, developmental criminology, neuropsychology of juvenile delinquency, police crackdowns, crime displacement, youth games, and criminal fines.

Volume 13
Comprehensive in its scope, Drugs and Crime illuminates the complex relations between drug use and crime and the challenges that confront efforts to reduce them. As they evaluate prevention, treatment, and law-enforcement policies, the contributors offer dynamic analyses of the strategies deployed in the "War on Drugs." Drawing on the best available scholarly evidence, the authors examine the relations between drug use and violent crime, aggression, and consensual crime; the technologies and uses of drug testing; and the corrosive effects of drug trafficking on the quality of life in inner-city minority communities.

Volume 14
The following topics are covered in Volume 14: The Technology of Personal Violence, Philip J. Cook; Burglary, Neal Shover; Sociological Perspectives on Punishment, David Garland; Drug-Control Policies in Britain, Geoffrey Pearson; Drugs and Drug Policy in the Netherlands, Ed Leuw; The Motivation of the Persistent Robber, Jack Katz; Women, Crime, and Penal Responses: A Historical Account, Lucia Zedner; The Needs and Rights of Victims of Crime, Mike Maguire.

Criminal Law Review. Anthology of some of the most significant articles published during the preceding year. Each volume includes selections in the four areas of substantive criminal law, constitutional rights and remedies, trial and sentencing, and professional responsibility. Each year there is a very useful introductory survey of significant court decisions dealing with criminal law. (New York: Clark Boardman, 1979-date).

Criminal Justice System Review. Emphasizes the legal aspects of the criminal justice system and unlike other annuals, contains some previously unpublished material. (Buffalo, NY: William S. Hein).

Annuals

Annual Editions are published by Dushkin Publishing Group, Inc., Guildford, Connecticut.

Annual Editions: Criminal Justice. An organized collection of articles, indexed, and reproduced in a low-cost format which provides easy and permanent access to the most current literature in the criminal justice field. Published annually since 1977.

Annual Editions: Drugs, Society and Behavior. For use in introductory courses dealing with drugs and society. Published annually since 1985.

Annual Editions: Social Problems. For use in social problems courses. Published annually since 1972.

Annual Editions: Violence and Terrorism. For use in political terrorism courses. Published annually since 1990.

Facts On File Yearbooks

Each week since January 1941 Facts on File has summarized, recorded and indexed the news of the nation and the world. This indexed record of the events of the past 41 years is preserved for permanent reference use in the library of bound Facts on File Yearbooks. Published at the end of each year, these volumes contain all the year's 52 weekly news digests and an annual index that makes it possible to pinpoint information on any major news event or person prominent in the year's news.

Set 1   America in World War II (1941-45)
Set 2   The Truman Administration and the Growth of the Cold War (1946-52)
Set 3   The Eisenhower Decade (1953-60)
Set 4   The Kennedy/Johnson Years (1961-68)
Set 5   The Nixon/Ford Years (1969-76)
Set 6   The Carter Years (1977-80)

Guide to Resources and Services. This 525-page guide lists and annotates numerous research studies of value to the criminal justice researcher. Of great importance is the criminal justice archive and information network which is housed by the Inter-University Consortium. Annual. (Ann Arbor, MI: Inter-University Consortium for Political and Social Research).

The Mental Measurements Yearbook. Oscar K. Buros. A bibliography of books on psychological measurement and of psychological tests published in all English-speaking countries. The section entitled "Books and Reviews" consists of a list of recent books, most of which are followed by excerpts from two or more critical reviews whose sources are cited in full. (Highland Park, NJ: Gryphon Press, 196 5).

Police Yearbook. Annual. Reports the proceedings of the IACP's yearly conference. (Gaithersburg, MD: International Association of Chiefs of Police).

Proceedings of the American Correctional Association. Annual report on the content of presentations given at the ACA's yearly meeting. Major developments and trends during the previous year are usually the topics addressed at this meeting. (College Park, MD: American Correctional Association).

Sage Research Progress Series in Criminology. The following annuals are published in cooperation with the American Society of Criminology. (Beverly Hills, CA: Sage Publications).

Volume 1
Theory in Criminology: Contemporary Views. Robert F. Meier (ed.) Examines the historical bases and current status of major theories, stressing the need to move beyond accepted hypotheses and improve the utility of contemporary criminological frameworks. 1977.

Volume 2
Juvenile Delinquency: Little Brother Grows Up. Theodore N. Ferdinand (ed.) Addresses such major concerns as the roles played by police and the courts in determining the outcomes of juvenile cases, the relationship between the theory of "naturalization" and "delinquency"; and the juvenile institutions. 1977.

Volume 3
Contemporary Corrections: Social Control and Conflict. C. Ronald Huff (ed.) Focuses on the sociological, legal, psychological, and policy issues posed by formal systems of legal control. 1977.

Volume 4
Criminal Justice Planning and Development. Alvin W. Cohn (ed.) Approaches the question of what constitutes effective planning and goal setting in the criminal justice area from the vantage points of the major actors in the justice system. 1977.

Volume 5
Violent Crime: Historical and Contemporary Issues. James A. Inciardi and Anne E. Pottieger (eds.) Explores the nature and historical roots of crimes and violence, discussing such topics as robbery outlawry on the U.S. frontier, the southern culture of violence, prison violence as exemplified in the George Jackson case, and Americans' fascination with handguns. 1978.

Volume 6
Crime, Law, and Sanctions: Theoretical Perspectives. Marvin D. Krohn and Ronald L. Akers (eds.) Presents cutting edge perspectives on vital areas of criminological theory, including labelling, law, crime, deterrence, and sanctions. 1978.

Volume 7
The Evolution of Criminal Justice: A Guide for Practical Criminologists. John P. Conrad (ed.) Recommends innovations in the use of empirically tested knowledge to change the justice system, discussing specific issues ranging from white collar crime and prison reform to deterrence and victim compensation. 1978.

Volume 8
Quantitative Studies in Criminology. Charles Wellford (ed.) Examines criminological problems to which statistical techniques can be usefully applied and demonstrates the value of a rigorous methodology in criminological research. 1978.

Volume 9
Discretion and Control. Margaret Evans (ed.) Discusses the relationship among legislation, the courts, and corrections in discretionary sentencing . . . and examines ongoing debates about the impact of discretion on the administration of justice. 1978.

Volume 10
Biology and Crime. C.R. Jeffery (ed.) Throws fresh light upon the controversial linkages among biological factors, human behavior, and crime. 1979.

Volume 11
Perspectives on Victimology. William H. Parsonage (ed.) Provides a stimulating overview of major issues in victimology, including the characteristics of special types of victims and offenders, and means of dealing with the social and personal effects of crime and victimization. 1979.

Volume 12
Police Work: Strategies and Outcomes in Law Enforcement. David M. Petersen (ed.) Probes the challenges confronting contemporary police as they serve diverse functions in law enforcement, crime prevention, and the public service sector, outlining innovative strategies to improve their performance. 1979.

Volume 13
Structure, Law, and Power Essays in the Sociology of Law. Paul J. Brantingham and Jack M. Kress (eds.) Explores the interplay of social structure, legal ideology, and political processes in the creation and enforcement of criminal law. 1979.

Volume 14
Courts and Diversion Policy and Operations Studies. Patricia L. Brantingham and Thomas G. Blomberg (eds.) Presents cutting edge efforts to link justice data, theory, and policy, stressing such topics as alternatives to processing through

the judicial system and the relationship between the availability of court services and crime control. 1979.

Volume 15
Taboos in Criminology. Edward Sagarin (ed.) Presents an insightful and heated discussion of these issues in criminology labeled "taboo" by the scholarly community. Six eminent contributors offer diverse viewpoints on such controversial issues as the relationship between the women's movement and female crime and the effects of race and I.Q. on delinquency. 1980.

Volume 16
Criminal Justice Research New Models and Findings. Barbara Raffel Price and Phyllis Jo Baunach (eds.) Explores major issues in applied criminology, dealing in particular with evaluation and policy analysis. Each chapter highlights new directions in areas where research has been limited to legal objections to experimental design, victimization, prosecutorial discretion, probation diversion, and model development for program evaluation. 1980.

Volume 17
Improving Management in Criminal Justice. Alvin W. Cohn and Benjamin Ward (eds.) Acknowledges the need for such tools as goal setting, effective management, and planning in all organizations. Contributors examine pressing issues of management and administration in the criminal justice system, evaluate the effectiveness of specific policies and practices, and offer suggestions for improvement. 1980.

Volume 18
Understanding Crime: Current Theory and Research. Travis Hirschi and Michael Gottfredson (eds.) Why do people commit crimes? Contributors representing a wide spectrum of opinions provide fresh insights into this controversial issue. The editors' comprehensive introduction puts the current theory and research reported here into the context of ongoing debates. 1980.

Volume 19
Evaluation and Criminal Justice Police. Ronald Roesch and Raymond R. Corrado (eds.) Addresses fundamental concerns posed by the methodologies, goals, materials, and uses of evaluation research in the criminal justice system. Discusses issues involving differing methodologies and approaches, the sensitive nature of many of the programs examined, and the policy applications of evaluation data. 1981.

Volume 20
Contemporary Issues in Law Enforcement. James J. Fyfe (ed.) An enlightening overview of current issues and research on police conduct, techniques, and interaction with the community. Examines such specific concerns as the

need to establish realistic expectations for police performance, public accountability of law enforcement agencies, and controversies regarding police treatment of minorities. 1981.

Volume 21

Comparing Female and Male Offenders. Marguerite Q. Warren (ed.) Sheds new light on the importance of gender in studying crime and the criminal justice system . . . while challenging many of the myths and sex stereotypes involved in such study. Proposes new hypotheses regarding the gender-related differences that do exist. 1981.

Volume 22

Sociology of Delinquency: Current Issues. Gary F. Jensen (ed.) Original articles represent traditional sociological positions as well as diverse critical and cross-cultural viewpoints creating an exciting overview of contemporary delinquency research and conceptualization. 1981.

Volume 23

Crime Spillover. Simon Hakim and George F. Rengert (eds.) Pioneers in the emerging field of criminal mobility draw upon criminological, economic, and geographical insights to explicate questions related to where crimes take place and why certain neighborhoods have higher crime rates than others. 1981.

Volume 24

Quantitative Criminology Innovations and Applications. John Jagan (ed.) These stimulating essays examine creative methodologies, test important hypotheses, and cast new light on major concerns in criminology and criminal justice. They exemplify the growing importance of quantitative criminology as a critical context (in which novel ideas are matched with new kinds of data and new modes of analysis.) 1982.

Volume 25

Law and the Legal Process. Victoria L. Swigert (ed.) In this provocative volume, original studies illuminate issues central to continuing debates over the relationship between law and society, differential legal treatment, the operation of the criminal justice system, the impacts of legal processes on individuals, and the implications of law for social organizations. 1982.

Volume 26

Implementing Criminal Justice Policies. Merry Morash (ed.) Contributors address disturbing instances of implementation failure in such areas as gun control, juvenile diversion, and parole programs. They clarify the individual, organizational, and group dynamics that account for implementation difficulties, and pinpoint directions for future research. 1982.

Volume 27

Rethinking Criminology. Harold E. Pepinsky (ed.) Pepinsky contends that professionals need to surpass the boundaries of traditional criminological research which has provided few answers for policymakers and move toward a new understanding of the field. These insightful studies, conducted in independent new ways, underline the potential of innovative research premises and directions. 1982.

Volume 28

Deterrence Reconsidered: Methodological Innovations. John Hagan (ed.) Leading figures in quantitative criminology consider deterrence in new and creative ways. They show how advances in research design and statistical techniques, coupled with theoretical innovation, have had a major impact on our understanding of an enduring policy problem. 1982.

Volume 29

Evaluating Juvenile Justice. James R. Kluegel (ed.) Rapid political shifts have alternately favored liberal approaches aimed at "diverting" some juvenile delinquents from the criminal justice system and conservative, more punitive approaches to dealing with juveniles. Focusing on a range of programs that reflects these political changes, the authors rigorously evaluate how they work. Kluegel's overview illuminates the current state, and prospects, of programs dealing with juvenile delinquents. Together, they offer policymakers, researchers, students, and professionals a useful basis for decisions concerning the treatment of juvenile delinquents. 1983.

Volume 30

Career Criminals. Gordon P. Waldo (ed.) The pick-pocket, the Mafioso, the corporate executive illegally dumping chemicals into a nearby river, the "career criminal" is seldom caught . . . and comparatively unstudied. These original essays, by such researchers as James A. Inciardi, Julian B. Roebuck, and Frank R. Scarpitti, make a major contribution to the scarce literature on career criminals. Through use of a variety of innovative methods and approaches, the authors enhance our understanding of whether or not there is a national crime conspiracy in the United States, the use of "social network analysis" to study organized criminals, the use of serendipitous participant observation and field methods to study organized crime. A record of significant advances in the study of the career criminal, this stimulating book will interest professionals, researchers, and students in criminology and criminal justice. 1983.

Volume 31

Comparative Criminology Theory and Applications. Israel L. Barak Glantz and Elmer H. Johnson (eds.) Can study of crimes against the centrally planned economies of Poland

and the USSR offer new insights into white collar crime in the United States? Do Dutch crime statistics indicate that "female emancipation" can be linked to rising crime rates for American women? What can comparative research tell us about such practical concerns as police training and alleviating stresses on prison guards? In analyses addressing these and other timely topics, the authors show that comparative criminology can play an important role in understanding criminal behavior and improving criminal justice policies and practices. 1983.

Volume 32
Measurement Issues in Criminal Justice. Gordon P. Waldo (ed.) Waldo and his colleagues address a problem typical of criminological research: attaining reliability and validity in measuring data obtained under imperfectly controlled conditions. They discuss appropriate operational definitions to use in measuring concepts, the selection of samples, items, and the data collection process, and differing forms of analysis. Topics include the development of a perpetually based offense seriousness scale, the use of self reports to measure crime, the roles of substantive and statistical significance in evaluating research results. Measurement Issues in Criminal Justice is a copious source of insights into measurement challenges in the social sciences. 1983.

Sage Annual Reviews of Studies in Deviance

Deviance and Mass Media. Charles Winick (ed.) Deviance and Mass Media represents a sound if selective collection of theory and research. It may well serve as one of several texts for undergraduate teaching purposes. 1978.

Deviance and Mental Illness. Walter R. Gove (ed.) Intensively examines this important form of deviance and related issues associated with caregivers, patients, and society as a whole. The authors' insightful analyses, many of which challenge the major paradigm presently used to explain mental illness (labelling theory), address such central concerns as the causes of insanity, modern trends in psychiatric research and treatment, and the impact of mental illness on personal relationships. 1982.

Deviants: Victims or Victimizers? Donal E.J. MacNamara and Andrew Karmen (eds.) Prisoners, homosexuals, drug addicts, and prostitutes, are they victims of society? Or victimizers? Experts in criminology, victimology, and deviance studies pursue this hotly debated issue, presenting in-depth arguments and conflicting perspectives on the problems surrounding social deviants. Some view deviants as a threat to other citizens; some argue that deviants are mistreated by society. 1983.

Law and Deviance. H. Laurence Ross (ed.) Discusses the relationships among labelling, deviance, and criminal and civil law. Considering the nature of law (as contrasted with custom and morality), contributors place this view of law and deviance in the context of theoretical developments in both social science and legal scholarship. 1981.

The Yearbook of Drug and Substance Abuse (series). (New York: Human Sciences Press).

The Yearbook of Drug Abuse, Volume 1. Leon Brill and Ernest Harms (eds.) 1973.

The Yearbook of Substance Use and Abuse, Volume II. Leon Brill and Charles Winick (eds.) 1980.

The Yearbook of Substance Use and Abuse, Volume III. Leon Brill and Charles Winick (eds.) 1984.

AMERICAN CORRECTIONAL ASSOCIATION PUBLICATIONS

Adult Standards

Standards for Adult Local Detention Facilities, Third edition. 425 standards covering 32 program areas for adult local detention facilities. 1991.

1990 Correctional Standards Supplement. This vital supplement updates all adult and juvenile standards with every approved addition, revision, deletion, and/or interpretation. 1990.

Standards for Adult Community Residential Services, Second edition. 191 standards covering 15 program areas ensure that community corrections is a viable and cost-effective alternative to confinement. 1981.

Standards for Adult Correctional Institutions, Third edition. 495 standards covering 27 critical program areas for effective institutional management, including safety and emergency procedures, security and control, inmate rules and discipline, staff development, physical plant, and medical and health care services. 1990.

Standards for Adult Local Detention Facilities, Second edition. 392 standards addressing the special needs of local jails. Focuses on 22 program areas including personnel, training, safety, sanitation, security, health care, reception, and inmate supervision. 1981.

Standards for Adult Parole Authorities, Second edition. 129 standards covering 13 program areas associated with parole decision making. 1981.

Standards for Adult Probation and Parole Field Services, Second edition. 208 standards concerning 11 important areas for sound and progressive non-institutional services. 1981.

Standards for the Administration of Correctional Agencies. 159 standards covering 12 vital areas of the operation of the administrative unit in correctional systems. 1979.

Standards for Correctional Industries. 74 standards providing a clear set of guidelines on the purpose, day-to-day operation, and long-term planning of correctional industries. 1981.

Standards for Small Jail Facilities. Sixty-three percent of the jails in the United States have capacities of 50 inmates or less. This comprehensive book contains 207 standards for safety and emergency procedures, security and control, food service, sanitation, hygiene, health care services, personnel, recordkeeping, visitation, and more. 1989.

Certification Standards

Certification Standards for Food Service Programs. 57 standards guide agencies to certification of this vital area while working toward eventual accreditation. Includes sanitation, fiscal and personnel procedures, security, and training for food service programs in juvenile training schools and detention facilities and in adult correctional institutions and local detention facilities. 1989.

Certification Standards for Health Care Programs. 92 standards spell out requirements for certification in this essential area by institutions working toward accreditation. Applies to juvenile training schools and detention facilities and to adult correctional institutions and local detention facilities. Includes safety and emergency procedures, sanitation, security, and medical standards. 1989.

Correctional Officer Resource Guide. This revised manual continues to be an essential reference on all aspects of a correctional officer's job. An excellent training and reference book, covering such topics as officer's legal liabilities, inmate programming, security, AIDS, and other health issues, use of firearms, segregation, methods of restraining inmates, emergency procedures, officer support programs, and contraband. 1989.

Foundation/Core Standards

Foundation/Core Standards for Adult Local Detention Facilities. A new, alternate approach to accreditation allows certain accredited facilities to prove they comply with all mandatory ACA standards—standards that go beyond the life safety area and address every area of correctional operations. Applicants can benefit from paperwork reduction and the expanded time ACA audit teams can devote to these mandatory standards. 1989.

Foundation/Core Standards for Adult Community Residential Services. Adult community residential services can realize reduced paperwork and experience more detailed compliance reviews for all mandatory standards by ACA audit teams under this new, alternate approach to accreditation. 1989.

Foundation/Core Standards for Adult Correctional Institutions. This new, alternate approach to accreditation allows certain accredited adult correctional facilities to prove compliance with all mandatory ACA standards. These standards address every correctional operations area. Reduced paperwork and expanded time devoted to these standards by ACA audit teams will be pluses for applicants. 1989.

Juvenile Standards

Standards for Juvenile Community Residential Facilities, Second edition. 216 standards focusing on 13 important areas for operating programs and outlining residents' access to the surrounding community. 1983.

Standards for Juvenile Probation and Aftercare Services, Second edition. 228 standards on how to choose the juveniles who should be processed through the court and who should be diverted to other organizations. 1983.

Standards for Juvenile Training Schools, Third edition. 326 standards covering 31 program areas for long-term juvenile incarceration. Now with an easy-to-use numbering system. 1991.

Standards for Juvenile Detention Facilities, Second edition. 422 standards addressing the special needs of short-term juvenile detention. 1983.

Guidelines—Adult

Guidelines for the Development of Policies and Procedures—Adult Community Residential Services. Applicable policies and procedures for the effective management and administration of community facilities. 1981.

Guidelines for the Development of Policies and Procedures—Adult Correctional Institutions and Adult Local Detention Facilities. Offers clear examples for formulating day-to-day policies and procedures. Sample policies cover all aspects of facility operation. Includes a guide to developing policies and procedures by tailoring the sample documents to the needs of your facility. 1987.

Guidelines for the Development of Policies and Procedures—Adult Parole Authorities/Adult Probation and Parole Field Services. Model policies and procedures relating to both probation and parole field services and parole authorities. 1981.

Guidelines for the Development of a Security Program. W. Hardy Rauch. Presents ideas and concepts for designing or updating a comprehensive security program. Includes discussions of security basics, specific duties and responsibilities, and emergency preparedness. 1988.

Guidelines—Juvenile

ACA's correctional guidelines provide step-by-step instructions for translating standards into effective and practical procedures. Each guidelines book includes sample forms and policies for universal use. All are invaluable aids for institutions working toward accreditation and for those upgrading everyday operations.

Guidelines for the Development of Policies and Procedures—Juvenile Community Residential Facilities. Contains definitions, sample policies and references for the management and administration of juvenile community residential facilities. 1990.

Guidelines for the Development of Policies and Procedures—Juvenile Training Schools. A guide based on the practical experience of many agencies and facilities for the development of consistent and efficient operational policies and procedures. 1987.

CAREER INFORMATION GUIDES

Career and occupational literature exists to advise students and job seekers at all levels on career selection or job change, addressing such aspects of employment as job requirements, current job availability, work environment, security, and advancement.

Career Planning in Criminal Justice. Robert C. DeLucia and Thomas J. Doyle. A practical, easy-to-use reference, this guide explores the variety of occupations available, including specific job responsibilities and qualifications for many criminal justice career areas. It offers information on internships, graduate school, law school, resumé writing and interviewing techniques (Cincinnati, OH: Anderson Publishing Co., 1990).

Careers in the Criminal Justice System. Describes personnel practices, recruiting, educational requirements, and job descriptions of positions in the areas of corrections, police, and courts. (Washington, DC: United States Department of Justice, Law Enforcement Assistance Administration, National Institute of Law Enforcement and Criminal Justice, 1975).

Careers in Law Enforcement. Briefly describes several entry-level positions available in police agencies at the state and local level, i.e., criminal investigator, crime prevention officer, training officer, communications officer, jail officer, bailiff, and police agent. (Washington, DC: United States Department of Justice, NCJRS, 1977).

Careers in Law Enforcement. Lists employment opportunities at the federal level is also available. Law enforcement employment opportunities are listed for the Department of Defense, Department of the Interior, Department of Justice, Department of the Treasury, General Services Administration, and United States Postal Service. Addresses for each department and the agencies within are provided. (Washington, DC: Office of Criminal Justice Education and Training, Law Enforcement Assistance Administration).

Chronicle Guidance Publications:

> Correctional Officers. Brief 467.
> Criminologists. Brief 456.
> Psychologists. Brief 144.
> School Counselors. Brief 145.
> School Social Workers. Brief 432.
> Social Workers. Brief 84.
> Sociologists. Brief 316.
> Chronicle Occupational Brief and Reprint List. Over 500 briefs and over 100 reprints. Free upon request.

(Moravia, NY: Chronicle Guidance Publications).

Concise Handbook of Occupations. Joan Costello and Rita P. Wolfson. Offers detailed information on most occupations. (Chicago, IL: J.G. Ferguson Publishing Company, 1971).

Criminal Justice Careers Guidebook. Provides background on the development and structure of the criminal justice system in the U.S., and describes criminal justice jobs, requirements, and employment opportunities at the federal, state, and local levels. A cooperative publication of the Departments of Labor and Justice. (Washington, DC: U.S. Department of Labor, 1982-date).

Current Career and Occupational Literature 1984. Leonard H. Goodman. Renowned as a bibliographic key to significant material published on vocational opportunities and counseling, the all new 1984 volume of Current Career and Occupational Literature indexes a wide selection of inexpensive pamphlets, books, and periodicals published by commercial publishers, professional associations, and government agencies, all providing critical information on jobs in over 700 contemporary occupations. Teachers, career counselors, librarians, and parents use Current. (Bronx, NY: H.W. Wilson Co., 1984).

The Encyclopedia of Vocational Guidance. William E. Hopke (ed.) Designed to help individuals make an assessment of occupational opportunities and demands. Virtually all fields and individual vocations are addressed. (Chicago: J.G. Ferguson Publishing Company, 1975).

Federal Employment Information Directory. National employment listing service for the criminal justice system. Offers information on entrance requirements, application procedures, salary levels, and job descriptions for all Federal agencies. (Huntsville, TX: National Employment Listing Service, 1978-date).

Good Works: A Guide to Social Change. Ralph Nader. Provides details on 275 citizen groups for people interested in voluntary or paid employment. (Washington, DC: Center for Responsive Law, 1980).

Jobs for Justice. (Concordville, PA).

National Employment Listing Service (NELS) Bulletin. A monthly publication which lists currently available job opportunities in law enforcement. Areas represented are academia, courts, corrections, human services, and private security. (Huntsville, TX: Texas Criminal Justice Center, Sam Houston State University).

Occupational Outlook Handbook. Describes the nature of occupations, places of employment, training qualifications and advancement, employment outlook, earnings and working conditions, and additional sources of information for nearly every field of employment and type of work. Annual. (Washington, DC: Bureau of Labor Statistics Division of Occupational Outlook).

In addition to the above guides, the following sources will also be helpful.

Pathway to Your Future. Kenneth R. Adler. Details elements of a job resume, preparation of a resume, and letters of application. (Arlington, MA: Bellman Publishing Company, 1971).

VGM Career Books:

Opportunities in Law Enforcement and Criminal Justice. James Stinchomb.

Opportunities in State and Local Government Careers. Neale Baxter.

Opportunities in Federal Government Careers. Neale Baxter. (Lincolnwood, IL: National Textbook Company).

Why and How To Prepare An Effective Job Resume. Juvenal L. Angel. Describes the various steps a job seeker must take in order to prepare an effective resume. (New York: World Trade Academy Press, Inc., 1972).

Bibliographies

Bibliographies are compilations of sources relating to a particular subject. Bibliographies provide readers with additional sources of information on a topic, and also acquaint the researcher with major authors in the field. Most textbooks, articles, encyclopedias, etc., will contain bibliographies. These can be a very good source for further exploration but are often overlooked by students in their search for information. Because of the vast amount of literature pertaining to criminal justice, there have been many bibliographies compiled that have attempted to organize and categorize the literature. These do provide very valuable tools for the criminal justice student. The most important bibliography is *Bibliographies in Criminal Justice*.

The National Criminal Justice Reference Service (NCJRS) offers custom and prepackaged topical searches and bibliographies. Other major sources of bibliographies are *Bibliographical Index,* published by the H.W. Wilson Company, *The American Correctional Association* for correctional related bibliographies, *Criminological Bibliographies* published by Greenwood Press. Also be sure to check *The Subject Guide to Books in Print.*

Abstracts on Evaluative Research. Weiss, C.H., J.A. Weiss, P.C. Kleinman and S.T. Hillsman. (Washington, DC: National Criminal Justice Reference Service Microfiche Program, 1975).

Abuse of Women: Legislation, Reporting, and Prevention. Joseph J. Costa. (Lexington, MA: Lexington Books, 1983).

The Administration of Justice in the Courts: A Selected Annotated Bibliography. Fannie J. Klein. (New York: Oceana, 1976).

After the Fact: The Art of Historical Detection. James W. Davidson and Mark H. Lytle. 2 vols. 2nd ed. 1985 Vol. 1. Vol. 2. 1985.

Alternatives to Institutionalization: A Definitive Bibliography. James R. Brantley and Marjorie Kravitz. (Rockville, MD: National Institute of Law Enforcement and Criminal Justice, 1979).

Alternatives to Institutionalization. (Washington, DC: United States Department of Justice, Law Enforcement Assistance Administration, 1980).

Annotated Bibliography for Criminal Justice Planning. Charles R. Davoli and Patrick J. Michaud. (Tallahassee, FL: Florida Bureau of Criminal Justice Planning and Assistance, 1975).

An Annotated Bibliography of Homosexuality. Vern L. Bullough., W. Dorr Legg, and Barrett W. Elcano. (New York: Garland, 1976).

Annotated Bibliography of Research Reports and Program Studies, Volume II. New York, 1974. Volume III. 1976.

Auxiliary Police Forces; A Selected Bibliography. Anthony G. White. (Public administration series, bibliography) Vance Bibliographies. 1989.

The Battered Child: A Review of Studies and Research in the Area of Child Abuse. Emilio C. Viano. In Israel Drapkin and Emilio C. Viano, *Victimology: A New Focus, v. 4.* (Lexington, MA: Lexington Books, 1975).

Battered Wives; A Comprehensive Annotated Bibliography of Articles, Books, and Statutes in the United States of America. Nathan Aaron Rosen. (National Center for Women & Family Law, 1975).

Behavior and Psychology as Related to Law Enforcement and Criminology; A Bibliography with Abstracts. Mary E. Young and Edward J. Lehmann. (Springfield, VA: U.S. National Technical Information Service, 1975).

Bibliographies in Criminal Justice. This "bibliography of bibliographies" briefly describes over 200 published bibliographies which pertain to criminal justice. Although it is not entirely comprehensive, its coverage represents almost all specialty areas within the field. The alphabetized subject index contains entries from adult offenders to work attitudes. An alphabetized title index is also included. Students should consider this work a very important research source, and if possible, consult it early in the research process. Descriptive annotations of each bibliography provide the user with a concise summary of the contents. Therefore it is an excellent tool for scanning the majority of criminal justice bibliographies which in turn will lead the researcher to appropriate materials. (Washington, DC: United States Department of Justice. NCJRS, 1980).

The following five bibliographies are available from The Information Resource Center (IRC) of The American Society for Industrial Security (ASIS), 1655 North Fort Myer Drive, Suite 1200, Arlington, VA 22209: *Bibliography of Security Salaries and Wages.* (November 1990) *Bibliography of Sources on Software/Security Applications* (June 1990). *Bibliography on Strikes* (September 1990) *Bibliography on Security for Multi-Tenant/High-Rise Buildings* (September 1990) *Bibliography on Security Lighting* (January 1991).

A Bibliography of Correctional Law. An excellent list of correctional legal materials. The titles reflect the opinions of nearly 25 councils representing correctional agencies, who were asked to list the research tools they found most useful. (Laurel, MD: American Correctional Association, 1987).

Bibliography on Dangerousness; Its Prediction and Treatment. United Nations. Social Defence Research Institute. (Washington, DC: National Criminal Justice Reference Service Microfiche Program, 1975).

A Bibliography on General Deterrence Research. Deryck Beyleveld. (Lexington, MA: Lexington Books, 1980.)

Bibliography on Runaway Youth. U.S. Department of Health, Education and Welfare. (U.S. Children's Bureau) Office of Youth Development. (Washington, DC: National Criminal Justice Reference Service Microfiche Program, 1975).

A Bibliography of Selected RAND Publications: Criminal Justice. This bibliography serves as a complete guide to all of the research completed by the RAND Corporation. This is one of the most excellent sources of state of the art research now being conducted in the field of Criminal Justice. This bibliography is a must for any serious researcher in criminal justice. (Santa Monica, CA: RAND Corporation, 1983).

Bibliography on Shoplifting. Patronic Systems Corp. Computer Science and Environmental Technology Division. Final report. Panorama City, California, 19 Sept. 1975.

Capital Punishment in America; an Annotated Bibliography. Michael L. Radelet and Margaret Vandiver. (New York: Garland 1988).

Capital Punishment Dilemma 1950-1977: A Subject Bibliography. Charles Triche. (New York: Whitson, Inc., 1979).

Child Abuse: An Annotated Bibliography. Dorothy P. Wells. (Metuchen, NJ: Scarecrow Press, 1980).

Child Abuse and Neglect, an Annotated Bibliography. Beatrice J. Kalisch. (Westport, CT: Greenwood Press, 1978).

A Collection of Bibliographic and Research Resources. (Dobbs Ferry, NY: Oceana, 1984-date).

Correctional Law: A Bibliography of Selected Books and Articles. William C. Collins. Covers a wide range of topics and legal issues related to corrections. Categories include criminal law, access to courts and counsel access to media behavior modification, civil disabilities, and rights of ex-offenders, civil rights, litigation, cruel and unusual punishment and detainment, grievance procedures, habeas corpus, and several others. (College Park, MD: American Correctional Association, 1987).

Community Crime Prevention: An Annotated Bibliography. National Council on Crime & Delinquency Staff. (Natl. Coun. Crime, 1987).

Court Reporting; A Selected Bibliography. By Kevin E. O'Brien, Marvin Marcus and Robert J. Wheaton. (Washington, DC: National Institute of Law Enforcement and Criminal Justice, 1976).

Crime, Vol. 4. Eleanor C. Goldstein, (ed.) (Incl. 1988-1989 Supplements) (Social Issues Resource Ser.). 1990. Soc. Issues.

Crime Analysis, Selected Bibliography. M.N. Emig, R.O. Heck, and M. Kravitz (eds.). This bibliography features 50 citations clarifying the role of crime analysis and presenting operational and administrative policies. The documents cited describe its application for resource deployment, investigation, and apprehension. There are three chapters: Tactical Use, Strategic Use, and Long-Range Planning. Microfiche. (Washington, DC: National Institute of Justice/NCJRS, 1980).

Crime and Juvenile Delinquency: A Bibliographic Guide to the Basic Microform Collection. This publication represents important or significant documents held in the library of the National Council on Crime and Delinquency (NCCD), which are not likely to be widely distributed in any other fashion. This is probably the largest single collection of reports and documents available from one source. (Glen Rock, NJ: Microfilming Corporation of America, 1977).

Crime Prevention and Law Enforcement Through Community Relations; A Bibliography with Abstracts. Mary E. Young. (Springfield, Virginia, U.S. National Technical Information Service, 1981).

Crime and Punishment in America: A Historical Bibliography. (Santa Barbara, CA: ABC-Clio, 1984).

Crime and the Elderly; An Annotated Bibliography. Ron H. Aday. (Westport, CT: Greenwood Press, 1988).

Crime in the Black Community; An Exploratory Bibliography. Lenwood G. Davis. (Monticello, IL: Council of Planning Librarians, 1975).

Crime in the United States: A Selected Bibliography. Robert Goehlert. (Monticello, IL: Vance Bibliographies, 1988).

Criminal Investigation: A Selected Bibliography. Robert Goehlert. (Monticello, IL: Vance Bibliographies, 1987).

Criminal Justice Bibliography. Marvin Marcus. Lists more than 6,000 entries and at the time of its publication was one of the most comprehensive bibliographies of criminal justice, consisting primarily of books, monographs, and government documents. (Atlanta: Georgia State University, School of Urban Life, 1976).

Criminal Justice Evaluation; An Annotated Bibliography. U.S. National Institute of Law Enforcement and Criminal Justice. (Washington, DC: National Criminal Justice Reference Service, 1975).

Criminal Justice History: An International Annual. Vol. 11. Louis A. Knafla (ed.) (Chicago: Greenwood Publishing, 1990).

Criminal Justice Information Systems Selected Bibliography. C. Klein and N. Arnesen (eds.) There are 197 citations in this bibliography addressing issues, concepts, and assessments of information systems; State plans developed in compliance with Federal regulations; issues of individual rights and the Privacy Act of 1975; and security and privacy plans for information systems. Citations also cover computerized criminal histories, offender-based transaction statistics, and the Prosecutor's Management Information System (PROMIS). (Washington, DC: National Institute of Justice/NCJRS, 1980).

Criminal Justice Research in Libraries: Strategies & Resources. Marilyn Lutzker. (Westport, CT: Greenwood Press, 1986).

Criminological Bibliographies and Uniform Citations to Bibliographies, Indexes and Review Articles of the Literature of Crime Study in the U.S. Bruce L. Davis. (Westport, CT: Greenwood Press, 1978).

Criminological Research: A Selected Bibliography. (Public Administration Ser.: P 2369). (Monticello, IL: Vance Bibliographies, 1988).

Criminology and Forensic Sciences: An International Bibliography. Rudolfe vom Ende. 1950-1980. (Detroit, MI: K.G. Saur, 1981).

Criminology Index; Research and Theory in Criminology in the United States, 1945-1972. Marvin E. Wolfgang (ed.) 2 vols. (New York: Elsevier, 1975).

Decision-Making In the Criminal Justice System. Don M. Gottfredson. (New York: Plenum, 1987).

Drug Abuse Bibliography. (Troy, NY: Whitson Publishing Co., 1970-present).

Drug Use and Abuse Among U.S. Minorities; An Annotated Bibliography. Patti Iiyama, Setsuko M. Nishi, and Bruce D. Johnson. New York, Praeger, 1976.

Drugs of Addiction and Non-Addiction Their Use and Abuse; A Comprehensive Bibliography, Menditto, Joseph. 1960-1969. Troy, New York, Whitston, 1970. NALU; supp., by Jean C. Advena. *Drug Abuse Bibliography for 1970.* 1971. 197p. NALU; supp., . . . *For 1971.* 1972.; . . . *For 1973.* 1975.; supp., by Charles W. Triche and Diane S. Triche. . . . *For 1974.* 1976.

Education of Prisoners: A Selected Bibliography of Journal Articles, 1984-1987. Verna Casey. (Monticello, IL: Vance Bibliographies, 1988).

The Effectiveness of General Deterrents Against Crime: An Annotated Bibliography of Evaluative Research. Deryck Beyleveld. (Cambridge, UK: University of Cambridge Institute of Criminology, 1978).

Electronic Detention-House Arrest As a Correctional Alternative: A Selected Bibliography. Verna Casey. (Monticello, IL: Vance Bibliographies, 1988).

Ethics in Local Government: A Selected Bibliography. Council of Planning Librarians. Anthony G. White. (Monticello, IL: Vance Bibliographies, 1977).

The Etiology of Criminality: Non-behavorial Science Perspectives. James R. Brantley. A bibliography which focuses on the efforts of bibliogical and physical scientists to determine the underlying nature of criminality. Entries are representative of a biological approach to the study of criminality but are not intended to advocate biological influences at the expense of social factors. Rather they make information available on those factors which may contribute to crime but which will rarely be included in social science literature. (Washington, DC: United States Department of Justice, Law Enforcement Assistance Administration, National Institute of Law Enforcement and Criminal Justice, 1979).

Etiology and Treatment of Homosexuality: Frank Acosta. Archives of Sexual Behavior. A Review. Jan. 1975.

The Female Offender. Margery Velimesis. *Crime and Delinquency Literature,* March 1975.

The Female Offender: A Guide to Published Materials. Eugen Doleschal. 1970. NALU; supp., Bibliography; The Female Offender: 1970-1974. (Hackensack, NJ: National Council on Crime and Delinquency, Information Center, 1975).

Homicide: A Bibliography of Over 4,500 Items. Bal K. Jerath, Paul E. Larson and Jesse F. Lewis. (Augusta, GA: Pine Tree Pubns., 1982).

The Impact of Crime. John E. Conklin. (New York: Macmillan, 1975).

Index to Minorities & Criminal Justice: an index to periodical and books relating to minorities and criminal justice in the United States. Scott Christianson. cumulative ed. (Albany, NY: Center on Minorities and Criminal Justice, School of Criminal Justice, State Univ. of New York at Albany, 1981).

Indian Justice: A Research Bibliography. Council of Planning Librarians. (Monticello, IL: Vance Bibliographies, 1976).

International Bibliography & Medical Subject Index of Crime Publications. American Health Research Institute Staff. John C. Barton. (ABBE Pubs Assn., 1982).

International Terrorism: An Annotated Bibliography and Research Guide. August R. Norton and Martin H. Greenberg. (Boulder, CO: Westview Press, 1980).

Judicial Administration and the Legal Profession: A Bibliography. Fannie J. Klein. *The Administration of Justice in the Courts: A Selected Annotated Bibliography Updating and Expanding Klein, Judicial Administration. . . .* (Dobbs Ferry, NY: Oceana, 1976).

The Judiciary and The Criminal Justice System. U.S. National Criminal Justice Reference Service. A report presented as the National Conference of State Criminal Justice Planning Adminstrators, annual meeting, July 18-20, 1976. (Seattle, WA: NCJRS, 1976).

Juvenile Delinquency. (Washington, DC: U.S. National Technical Information Service, 1975).

Juvenile Delinquency; A Bibliography with Abstracts. Mary E. Young. (Springfield, VA: U.S. National Technical Information Service, 1976).

Juvenile Delinquency in the Black Community. Council of Planning Librarians. Eleanor Dorton and Lenwood G. Davis. (Monticello, IL: Vance Bibliographies, 1975).

Juvenile Diversion; A Selected Bibliography. U.S. National Institute of Law Enforcement and Criminal Justice. Kevin E. O'Brien and Marvin Marcus. (Washington, DC: National Institute of Law Enforcement and Criminal Justice, 1976).

Juvenile Gangs; A Bibliography. U.S. National Criminal Justice Reference Service. C.A. Riccio. Washington, National Criminal Justice Reference Service Microfiche Program (1975). NCJ-18039.

Law Enforcement: A Selected Bibliography, B.R. Felkenes and H.K. Becker. Contains thousands of listings which deal with the entire criminal justice system. Many of these are annotated. Books and articles are listed in alphabetical order by subject. (Metuchen, NJ: Scarecrow Press, 1977).

Law, Medicine and Health Care: A Bibliography, Dr. James T. Ziegenfuss, Jr. malpractice suits and a multiplicity of other medical and health care issues today are embroiling lawyers, health care officials and doctors. *Law, Medicine and Health Care* offers a complete listing of recent issues, their litigation and decisions both in and out of the courts. The book is divided into sections of specialty concern and each is supplemented with introductory text outlining the scope and relevance of the subject area to the overall health care field. Also provided is an essential listing of the lawyers involved in health care and medical issues throughout the 50 states. (New York: Facts on File, 1984).

LEAA and Criminal Justice Planning: A Partial Bibliography of Documents and Articles. Council of Planning Librarians. James C. Starbuck. (Monticello, IL: Vance Bibliographies, 1976).

Legal Bibliography, Current. (Cambridge, MA: Harvard Law Library).

The Library Catalogue of the Radzinowicz Library. Radzinowicz Library. Institute of Criminology, University of Cambridge, England. (Boston: G.K. Hall, 1979).

The Literature of Higher Education in Criminology and Criminal Justice: An Annotated Bibliography. Carolyn Johnson. (Chicago: Joint Commission on Criminology and Criminal Justice Education and Standards, 1979).

The Literature of Police Corruption, Volume I: A Guide to Bibliography and Theory. Anthony E. Simpson. (New York: The John Jay Press, 1980).

The Literature of Terrorism: A Selectively Annotated Bibliography. Edward F. Mickolus. "Mickolus has compiled the definitive bibliography on terrorism, superseding Augustus R. Norton's International Terrorism. Mickolus has been affiliated with the CIA for many years and knows his subject well. He provides extensive coverage . . . He has succeeded in imposing some order on the avalanche of material about terrorism. His tightly organized and well indexed bibliography is highly recommended for academic and large public libraries." (Westport, CT: Greenwood Press, 1980).

Mafia: A Selected Annotated Bibliography. Lloyd Trott. (Cambridge, U.K.: Institute of Criminology, 1977).

Memoirs of American Prisons: An Annotated Bibliography. Daniel Sunack. (Metuchen, NJ: Scarecrow Press, 1979).

Observing the Law: Applications of Field Methods to the Study of the Criminal Justice System. U.S. National Institute of Mental Health. Center for Studies of Crime and Delinquency. George J. McCall. (Washington, DC: National Institute of Mental Health, 1974).

Organized Crime: A Bibliography. Provides references of contemporary writings on the problems of organized crime. (Gaithersburg, MD: International Association of Chiefs of Police).

Physical Design and Urban Crime: A Selected Bibliography. Council of Planning Librarians. Anthony G. White. (Monticello, IL: Vance Bibliographies, 1976).

Physical and Sexual Abuse of Children: Causes and Treatment. David R. Walters. (Bloomington, IN: University Press, 1975).

Plea Bargaining; A Selected Bibliography. U.S. National Institute of Law Enforcement and Criminal Justice. Marvin Marcus and Robert J. Wheaton. (Washington, DC: National Institute of Law Enforcement and Criminal Justice, 1976).

Police Administration: A Bibliography. Cites over 1,100 references dealing with various aspects of police administration. Entries are listed alphabetically and categories include accountability and discretion, corruption, detectives and criminal investigation, discipline, firearms and deadly force, job hazards, pedestrian and bicycle safety, police management, police chiefs and relationships with local government, productivity and performance measurement, recruitment, team policing, traffic and highway safety, and traffic engineering. An author index and an appendix listing publishers and periodicals is included. (Evanston, IL: Northwestern University, The Traffic Institute.)

Police Bibliography. Jack E. Whitehouse. This comprehensive 500 page bibliography organizes approximately 17,000 published and unpublished criminal justice information sources into 1,100 subject headings with page references and cross indexes. (New York: AMS Press, Inc., 1980).

Police Consolidation; A Selected Bibliography. U.S. National Institute of Law Enforcement and Criminal Justice. Marvin Marcus, James M. Edgar, Robert J. Wheaton and Robert C. Hicox. (Washington, DC: National Institute of Law Enforcement and Criminal Justice, 1976).

Police; Operations, Management, Training, Behavior, Equipment: A Bibliography with Abstracts (1964-March 1976). Mary E. Young. (Springfield, VA: U.S. Technical Information Service, 1976).

Police Personnel Mangement, Selected References. Annotates over 700 citations from the following subject areas: personnel management, professionalization, employee and groups, labor relations, uniforms, problems on the job, and attitudes of police and public. (Evanston, IL: Northwestern University, The Traffic Institute, 1972).

Police Research and Evaluation Studies: A Working Bibliography. Council of Planning Librarians. Police Study Group, Northwestern University. (Monticello, IL: Council of Planning Librarians, 1976).

Police Science, 1964-1984, a Selected Annotated Bibliography. William G. Bailey. (New York: Garland Publishing, 1986).

Police Training. Highlights the literature on police training. The citations relate specifically to general issues of police training, descriptions of training programs in the United States and abroad, descriptions of modular programs, laboratory training, use of closed-circuit televisions, and evaluation of specific programs. The documents listed are part of the NCJRS collection and may be borrowed through interlibrary loan, or if available on microfiche, obtained free of charge. (Washington, DC: United States Department of Justice, NCJRS, 1980). (For more information on other government documents and NCJRS, please see Chapter 10, "Government Documents").

Police Unionization and Bargaining. Selected references concerning police unions, associations, and collective bargaining and public employee labor-management relations. (Evanston, IL: Northwestern University, The Traffic Institute, 1976).

The Policewoman in American Society: A Preliminary Survey. Council of Planning Librarians. Lenwood G. Davis. Monticello, Illinois, May 1976.

Political Violence in the United States, 1875-1974. Jarol B. Manheim and Melanie Wallace. (New York: Stein, 1975).

The Politics of Rape; the Victim's Perspective. Barbara Fagan, Diana E.H. Russell and Margaret Stone. Bibliography. (New York: Stein, 1975).

A Preliminary Bibliography of Modern Criminal Law & Criminology. xxi, Repr. of 1909 ed. lib. bdg. (Littleton, CO: Rothman, 1981).

Poly Drug Use, Annotated Bibliography. U.S. National Institute on Drug Abuse. National Clearinghouse for Drug Abuse Information. (Washington, DC: National Institute on Drug Abuse, 1975).

Prescriptive Packages. (Washington, DC: U.S. National Institute of Law Enforcement and Criminal Justice, 1975).

Problems and Planning of Police Community-Relationships; a Selected Research Bibliography. Council of Planning Librarians. Prakash C. Sharma. (Monticello, IL: National Council of Planning Librarians, 1975).

Protecting the President: A Selective Bibliography. Larry D. Benson. (Monticello, IL: Vance Bibliograhies, 1989).

Protest and Crime in China: a Bibliography of Secret Associations, Popular Uprisings, Peasant Rebellions. Ssu-yu Teng. (New York: Garland, 1981).

Public Perceptions of Criminal Behavior: A Review of the Literature. Graeme Newman and Carol Trilling. *Criminal Justice and Behavior,* Sept. 1975.

Publications of the National Institute of Law Enforcement and Criminal Justice. A comprehensive bibliography designed to provide criminal justice professionals with access to research sponsored and published by National Institute during 1968 and 1977. (Washington, DC: United States Department of Justice, Law Enforcement Assistance Administration, National Institute of Law Enforcement and Criminal Justice, 1979).

Publication of the National Institute of Law Enforcement and Criminal Justice, 1979 Supplement. This is a supplement to the 1978 catalog and contains citations for documents published in 1978 for distribution through the GPO or the NCJRS. Subject and title indexes are included. Part I lists citations in NCJ number order and abstracts are provided for each publication. Part II contains listings and annotations of several specialized types of publications such as program models, national evaluation programs, exemplary projects, and selected bibliographies. (Washington, DC: National Institute of Law Enforcement and Criminal Justice, 1979). (See Chapter 10, "Government Documents," under exemplary projects.)

Readers Advisory Service: Selected Topics. Leonard Cohan (ed.) (Broadway, NY: Science Associates International, 1983).

Recidivism: A Selected Bibliography. Robert J. Trudel, Marvin Marcus, and Robert J. Wheaton. (Washington, DC: National Institute of Law Enforcement and Criminal Justice, 1976).

Rehabilitation of Criminals: A Bibliography. Mary Vance. (Monticello, IL: Vance Bibliographies, 1988).

Rehabilitation And The Retarded Offender. Philip L. Browning. Springfield, Illinois, Thomas, 1976.

Research Approaches In Illicit Drug Use; S.W. Sadava. A critical Review. Genetic psychology monographs, Feb. 1975.

Restitution As A Criminal Sentence: Anthony G. White. (Monticello, IL: Council of Planning Librarians, 1977).

A Selected Bibliography of Security and Loss Prevention. An excellent bibliography of private security topics. Included are books, publications of the government, learned societies, and other organizations. Films and audio-visual materials, periodicals, related bibliographies and selected publishers. (Washington, DC: American Society for Industrial Security, 1981).

Security and Privacy of Criminal Justice Information: A Bibliography. This 126-page bibliography presents a wide range of literature dealing with various aspects of the subject of privacy and the security of information obtained on individuals who have had contact with the criminal justice system. (Sacramento, CA: Search Group, Inc., 1979).

A Selective Bibliography on the Economic Costs of Crime. Michael J. Slinger. (Monticello, IL: Vance Bibliographies, 1989).

Selected Literature on Evaluation. (Washington, DC: U.S. National Institute of Law Enforcement and Criminal Justice, 1975).

Skid Row. J. Randolph Gregson II. Council of Planning Librarians. A wide-ranging bibliography. (Monticello, IL: Vance Bibliographies, 1977).

Social Class and Delinquency. C.A. Riccio. U.S. National Criminal Justice Reference Service. (Washington, DC: National Criminal Justice Reference Service Microfiche Program, 1975).

Soviet Prisons and Concentration Camps, Zorin Libushe. An annotated bibliography, 1917-1980. (Newtonville, MA: Oriental Research Partners, 1980). (Russian bibliography Ser., no. 3).

The Spatial Analysis of Crime. Perry O. Hansen and Barbara Boehnke. (Monticello, IL: Council of Planning Librarians, 1976).

Spies and All That . . . Intelligence Agencies and Operations: A Bibliography. Ronald M. DeVore. Cites over 500 monographs, reports, and articles pertaining to espionage, intelligence operations, and related subjects. (Los Angeles: Center for the Study of Armament and Disarmament, California State University, 1977).

Strategic Criminal Justice Planning. Daniel Glaser. U.S. National Institute of Mental Health. Center for Studies in Crime and Delinquency. (Washington, DC: Center for Studies in Crime and Delinquency, 1975).

Stress Factors As Identified By Research In Prisons. Debra M. Hydge and Donald Conway. (Monticello, IL: CPL Bibliographies, 1977).

Suicide; A Guide to Information Sources. David Lester and Betty H. Sell (eds.) (Detroit: Gale Research Co., 1980).

Suicides In The Black Community; A Preliminary Survey. Edward E. Hubbard. (Monticello, IL: Council of Planning Librarians, 1975).

Toward the Prevention of Rape: A Partially Annotated Bibliography. Marcia J. Walker. University of Alabama. Department of Psychology. Center for Correctional Psychology. (Washington, DC: National Criminal Justice Reference Service Microfiche Program, 1975).

The Urban Police: An Annotated Bibliography of the Social Science Literature, 1960-1973. Donald Ostrom. (Monticello, IL: Council of Planning Librarians, 1975).

Victim Compensation and Offender Restitution; A Selected Bibliography. Marvin Marcus, Robert J. Trudel and Robert J. Wheaton. (Washington, DC: U.S. National Criminal Justice Reference Service, 1975).

Violence in the Family: An Annotated Bibliography. Elizabeth Jane Kemmer. Comprises 1,055 citations to English-language publications, 1960-82. Main-entry arrangement; subject and author indexes. (New York: Garland, 1984).

Violence at Home. Mary H. Lystad. A review of the literature. *American Journal of Orthopsychiatry,* Apr. 1975.

Violence in the Home: Interdisciplinary Perspectives. Mary H. Lystad. (New York: Brunner-Mazel, 1986).

NCJRS Custom Searches

A cost-effective way to gather complete, targeted information. Following a search strategy based on your needs, the NCJRS reference specialist conducts a data base search to identify citations that address your area of interest.

• Requester-specified areas and parameters ensure pertinent information.

• Contains up to 400 citations including bibliographic information and summaries of content.

Custom searches are available in hard copy as printouts or on diskette to use on an IBM-compatible personal computer.

The printouts include all abstracts and bibliographic citations in the NCJRS document data base on your topic. You will also receive instructions for interpreting.

NCJRS data base searches do it for you. They provide overviews of published and unpublished materials on the topic of your choice compiled from the NCJRS data base of almost 100,000 documents, the largest criminal justice data base in the world.

Highly trained information specialists with direct online access to NCJRS's unparalleled criminal justice data base can help answer your information requests in all these areas:

• AIDS	• Juvenile justice
• Corrections	• Law enforcement
• Courts	• Victims
• Criminology	• Drugs
• Crime prevention	• Statistics

Three types of NCJRS data base searches are available: topical searches, topical bibliographies, and custom searches. Call NCJRS to find out if the information you want has already been compiled, or to request a custom search to meet your specific needs.

Topical Searches

Topical searches and topical bibliographies are prepackaged computerized searches of the NCJRS data base— the largest criminal justice data base in the world. They provide reviews of published and unpublished materials on many criminal justice topics. Each includes bibliographic information, availability, and a summary. Attached is a listing of all topical searches and topical bibliographies available from NCJRS. Topical searches contain 30 citations and are updated every 6 months. Topical bibliographies contain up to 200 citations with subject and title indexes and are updated annually. The following is a list of prepared topical searches and their topical search (TS) numbers, available from NCJRS. They can be ordered from:

NCJRS
Attention: AIO
Department F
Box 6000
Rockville, MD 20850.

AIDS

AIDS and Intravenous Drug Use
(TS011647)

AIDS and Its Impact on Corrections
(TS011644)

AIDS and Youth
(TS011651)

Corrections

Adult Female Offender
(TS010103)

Capital Punishment
(TS010302)

Corrections Construction
(TS011105)

Corrections Personnel: Selection, Training, and Performance
(TS011650)

Crowding in Prisons and Jails
(TS011108)

Educational and Vocational Programs in Corrections
(TS011649)

Effectiveness of Probation and Parole
(TS011643)

Electronic Monitoring/House Arrest
(TS011662)

Health Care in Correctional Facilities
(TS011106)

Inmates and Their Families
(TS011103)

Intermediate Supervision
(TS011107)

Mentally Disordered/Disabled Offenders
(TS011627)

Prison Violence
(TS011633)

Private Sector Involvement in Corrections
(TS011628)

Recidivism
(TS011615)

Restitution
(TS011104)

Sex Offenses and Offenders
(TS011617)

Siting of New Correctional Facilities
(TS011663)

Courts

Court Management
(TS011638)

Exclusionary Rule
(TS011620)

Habeas Corpus
(TS011646)

Insanity Defense
(TS010301)

Jury Selection
(TS011634)

Plea Bargaining
(TS011635)

Pretrial Issues
(TS011639)

Sentencing Disparity
(TS010303)

Sentencing Guidelines
(TS011654)

Crime Prevention

Community Crime Prevention Programs
(TS010201)

Computer Crime and Security
(TS011602)

Crime Prevention Through Environmental
Design
(TS011210)

Crimes Against Business
(TS011205)

Employee Theft
(TS011203)

Evaluation of Crime Prevention Programs
(TS011201)

Private Police/Security Police
(TS011202)

Shoplifting
(TS011209)

Drugs

Asset Seizure and Forfeiture
(TS011652)

Cocaine and Crack
(TS011648)

Drinking and Driving
(TS011619)

Drug Abuse Programs for Offenders
(TS011636)

Drug Law Enforcement
(TS011642)

Drug Legalization
(TS011653)

Drug Testing
(TS011640)

Drug Trafficking
(TS011641)

Drugs in the Workplace
(TS011645)

Juvenile Justice

Child Abuse and Its Link to Delinquency
(TS021516)

Child Sexual Exploitation
(TS021507)

Deinstitutionalization of Status Offenders
(TS021525)

Juvenile Classification
(TS021523)

Juvenile Correctional Education
(TS021524)

Juvenile Detention
(TS021511)

Juvenile Diversion Programs
(TS021513)

Juvenile Gangs
(TS020501)

Juvenile Probation Services
(TS021518)

Juvenile Restitution
(TS021508)

Juvenile Substance Abuse
(TS021504)

Juveniles in Adult Jails and Lockups
(TS021503)

Learning Disabled Youth
(TS021510)

Runaway, Missing, and Abducted Children
(TS021519)

Violence and Vandalism in Schools
(TS020503)

Serious Juvenile Offenders
(TS020502)

Waiver of Juvenile Court Jurisdiction
(TS020515)

Law Enforcement

Campus Crime and Police
(TS011204)

Crime Analysis
(TS011610)

Criminal Investigations Management
(TS011637)

DNA (Deoxyribonucleic Acid)
(TS011655)

Foot Patrol
(TS011625)

Gun Control
(TS011621)

Minorities in Law Enforcement
(TS011660)

Motorcycle Gangs and Drugs
(TS011656)

One Officer Patrols and Take Home Vehicles
(TS011657)

Organized Crime
(TS011603)

Police Discipline and Internal Affairs
(TS011605)

Police Dogs
(TS011624)

Police Firearms Training
(TS011613)

Police/Fire Consolidation
(TS011611)

Police Manpower Allocations and Work
Scheduling
(TS011601)

Police Mobile Computers and Terminals
(TS011658)

Police Personnel Selection
(TS010601)

Police Physical Fitness
(TS011606)

Police Pistols and Revolvers
(TS011659)

Police Promotion/Career Development
(TS011604)

Police Pursuit Driving
(TS011614)

Police Stress and Stress Management
(TS011612)

Police Use of Force
(TS010604)

Search and Seizure
(TS011661)

Serial/Mass Murder
(TS011664)

SWAT and Hostage Negotiations
(TS010603)

Terrorism
(TS011631)

Statistics

Prison Population Projections
(TS030001)

Victims

Battered Women
(TS011213)

Bias-Related Violence
(TS040011)

Child Sexual Abuse: Programs and Curricula
(TS040008)

Crime and the Elderly
(TS010202)

Crime Victims and the Criminal Justice
System
(TS040003)

Effects of Violence on Children
(TS040014)

Homicide Victims
(TS040016)

Marital Rape and Date/Acquaintance Rape
(TS040010)

Police Response to Domestic Violence
(TS011622)

Psychological Effect of Victimization
(TS040004)

Rape
(TS040005)

Sexual Assault
(TS040013)

Survivors of Sexual Abuse
(TS040015)

Treatment of the Child Victim
(TS040002)

Victim Compensation
(TS040006)

Victims of Child Sexual Abuse
(TS040007)

Victims Rights
(TS040012)

Victim Services
(TS040001)

Topical Bibliographies

AIDS

AIDS and the Criminal Justice System
(TB010618)

Corrections

Adult Female Offender
(TB010103)

Capital Punishment
(TB010302)

Crowding in Prisons and Jails
(TB010101)

Prison Industry
(TB010102)

Prison Violence
(TB010610)

Trends and Alternatives to Incarceration
(TB010619)

Courts

Alternative Dispute Resolution
(TB050001)

Insanity Defense/Competency to Stand Trial
(TB010301)

Pretrial Issues and Practices
(TB010613)

Sentencing Disparity
(TB010303)

Crime Prevention

Community Crime Prevention Programs
(TB010201)

Private Security: Training and Management
(TB010608)

Drugs

Drugs and Crime
(TB010614)

Drug Law Enforcement
(TB010616)

Drugs in the Workplace
(TB010620)

Drug Treatment in Criminal Justice Settings
(TB010623)

Juvenile Justice

Alternatives to Institutionalization
(TB020506)

Juvenile Illegal Drug Use
(TB020505)

Juvenile Gangs
(TB020501)

Juvenile Restitution
(TB020508)

Publications of the Office of Juvenile Justice
and Delinquency Prevention
(TB020510)

Sexual Exploitation of Children
(TB020504)

Violence and Vandalism in Schools
(TB020503)

Serious Juvenile Offender
(TB020502)

Law Enforcement

Arson
(TB010203)

Community Policing
(TB010621)

Computer Crime
(TB010622)

Police Personnel Selection
(TB010601)

Police Use of Force
(TB010604)

SWAT and Hostage Negotiations
(TB010603)

Terrorism
(TB010611)

White Collar Crime
(TB010615)

Statistics

Publications of the Bureau of Justice
Statistics, 1971-1984
(TB030012)

Victims

Crime and the Elderly
(TB010202)

Crime Victims and the Criminal Justice
System
(TB040002)

Criminal Justice Response to Child Abuse
(TB040005)

Victim Compensation
(TB040003)

Victim Services
(TB040001)

Victims: Family Violence
(TB040004)

8

Directories

Directories are a major source of information for students. Directories are usually in book form, although now many directories also exist on computer disks and in computer data bases. Directories most often will cover a specific subject matter and are listed in alphabetical order.

There are thousands of directories that provide you with direct information to addresses, phone numbers, and other data that you may be seeking.

The following is a listing of directories related to Criminal Justice.

Access: A Resource Guide to Legal Automation. Rees W. Morrison. Publishers of legal publications, consultants, seminars, bulletin board systems, and user groups involved in legal automation. (Chicago: American Bar Association, 1991).

American Combatting Terrorism (ACT) Directory. Approximately 450 corporate, government, nonprofit, media, and individual members maintaining specialized information on policies and activities concerning terrorism. (Telluride, CO: American Combatting Terrorism).

American Association of Motor Vehicle Administrators (AAMVA)—Membership Directory. (Arlington, VA: American Association of Motor Vehicle Administrators).

Almanac of American Politics. Governors, United States senators, and members of the United States House of Representatives, voting records of major issues, ratings from liberal and conservative organizations; election votes; campaign contributions by source. Annual. (Washington, DC: Government Research Corporation).

American Academy of Forensic Sciences—Membership Directory. 3,400 persons qualified in forensic sciences, including law, pathology, biology, odontology, physical anthropology, psychiatry, questioned documents, criminalistics, engineering, and toxicology. Entries include: Name, office address and phone, highest degree held, professional title, type of certification. Annual, May. (Colorado Springs, CO: American Academy of Forensic Sciences).

American Academy of Matrimonial Lawyers—List of Certified Fellows. 1,200 lawyers. Annual, July. Members only. (Chicago, IL: American Academy of Matrimonial Lawyers).

The American Bar. 85,000 lawyers in the United States and over 100 countries abroad; selected state administrative offices. Entries include: Firm name, type of practice, address, phone, names, educational data, and memberships of partners and associates. State offices' listings include address, phone. Annual, March. (Sacramento, CA: Forster-Long, Inc. 95827).

American Correctional Association Directory; State and Federal Correctional Institutions. (College Park, MD: American Correctional Association).

American Lawyers Quarterly. Semiannual, January and July; monthly supplements. (Cleveland, OH: The American Lawyers Company).

American Polygraph Association—Membership Directory. Approximately 2,000 member individuals and companies involved in the polygraph field. (Chattanooga, TN: American Polygraph Association).

American Society of Criminology—Membership Directory. 2,200 professional and academic criminologists, students of criminology in accredited universities, psychiatrists, psychologists, and sociologists. Reported as annual; previous edition 1987; latest edition May 1990. (Columbus, OH: American Society of Criminology).

Annual Directory of Sheriffs of the United States. (Washington, DC: National Sheriffs' Association).

Arms Control Fact Book. Dennis Menos. (Jefferson, NC: McFarland & Company, Inc., 1985).

Arson Control: Directory. (New York: Insurance Committee for Arson Control).

Arson Resource Directory. National, state, and local anti-arson organizations and agencies, and information, research, courses, and training programs; publishers and producers of periodicals, audiovisuals. (Emmittsburg, MD: United States Fire Administration).

Association of Federal Investigators Directory. (Washington, DC: Association of Federal Investigators).

Association of Former Agents of the U.S. Secret Service— Membership Directory. (Alexandria, VA: Association of Former Agents of the U.S. Secret Service).

Associated Public-Safety Communications Officers— Membership Directory. Approximately 7,500 member firemen, police officers, civil defense and governmental officials involved with public safety communications, as well as manufacturers and distributors of communications products. Annual, January. (New Smyrna Beach, FL: Associated Public-Safety Communications Officers).

Attorneys and Agents Registered to Practice before the United States Patent and Trademark Office. About 11,000 attorneys and agents. (Washington, DC: U.S. Patent and Trademark Office, Department of Commerce).

Barron's Guide to Law Schools. About 200 American Bar Association approved law schools. List of top law schools ranked for prestige is also included. Irregular; previous edition 1988; latest edition 1990. (Hauppauge, NY: Barron's Educational Series, Inc.).

Barter Associations, Organizations & Businesses in the United States [Microfiche]. Association or company name and address. Triennial; latest edition 1990. (Houston, TX: Barter Publishing).

Battered Women's Directory. Over 2,000 shelters, hotlines, YWCA's, hospitals, mental health services, legal services agencies, and other organizations and agencies which offer services to abused wives in the United States and abroad; includes listings of many educational resources on the problem. Irregular; latest edition spring 1989. (Richmond, IN: Terry Mehlman).

Books on Trial: A Survey of Recent Cases. List of about 25 attorneys who have participated in school district book censorship litigation. Irregular; latest edition October 1987; update, September 1989. Main content is narrative reporting of litigation surrounding attempts at censorship of published works, with recent decisions indexed by state and banned books indexed by author. [Censorship litigation]. (New York: National Coalition Against Censorship).

Campus Gang Rape: Party Games? List of about 10 publishers and organizations concerned with gang rape on college campuses. Published November 1985. (Washington, DC: Project on the Status and Education of Women, Association of American Colleges).

Child Abuse and Neglect and Family Violence Audiovisual Catalog. Distributors of over 300 films, videotapes, filmstrips with tapes, slides with tapes, and audiovisual packages about child abuse and neglect and family violence. Irregular; latest edition February 1990; new edition expected 1991. (Washington, DC: Clearinghouse on Family Violence Information).

Child Find Photo Directory of Missing Children. Nearly 570 children reported as missing in the United States. Name, photograph, description, date of birth, date abducted or became missing, location where last seen. Irregular; latest edition spring 1988; new edition expected fall 1990. (New Paltz, NY: Child Find of America).

Congressional Yellow Book Directory. Supplies up-to-date information on members of Congress, their key aides and nearly 300 Congressional committees and subcommittees. (Washington, DC: The Washington Monitor, Inc.).

Contacts [Alcoholic beverage control]. Government officials in 19 control state jurisdictions concerned with alcoholic beverage regulation; association members in the alcoholic beverage industries; trade associations. Annual; updated quarterly. (Alexandria, VA: National Alcoholic Beverage Control Association).

Correctional and Juvenile Justice Training Directory of North America. A profile of training in each state and province as well as federal agencies in both the U.S. and Canada. Identifies training standards and oversight commissions, the number of full and part-time trainers in each jurisdiction and minimum annual training requirements. (Richmond, KY: Eastern Kentucky University).

Crime Stoppers International—Directory. Over 700 agencies and organizations which sponsor "Crime Stoppers," "Crime Solvers," or similarly named programs offering anonymity and rewards for information leading to the solution of serious crimes; coverage also includes Canada, Puerto Rico, Guam, Great Britain, Australia, the Netherlands, and West Africa. (Albuquerque, NM: Crime Stoppers International).

Criminal Justice Agencies. Names and addresses of all state and local criminal justice agencies in the U.S. (Washington, DC: National Criminal Justice Information and Statistics Service).

Criminal Justice Education Directory. Presents the number and types of institutions granting degrees in the field of criminal justice. Annual. (Gaithersburg, MD: International Association of Chiefs of Police).

Criminal Justice Information Exchange Directory. About 90 libraries that are members of the Criminal Justice Information Exchange Group; coverage includes Canada. (Rockville, MD: National Institute of Justice).

Detective Agencies. 4,300. Nationwide. (Omaha, NE: American Business Directories, Inc., American Business Information, Inc.).

Directory of All Prison and Jail Addresses and Zip Codes. Over 7,000 federal, state, county, and municipal correctional institutions and facilities; also includes drug and alcohol centers. (Boynton Beach, FL: Fraud and Theft Information Bureau).

Directory of Automated Criminal Justice Information Systems. Over 100 computerized information systems serving over 600 police, courts, and correction agencies in federal, state, and local governments. (Washington, DC: Bureau of Justice Statistics).

Directory of Bar Associations. More than 55 state bar associations, 40 local bar associations represented in the American Bar Association House of Delegates, 170 other local associations with at least 300 members, and other associations represented in the ABA House of Delegates. (Chicago, IL: Division of Bar Services, American Bar Association).

Directory of British Associations. Addresses and brief descriptions of both profit and nonprofit associations in England. (Croydon, UK: C.B.D. Research Ltd., 1980).

Directory of California Justice Agencies Serving Juveniles and Adults. (Sacramento, CA: Department of Youth Authority).

Directory of Community Crime Prevention Programs, National and State Levels. James Lockard, et al. Designed to facilitate dissemination of knowledge and ideas about crime prevention. (Washington, DC: United States Department of Justice, 1978).

Directory of Computer Software Applications: Urban and Regional Technology & Development. (Springfield, VA: National Technical Information Service, Commerce Department).

Directory of Computerized Data Files. (Springfield, VA: National Technical Information Service, Commerce Department).

Directory of Corporate Counsel. Kenneth B. Miller (managing ed.) For some 4,000 companies, subsidiaries, and divisions, provides details on: law department's address, telephone number, and staffing; area of legal specialization; biographical data on individuals listed. Companies include publicly held corporations, privately owned businesses, utilities, insurance companies, and financial institutions. Annual. (New York: Prentice-Hall Law & Business, Inc., 1991).

Directory of Correctional Service Agencies. Lists voluntary, professional and private non-profit agencies in the United States that provide assistance, and job training to inmates, ex-prisoners, probationers, parolees, and their families. (Philadelphia, PA: Correctional Services Federation, USA).

Directory of Courses in the Field of Code Administration and Enforcement. A listing for those seeking information about colleges and universities that offer courses and curricula in Fire Science, Architectural Design, Building Construction Technology, and related disciplines. (McLean, VA: National Academy of Code Administration, 1979).

Directory of Criminal Justice Information Sources. Lists 149 agencies throughout the country which provide sources of information in the criminal justice area. Notations are also made as to whether special services such as computerized literature search services, interlibrary loan programs, reference services, and technical assistance to criminal justice professionals are provided. An index by criminal justice specialty is provided. (Washington, DC: NCJRS, 1982).

Directory of Criminal Justice Issues in the States. List of nearly 50 state Statistical Analysis Centers sponsoring about 420 criminal justice policy research studies. Annual, August. (Washington, DC: Criminal Justice Statistics Association).

Directory of Surveillance Equipment Supplies. Over 90 companies that supply equipment and services in the field of electronic surveillance. (Libertyville, IL: Full Disclosure).

Directory of European Associations. Address and description of each association. Annual. (Detroit: Gale Research Co.).

Directory of Expert Witnesses in Technology. Suspended indefinitely, last published in 1985. (Woodbridge, CT: Research Publications).

Directory of Federal Experts in Fire Technology and Related Fields. Lists federal personnel with expertise in the field of fire safety technology. Provides addresses, telephone numbers, organizational affiliation, and fields of expertise. (Washington, DC: U.S. Fire Administration, 1979).

Directory of Government Document Collections and Librarians. (Chicago, IL: Government Documents Round Table, American Library Association).

Directory of Halfway Houses and Group Homes for Troubled Children. A national directory of alternative treatment programs for youth. (Tallahassee, FL: State of Florida Department of Health and Rehabilitation Services, Division of Youth Services).

Directory of Institutions for Mentally Disordered Offenders. Lists mental health and correctional institutions providing psychiatric care to mentally disordered adult offenders in the United States. (Rockville, MD: Center for Studies of Crime and Delinquency, 1974).

Directory of Intellectual Property Lawyers and Patent Agents. More than 7,000 patent agents, lawyers, and law firms specializing in intellectual property law, including patents, trademarks, copyrights, unfair trade, and trade secrets. (New York: Clark Boardman Company Ltd.).

Directory of International Terrorism. Surveys more than a century of revolution, terror and counter-terror. ". . . it is the Middle East . . . which remains the world's most dangerous flash point." Over 1,000 entries. (Upland, PA: DIANE Publishing Co.).

Directory of Judges with Juvenile/Family Law Jurisdiction. (Reno, NV: National Council of Juvenile and Family Court Judges).

Directory of Juvenile and Adult Corrections Departments, Institutions, Agencies and Paroling Authorities. 4,000 juvenile and adult state and federal correctional departments, institutions, agencies, paroling authorities, and military correctional facilities in the United States and Canada. (Laurel, MD: American Correctional Association).

Directory of Juvenile Detention Homes. (Dunbar, WV: National Juvenile Detention Association).

Directory of Law Enforcement and Criminal Justice Associations and Research Centers. More than 200 international, national, regional, and local organizations and associations, research centers and government agencies active in law enforcement and criminal justice within the United States. (Gaithersburg, MD: Law Enforcement Standards Laboratory, National Institute of Standards and Technology, Department of Commerce).

Directory of Law Libraries. Published for the American Association of Law Libraries . . . by the Commerce Clearing House, 1940-date. Biennial. Title varies: Law libraries in the United States and Canada, 1940-62/63. Geographical listing of law libraries in the United States, Canada, and other foreign countries that are members of the Association. Gives name, librarian, and number of volumes. Personnel index.

Directory of Law Libraries. (Chicago, IL: American Association of Law Libraries).

Directory of Law-Related Education Projects. C.A. Kelly (ed.) Lists approximately 291 educational programs which focus on the law, legal system, and the legal process. (ABA Special Committee on Youth Education for Citizenship, 1978).

Directory of Lawyer Disciplinary Agencies and Clients' Security Funds. Disciplinary agencies responsible for handling complaints against lawyers; also covers agencies responsible for handling clients' security funds. (Chicago, IL: Center for Professional Responsibility, American Bar Association).

Directory of Legal Aid and Defender Offices in the United States, 1933-. Name of issuing body varies. Title varies slightly. Gives the names and addresses of all such known organizations in the United States, Canada, the Philippine Islands, and Puerto Rico, with a brief description of the types and limitations of the services provided by each. Annual. (Washington, DC: Legal Aid & Defender Association).

Directory, Legal Aid and Defender Offices. Attorneys that provide criminal representation to persons unable to retain a private counsel. Programs for special needs and legal support services. (Washington, DC: National Legal Aid and Defender Association, 1979).

Directory of Legal Aid and Defender Services. Annual directory listing names, addresses, and telephone numbers for sources of legal assistance and defender programs in the United States. (Chicago: National Legal Aid and Defender Association).

Directory of Legal and Law Enforcement Periodicals. (New York: Facts on File).

Directory of Opportunities in International Law. Several hundred possible employers of specialists in international law, United States and foreign law firms, United Nations agencies, governmental organizations and bodies; lists of law schools which include international law in their programs. (Charlottesville, VA: John Bassett Moore Society of International Law).

Directory of Probation, Parole, and Correctional Associations. Lists probation, parole, and correctional associations in the United States. (Hackensack, NJ: National Council on Crime and Delinquency, 1973).

Directory of Published Proceedings, Series SSH-Social Sciences/Humanities. Lists conference meetings on an international basis. Arranged by dates of conference meetings, a subject and sponsoring organization index. (Harrison, NY: Interdok).

Directory of Residential Treatment Centers. An annual, nationwide directory of juvenile and adult halfway houses. Halfway houses specializing in parole, probation, alcoholism, mental health, drug addiction pre-release, and work release. (Cincinnati, OH: International Halfway House Association).

Directory of Sheriffs of the United States. Annual. (Washington, DC: National Sheriff's Association).

Directory of Social and Health Agencies of New York City. Information about public and voluntary welfare and health agencies serving New York City (New York: Columbia University Press, 1981-82).

Directory of State and Local Judges. Furnishes an alphabetized state-by-state listing of state appellate, trial, county, and local judges within four jurisdictions of 50 states and the District of Columbia. The order of jurisdiction is as follows: court of last resort, intermediate appellate court, court of general jurisdiction, and court of special/limited jurisdiction. (Reno, NV: National College of the State Judiciary, United States Department of Justice, Law Enforcement Assistance Administration, National Institute of Law Enforcement and Criminal Justice, 1976).

Directory of State Officials [Food and drug enforcement]. Officials of state health and agriculture departments, boards of pharmacy, and other state departments charged with enforcement of food, drug, device, feed, and cosmetic laws. Annual, February. (Rockville, MD: Division of Federal-State Relations, Food and Drug Administration).

Directory for Successful Publishing in Legal Periodicals. Publishers of about 450 legal journals, periodicals, and reviews; international coverage. Irregular; latest edition February 1987. (Charleston, IL: Qucoda Publishing Company).

Directory Toward Criminal Justice. A nationwide directory of organizations involved with the criminal justice system. National, voluntary, professional, nonprofit, and citizen organizations in the United States. (New York: National Council of Churches).

Directory of United States Probation and Pretrial Services Officers. Arranged by district, kind of prison, then by city. Free. Annual, September. (Washington, DC: Probation Division, Administrative Office of the U.S. Courts).

Encyclopedia of Legal Information Sources. Over 19,000 books, periodicals, newsletters, law reviews and digests, newspapers, audiovisual materials, and other publications; research centers, institutes, and clearinghouses; professional associations and societies; databases; and other organizations and sources of information on 460 legal topics. (Detroit, MI: Gale Research Inc.).

Federal Criminal Investigators Association—Directory. 5,000 special agents and criminal investigators currently employed by or retired from the United States government). (Detroit, MI: Federal Criminal Investigators Association).

Federal Funding Guide. About 220 major federal aid programs for which local, county, and state governments are eligible; nonprofit organizations are also eligible for about two-thirds of the programs. Programs are in the areas of community development, economic development, energy, housing, jobs, transportation, health, environment, emergency services, social services, senior citizens, arts, cultural activities, law enforcement, and substance abuse. (Arlington, VA: Government Information Services).

Federal Information Centers. (Washington, DC: General Services Administration).

Federal Information Sources and Systems. (Washington, DC: General Accounting Office).

Federal Job Information Centers Directory. (Washington, DC: Office of Personnel Management).

Federal Prison System Facilities. Reference guide to the institutions of the Federal Prison Service. (Washington, DC: U.S. Bureau of Prisons, 1980).

Federal Regulatory Directory. Contains each agency's history, responsibilities, powers and authorities; biographies of commissioners; a detailed organizational description; sources of further information and location of regional offices. Annual. (Washington, DC: Congressional Quarterly Inc.).

Federal Yellow Book Directory. An organizational directory of the top level employees of Federal departments and agencies. (Washington, DC: The Washington Monitor, Inc.).

FEDFIND (Information sources of U.S. government). List of nearly 140 government agencies and other publishers which are sources of the over 700 federal information publications and services described. (Springfield, VA: ICUC Press).

Fire Marshals Association of North America—Membership Directory. Over 1,200 municipal, county, state and provincial fire marshals and fire prevention bureau officials. (Washington, DC: Fire Marshals Association of North America).

Fire Protection Reference Directory. Equipment reports and addresses of all manufacturers of fire prevention materials. (Quincy, MA: National Fire Protection Association, 1982).

Fire Research Specialists. Names, addresses, and telephone numbers of specialists from the U.S. and Canada who have made significant contributions to the teaching of fire science, or have participated in fire research programs. (Quincy, MA: National Fire Protection Association, 1982).

First Amendment Lawyers Association—Directory. Approximately 125 member lawyers who support and defend cases involving the First Amendment to the U.S. Constitution. Annual. (Chicago, IL: First Amendment Lawyers Association).

Forensic Sciences Certification Program Directory of Diplomats. (Colorado Springs, CO: Forensic Sciences Foundation).

Forensic Services Directory. About 5,000 individuals willing to serve as expert witnesses or consultants during litigation; also associations, societies, and institutes with specialized information. (Lawrenceville, NJ: National Forensic Center).

Handbook of Federal Police and Investigative Agencies. Over 60 federal police and investigative agencies. (Westport, CT: Greenwood Press, Inc.).

Hazard Control Information Handbook. (International Institute of Safety & Health, 1985).

How and Where to Check Driving Records and Report Accidents. Offices responsible for maintaining driving records and offices to which truck accidents are to be reported, in all states and Puerto Rico. (Alexandria, VA: American Trucking Association).

IACP World Membership Directory. A listing of the 15,000 IACP members. Includes the mailing addresses of thousands of the world's leading police executives, from Algeria to Zaire. Annual. (Arlington, VA: International Association of Chiefs of Police).

Inside the Law Schools: A Guide by Students for Students. About 100 law schools. School address, phone; median entrance scores and grade point averages, acceptance rate, transfer rate; enrollment; percentage minority, and women students; student-faculty ratio, expenses, financial aid, library facilities; and a description of student life, faculty, curriculum, reputation, and placement success. Irregular; previous edition 1982; latest edition November 1986. (New York: Plume, 1991).

Institute of Professional Investigators—Professional Register of Members in Private Practice. Nearly 300 member investigators working in private practice worldwide. (Blackburn, UK: Institute of Professional Investigators).

International Association of Arson Investigators— Constitution and Bylaws, Membership Directory. 7,500 member arson investigators. Annual, May. (Louisville, KY: International Association of Arson Investigators).

International Association of Assessing Officers—Membership Directory. About 8,200 state and local officials concerned with valuation of property for tax purposes. Annual, December. (Chicago, IL: International Association of Assessing Officers).

International Association of Chiefs of Police—World Membership Directory. 14,200 members in command and administrative positions in federal, state, and local law enforcement and related fields; includes county police and sheriffs; international, national, and regional law enforcement agencies and related organizations. (Arlington, VA: International Association of Chiefs of Police).

International Association for Identification—Membership Directory. About 2,500 police officials, identification personnel, and others engaged in forensic identification, investigation, and scientific crime detection work. Annual, September. (Alameda, CA: International Association for Identification).

International Association of Law Libraries, Directory. A list, arranged by country, of personal and institutional members. Indexed. (Marburg, Germany: International Association of Law Libraries, 1980-date).

International Bar Association—Directory of Members. About 12,000 members of the International Bar Association. (London, UK: International Bar Association).

International Bibliography of Police. 200,000 police officers, either on active service or retired, organized to establish ties of friendship and mutual aid. (Maidstone, UK: International Police Association).

International Council of Environmental Law—Directory. About 300 individuals and organizations in the fields of environmental law, policy, and administration organized to provide professional contacts and information on environmental conservation. Semiannual. (Bonn: International Council of Environmental Law).

International Defense Directory. About 15,000 suppliers of defense and military products and services; government armed forces, police, and customs agencies worldwide concerned with defense and procurement in 170 countries. (Geneva, Switzerland: Interavia S.A.).

International Directory of Correctional Administrations. Suspended indefinitely. Last edition published in 1987. (Laurel, MD: American Correctional Association).

International Directory of Prisoner's Aid Agencies. A worldwide directory which lists voluntary agencies concerned with providing aftercare for prisoners and their families. (Milwaukee, WI: International Prisoner's Aid Association).

International Exchange of Information on Current Criminological Research Projects in Member States of the Council of Europe. Centers conducting about 200 research projects in criminology. English, French. (Strasbourg, France: Publications Section, Division of Crime Problems, Directorate of Legal Affairs, Council of Europe).

International Institute of Comparative Linguistic Law— Membership Directory. Approximately 550 law and linguistics professors, jurists, lawyers, judges, linguists, and social scientists worldwide, whose objective is to promote the study of comparative linguistic law. French, English. Annual. Members only. (Montreal, Canada: International Institute of Comparative Law).

International Law and Practice—Directory. Over 12,800 member lawyers, judges, law students, and law clerks; international coverage. Annual. (Washington, DC: International Law and Practice, American Bar Association).

International Legal Aid Association. Directory of legal aid and advice facilities available throughout the world. (London and New York: International Legal Aid Association).

International Legal Aid Directory. List of organizations able to give preliminary legal advice. (London, UK: International Bar Association).

The International List. Attorney firms with collection practices, address, phone. (Williston Park, NY: The International Lawyers Company, Inc.).

International Narcotic Enforcement Officers Association— Directory. 7,500. Name affiliation, address, phone. Annual, January. Members only. (Albany, NY: International Narcotic Enforcement Officers Association).

International Security Directory. Defense and security companies in the United Kingdom and selected other nations; ministries of defense, police, and fire in each country profiled; defense/security trade associations worldwide. 1990. (Henley-on-Thames, UK: R. Hazell and Company).

International Society of Family Law—Directory of Members. Approximately 650 member individuals and organizations. Irregular. (Cambridge, UK: International Society of Family Law).

The Jeffers Directory of Law Enforcement Officers. The most comprehensive listings available for all law enforcement agencies in the United States. More than 17,000 agencies. A total of more than 38,000 names of law enforcement officers. (New York: Pace Publications).

Justice—Directory of Services. Nearly 2,000 police commissions, Royal Canadian Mounted Police divisions, human rights commissions, legal aid services, police colleges, courts, parole boards, correctional authorities, prisoner aid agencies, and professional and voluntary associations. (Ottawa, ON: Canadian Criminal Justice Association).

Juvenile and Adult Correctional Departments, Institutions, Agencies and Paroling Authorities, United States and Canada. Addresses, names of officials, and brief descriptions, with some statistical summaries. (College Park, MD: American Correctional Association, 1980).

The Law Schools of the World. Henry P. Tseng. A specialized directory listing all existing law schools on a worldwide basis. (Buffalo, NY: William S. Hein, 1977).

Law and Legal Information Directory. Approximately 29,000 national and international organizations, bar associations, federal courts, federal regulatory agencies, law schools, firms and organizations offering continuing legal education, paralegal education, sources of scholarships and grants, awards and prizes, special libraries, information systems and services, research centers, publishers of legal periodicals, books, and audiovisual materials, speaker bureaus, lawyer referral services, legal aid offices, public defender offices, legislature manuals and registers, corporation departments of states, and law enforcement agencies. Biennial, October of even years. (Detroit, MI: Gale Research Inc.).

Law and Order Magazine—Police Equipment Buyer's Guide Issue. List of manufacturers, dealers, and distributor products, and services for police departments. Entries include: Company name, address, phone, product codes, code showing what manufacturer or dealer. Annual, January. (Wilmette, IL: Hendon, Inc.).

Law Books and Serials in Print. List of publishers and producers of over 50,000 legal reference publications, periodicals, software, online databases, microforms, audio cassettes, and video cassettes. Base edition, annual, February; quarterly cumulative supplements. (New York: Bowker Legal Reference Publishing).

Law Books in Print. Approximately 900 publishers of law books in English; international coverage. Each volume of the six-volume set includes the publisher directory. Triennial; latest edition spring 1990. (Dobbs Ferry, NY: Glanville Publishers, Inc.).

Law & Business Directory of Corporate Counsel. About 5,000 corporations in the United States with in-house corporate counsel staff. Includes parent companies and subsidiaries of industrial firms, utilities, financial institutions, insurance companies, and service firms. Annual, April. (Englewood Cliffs, NJ: Prentice-Hall Law & Business).

Law Directory [Solicitors in Ireland]. About 4,200 member solicitors, court officials, members of the Honourable Society of Kings Inns, circuit barristers, notaries public, and relevant government departments in Ireland; also includes solicitors in Northern Ireland. Annual, February. (Dublin, Ireland: Incorporated Law Society of Ireland).

Law Databases. (ASLIB) Over 35 publicly available online data bases in the field of law, including full-text, referral, and indexing databases; international coverage. (London, UK: Association for Information Management).

Law Enforcement Technology—Directory Section. Each issue includes a directory of manufacturers and suppliers of one type of law enforcement equipment such as computers, weapons, training, Special Weapons and Tactics (SWAT) radio and communications equipment. Updated ten times during the year. (Woodbury, NY: PTN Publishing).

Law Librarian's New Product Directory. Publishers and suppliers of recently introduced law books and services. (New York: Garland Publishing, Inc.).

Law Office Economics & Management—Directory Computers for the Law Office Issue. List of about 100 suppliers of data processing equipment and software. Companies listed have more than one installation in a law firm or, if only one installation, have additional experience with law firm management needs. Annual, August; updated in quarterly issues. (Deerfield, IL: Callaghan & Company).

Law Office Guide in Computers Directory. Discontinued. (San Francisco, CA: L.O.G.I.C. Publishing Company).

Law Services Information Book—Canadian Edition. (Newtown, PA: Law School Admission Council/Law School Admission Services).

Lawyers' and Creditors' Service Directory. About 30,000 individuals and agencies involved in forwarding and collecting, including sheriffs, process servers, private investigators, repossessors, skip tracers, court reporters, litigation attorneys, courthouses, chambers of commerce, and collection agencies. Entries include: Firm name, address, phone. (Eau Claire, WI: Professional Education Systems, Inc.).

Lawyers' List. About 2,500 lawyers in practice in the United States. Annual, April. (Easton, MD: Commercial Publishing Company).

Lawyer's PC—Legal Software Directory Issue. List of more than 500 programs from 200 publishers designed for personal computer use by lawyers, including timekeeping and billing software. Annual, November. (Lexington, SC: Shepard's/McGraw-Hill, Inc.).

Lawyer's Register International by Specialties and Fields of Law Including a Directory of Corporate Counsel. Corporate legal staffs worldwide; legal firms; independent practicing attorneys each identified as specialist in one or more fields of law. Irregular. 1990. (Solon, OH: Lawyer's Register Publishing Company).

Legal Information Alert. List of publishers of books, databases, CD-ROM products, loose-leaf services, periodicals and journals, audio and videotapes, and microfilm covering the legal profession and reviewed or discussed in the issue. Ten issues per year. (Chicago, IL: Alert Publications, Inc.).

Legal Looseleafs in Print. (Infosources Publishing, 140 Norma Rd., Teaneck, NJ 07666). Over 320 publishers offering more than 3,500 loose-leaf legal information services; includes many publications of interest outside the legal field. Annual, March.

Legal Newsletters in Print. Over 1,750 legal, law related, legislative, or regulatory related newsletters, bulletins, and reporting services published in the United States. Annual, January. (Teaneck, NJ: Infosources Publishing).

Legal Software Directory [Law office software]. Over 300 suppliers of computer software used in legal offices. Annual, March. (Chicago, IL: American Bar Association).

Martindale-Hubbell Law Directory. An annual publication since 1968, this directory provides biographical sketches of United States lawyers. (New York: Martindale-Hubbell).

Municipal Yearbook. Listing of city officials, including police and fire chiefs. Information on salaries of municipal employees and separate mini-directories for various city-run agencies nationwide. Annual. (Chicago, IL: International City Manager's Association).

National Council of Juvenile Court Judges Directory. (Reno, NV: National Council of Juvenile and Family Court Judges).

National Directory of Black Law Firms. Discontinued. (Philadelphia, PA: Drexel University).

National Directory of Child Abuse Services and Information. Child abuse services and sources of information are listed. Governmental and private agencies, volunteer and professional organizations, and specific intervention programs such as referrals, prevention programs, hotlines. (Chicago, IL: National Committee for Prevention of Child Abuse).

National Directory of Correctional Education—State Administrators. Names and addresses of all state administrators in various agencies dealing with correctional education and social rehabilitation. (Vienna, IL: Correctional Education Association).

National Directory of Corrections Construction. Over 265 correctional institutions constructed since 1978. (Rockville, MD: National Criminal Justice Reference Service).

National Directory of Drug Abuse and Alcoholism Treatment Programs. "A compilation of over 9,000 federal, state and local agencies responsible for the administration of alcoholism or drug abuse services." (Rockville, MD: U.S. Department of Health, Education and Welfare, 1979).

National Directory of Hotlines, Switchboard and Related Services. Lists a variety of telephone intervention services, such as crisis hotlines and suicide prevention, free clinics for medical problems and legal assistance, and runaway programs and services. (Minneapolis, MN: National Crisis Intervention Clearinghouse).

National Directory of Law Enforcement Administrators and Correctional Institutions. Police departments and police chiefs in cities and towns with populations of more than 1,600; sheriffs and criminal prosecutors in all counties in the nation; state law enforcement and criminal investigation agencies; federal criminal investigation and related agencies; state and federal correctional institutions; campus law enforcement departments. (Stevens Point, WI: National Police Chiefs and Sheriffs Information Bureau).

National Directory of Prosecuting Attorneys. (Alexandria, VA: National District Attorneys' Association).

National Directory of Runaway Centers. Runaway programs in the United States which accept runaways and provide them with housing in group homes or other residential facilities. (Washington, DC: National Youth Alternative Project).

National Directory of Runaway Programs. I.G. Miles, et al. 212 runaway centers located throughout the country. Also included are reviews of literature on the runaway problem, sociological explanations, responses of the government to the problem, and motives of the runaway. (Washington, DC: National Youth Work Alliance, 1983).

National Directory of State Agencies. Nancy Wright, comp. All state agencies organized by state and by function in 93 categories. Includes U.S. possessions. (Washington, DC: Information Resources Press, 1977).

National District Attorneys Association Roster of Officers and Board of Directors. (Chicago, IL: National District Attorneys' Association).

National Ex-Offender Assistance Directory. 1,000 programs assisting the ex-offender with such problems as employment, housing and vocational training. (Lincoln, NE: CONTACT Inc., 1979-80).

National Jail and Adult Detention Directory. 3,000 facilities in the United States. Such vital data as operations budgets and capital expenditures, program and staff information, population size and movement, and more are included in an easy-to-use format. (Laurel, MD: American Correctional Association).

National Legal Aid and Defender Association. (Chicago, IL: American Bar Association).

National Prison Directory, Organizational Profiles of Prison Reform Groups in the United States. M.A. Bundy and K.R. Harmon (eds). 1975, with 1976 and 1977 supplements. Describes the goals, objectives, programs, and activities of several hundred prisons. (College Park, MD: Urban Information Interpreters, Inc.).

Nationwide Patrol [Missing children/crime watch]. About 25 individuals concerned with locating missing children through search and rescue patrols. (Wilkes-Barre, PA: Nationwide Patrol, Inc.).

National Victims Resource Directory. The National Victims Resource Center, sponsored by the Office for Victims of Crime, has developed the National Victims Resource Directory, a central listing and service description of organizations that provide national victims information. This directory is a useful resource for making referrals and exchanging information between organizations. It also provides information about who is conducting research, tracking legislation, offering training programs, or providing victim assistance, counseling, and crisis intervention. In addition, the directory includes a summary appendix for quick reference.

Police Chiefs' Directory. Names and addresses of members of the International Association of Chiefs of Police. (Published annually with the October issue of Police Chief magazine).

Police Employment Guide. Offers information about employment with police departments in all major U.S. cities. Entrance requirements, salaries, fringe benefits, training and application procedures are presented. Includes descriptions of all special programs. (Huntsville, TX: Sam Houston State University).

Probation and Parole Directory. Parole, pardon, and release boards; names, addresses, and telephone numbers of key personnel; data on probation and parole programs and services; statistics on budgets, beginning salaries, personnel, and client caseloads. (Laurel, MD: American Correctional Association).

Research Centers Directory. A guide to university-related and other non-profit research organizations and support services. (Detroit, MI: Gale Research Inc.).

Risk Retention Group Directory and Guide. (Pasadena, CA: Risk Retention Reporter).

Schroggins National Law Enforcement Directory. Annual. (Montrose, CA).

Sheriffs of the United States. State by state listing of all law enforcement administrators and county sheriffs. Annual. (Washington, DC: National Sheriffs Association).

State Drug Resources: A National Directory. A comprehensive guide to state agencies that address drug abuse concerns. Organized by state, the directory provides agency names, addresses, and telephone numbers. Also included are listings of federal agencies that people frequently contact for information, as well as several quick references of state agencies by area of specialty. The directory was compiled by the Drugs & Crime Data Center & Clearinghouse, which is a national resource center for drug-related crime information. (Rockville, MD: National Criminal Justice Reference Service, 1990).

A Survey of Educational Offerings in the Forensic Sciences. K. Field, B. Lipskin and M. Reich. A guide to courses and degree programs in the forensic sciences offered at American colleges and universities. (Washington, DC: Law Enforcement Assistance Administration, 1977).

U.S. Court Directory. A comprehensive listing of each and every court in the U.S., and includes: the Court of Appeals, Claims Court, Special Courts, Sentencing Commission, and U.S. District Courts and much more. (Upland, PA: Diane Publishing Co.).

United States Government Manual. The official handbook of the federal government; provides comprehensive information on the agencies of the legislative, judicial, and executive branches. Also includes information on boards, committees, commissions and international organizations in which the U.S. participates. Annual. (Washington, DC: Office of the Federal Register).

Washington Information Directory. Names, addresses and all pertinent information on federal and non-governmental organizations located in Washington, DC. Annual. (Washington, DC: Congressional Quarterly).

Who's Who in American Law Enforcement. (Miami, FL: American Law Enforcement Officers Association).

World Association of Detectives, Membership Directory. (San Mateo, CA: World Association of Detectives).

A World Directory of Criminological Institutes. 300 agencies in 53 countries. Gives addresses, names of staff members, projects and publications. (Rome: United Nations Social Defense Research Institute, 1978).

World Legal Directory, Second edition. (Washington, CA: World Peace Through Law Center, 1974).

World List of Forensic Science Labs. (North Yorkshire, UK: Forensic Science Society, 1984). Lists addresses, directors and fields of investigation for each lab.

Computerized Literature Searches

The prolific publication of books, journals, special reports, newspapers, and other written material since World War II has created an information explosion, resulting in the need for more sophisticated information handling systems. Computers are increasingly being used to meet this need. Most libraries have access to various computerized information systems. These information systems are composed of categorized units of information relating to a given field or body of knowledge known as data bases. Data bases are created when indexing and abstracting services put their data into machine-readable form. Computerized information systems vendors then make the data bases available to subscribers (e.g., libraries, industries, agencies) so they, in turn, can provide this information to researchers. Computerized literature searches are also referred to by librarians, information scientists, and researchers as "online information" searches. This denotes a comprehensive service in terms of the type and quantity of information available for searching. Access to many millions of records (books, directories, periodicals, reports, bibliographies, dissertations, newspaper features, patents, grants, reviews, legislative reports, conference proceedings, descriptions of documents, current research, pamphlets, and manuals) is possible via computer or online searches. Online searches fulfill many needs, including information gathering for reports, keeping up with new developments in a particular field, determining important issues, reviewing literature, avoiding duplication of research, obtaining background material on court cases, and gathering resources for writing papers, theses, and dissertations.

When an online search is initiated, a computer scans the appropriate data base and provides the researcher with a printed, annotated bibliography of citations on the topic. The larger the data base, the more citations a researcher is likely to get from a computerized search. Students contemplating a computerized literature search will need to contact the reference librarian for assistance. The librarian will work with the student to develop a strategy for searching the data bases appropriate for the topic and will then perform the online search.

Some libraries absorb part of the cost for computerized literature searches but the user will also be responsible for a portion of the fee. Charges vary according to the complexity of the search and the number of data bases scanned, and actual "online" computer usage time.

Literature searches through computers are faster and more efficient than manual searches of printed indexes, especially when research involves searching several subject concepts. Computerized searches make available far more documents and information sources than most libraries and other information centers could possibly purchase in printed form. The computerized data bases are also generally more current than printed abstracts and indexes and the researcher has access to the latest information before it appears in published form.

Obtaining information on topics related to criminal justice need not be limited to searching printed indexes and other reference books. In fact, many departments and professors now expect or require students, particularly master's and doctoral candidates, to use computer literature search services. It should be kept in mind, however, that computerized searches are most suitable for certain types of questions. Research questions with one or more of the following characteristics are most effectively searched with the computer:

1. Questions involving two or more distinct but interrelated topics, such as the relationship of school failure to drug abuse or the difference, if any, in the self-concept of male

inmates of prisons that allow conjugal visits as opposed to male inmates of prisons that do not allow such visits. The first example has two topics—school failure and drug abuse. The second example involves three topics—self-concept, male inmates, and conjugal visits.

2. Questions with topics so new that only limited material on the subject is available in printed form.

3. Topics that involve searching several different topic headings, or topics that could be stated in so many ways that searching printed indexes and abstracts would be extremely time-consuming. For example, a researcher studying an aspect of organized crime might be referred to several different subject headings in addition to organized crime, such as mafia, mob, mobsters, gangsters, professional criminals, subversive activities, underworld, syndicate, and even "family" before an adequate manual search of the literature could be accomplished.

Questions should be relatively specific, so as to result in a fairly small number of citations. A broad or vaguely stated question is likely to result in hundreds of citations, many of which may not directly refer to the problem the researcher is trying to solve. He will be inundated with references and will waste time reviewing them in order to determine which ones have a bearing on the study. This negates the time-saving benefit of using the computer in the first place. A librarian or other information specialist will usually ask the user to describe his or her topic in as detailed a fashion as possible. Key words likely to appear in titles or abstracts of articles on the subject being researched are noted. The online search will involve the use of these key words to obtain bibliographic citations from one or more data bases. The result is a printout and annotation of citations, usually more comprehensive than can be obtained by manual searching, in a fraction of the time.

The major source available for information on computerized on-line data bases is *The Directory of On-Line Data Bases*, published by Cuadra/Elsevier. This publication is updated on a regular basis and, at the time of this writing, listed and annotated 4,400 different computer data bases. *The Directory of On-Line Data Bases* classifies data bases in the following way:

Reference Databases: These point the user to other sources of information.

Bibliographic: Contains citations, abstracts, and indexes of journals, books, and other printed information.

Referral: Contains references to non-published information.

Source Database: These contain original source data.

Numeric: Contains survey data.

Textual-Numeric: Typically would contain data bases with dictionary on handbook-type data most often in chemical or physical fields.

Full-Text: Contains the complete text of newspaper articles, court decisions, or newsletters.

Software: Contains computer programs that can be downloaded with local computers.

Images: Contains photographs, maps, trademark logos, and other graphics.

Another major source available for information on computerized on-line data bases is *Access to Access: An On-Line User's Guide to IAC Databases*, 3rd edition. This guide is the definitive source to searching all of Information Access Company's (IAC's) data bases on BRS, Dialog, and LEXIS/NEXIS.

Another major source available for information on computerized data bases is:

American Psychological Association
P.O. Box 0107
Washington, D.C. 20055-0107

There are many data bases now in existence and more are being developed all the time. There are several on-line information system vendors. Perhaps the pioneer is Lockheed's DIALOG Information Retrieval Services, which supplies over 200 data bases. Database vendors include:

- *Dialog Information Services, Inc.*
  Marketing Development
  3460 Hillview Avenue
  Palo Alto, Calif. 94304
  1-800-3-Dialog

- *BRS Information Technologies*
  A division of Maxwell On-Line 1990 Database Catalog
  BRS 8000 Westpark Dr.
  McLean, VA 22101
  (703) 442-3870

- *The User's Directory of Computer Network*
  1990 Ed. Tracy L. LaQuey
  University of Texas System
  Austin, Texas

ORBIT, by System Development Corporation (SDC), Bibliographic Retrieval Services, Inc., Informatics, Inc., LEXIS and NEXIS from Mead and New York Times Information Bank. Most university and large public libraries subscribe to at least one of these systems. For those who may wish to contact these information systems directly, addresses and telephone numbers follow:

- System Development Corporation Search Center (SDC)
  2500 Colorado Avenue
  Santa Monica, California 90406
  (800) 421-7229

- Informatics, Inc.
  Database Services
  6011 Executive Blvd.
  Rockville, Maryland 20805
  (301) 770-3000

- New York Times Information Bank
  Mt. Pleasant Office Park
  1719 Route 10
  Parsippany, New Jersey 07054
  (201) 539-5850

- Bibliographic Retrieval Services, Inc. (BRS)
  Corporation Park
  Building 702
  Scotia, New York 12302
  (518) 374-5011

- Mead Data Central, Inc.
  9443 Springboro Pike
  Miamisburg, OH 45342
  (513) 865-1245

Various data bases of potential interest to criminal justice students are alphabetically presented and briefly described below. These are offered as suggestions—your library may have additional data bases from which to choose.

ABA Standards for Criminal Justice
Contains full text of guidelines and standards relating to the administration and development of the criminal justice system.

Academic American Encyclopedia
Contains full text of the 20-volume *Academic American Encyclopedia*.

Academic Index
Provides coverage of about 950 scholarly and general interest journals and periodicals most commonly referenced in undergraduate research.

ACAnet
Contains a variety of information services for corrections professionals. Contains citations, with abstracts, to approximately 500 reports on such topics as security and safety, prison crowding, personnel management, facility design, litigation, and juvenile corrections.

AgeLine
Contains about 28,000 citations, with abstracts, to the literature on social gerontology, with a focus on the social, psychological, and economic aspects of middle age and aging.

AIDS Abstracts from the Bureau of Hygiene and Tropical Diseases
Contains about 11,000 citations, most with abstracts to the worldwide literature on Acquired Immune Deficiency Syndrome (AIDS).

AIDS In Focus
Contains about 14,000 citations to the worldwide literature on Acquired Immune Deficiency Syndrome.

AIDS Knowledge Base
Contains full text of approximately 200 textbook chapters on Acquired Immune Deficiency Syndrome (AIDS) written by physicians and other health professionals associated with San Francisco General Hospital, the University of California, and affiliated institutions.

AIDS Newsletter
Contains full text of the *Aids Newsletter*, covering news and developments about Acquired Immune Deficiency Syndrome (AIDS) and HIV infection.

AIDS Policy and Law
Contains information on the legal and practical implications of Acquired Immune Deficiency Syndrome (AIDS) on government and private employment policies.

AIDSDrugs
Contains references to over 80 drugs being tested for use against Acquired Immune Deficiency Syndrome (AIDS), AIDS-Related Complex (ARC), and related opportunistic diseases.

AIDSScan
Contains about 600 annotated citations to the holdings of Ryerson Polytechnical Institute on treating and interacting with Acquired Immune Deficiency Syndrome (AIDS) patients.

AIDSLine
Contains about 30,000 citations, with some abstracts, to the worldwide literature on Acquired Immune Deficiency Syndrome (AIDS) from CANCERLIT literature on AIDS and HEALTH PLANNING AND ADMINISTRATION.

AIDSQuest Online
AIDS Periodical Information Database (AIDS P/D). Contains full text of over 8000 articles and book reviews on AIDS. AIDS Research Database (AIDS R/D). Contains descriptions of computer-readable and online AIDS data bases. Includes contact addresses and telephone numbers.

AIDSTrials
Contains references to about 230 clinical trials of agents being evaluated for use against Acquired Immune Deficiency Syndrome (AIDS), AIDS-Related Complex (ARC), and related opportunistic diseases.

Alcohol & Drugs in the Workplace Costs, Controls, and Controversies
Contains full text of *Alcohol & Drugs in the Workplace: Costs, Controls, and Controversies*, a special report covering drug and alcohol abuse in the workplace and strategies for employer and union responses.

Alcohol and Alcohol Problems Science Database
Contains about 65,000 citations with abstracts to the worldwide literature on alcoholism research.

Alcohol Information for Clinicians and Educators Database
Contains about 9000 citations to literature on alcohol use and abuse with an emphasis on educational materials for health-care providers.

Alcohol Outlook
Contains full text of *Alcohol Outlook*, a monthly newsletter providing data and analyses of alcohol fuels, with an emphasis on oxygenated fuels.

A.L.E.R.T. (A Law Enforcement RoundTable)
Contains news and information of interest to people in law enforcement and related occupations at the local, state, and federal levels.

America: History & Life
Contains citations, with abstracts, to literature on all aspects of U.S. and Canadian history, culture, and current affairs from prehistoric times to the present. 1964-present.

Applied Social Sciences Index & Abstracts
Contains over 68,000 citations, with abstracts, to the worldwide literature on the applied social sciences. 1987-present.

ASI (American Statistics Index)
Contains citations, with abstracts, to publications containing social, economic, demographic, and other statistical data collected and analyzed by the U.S. government. 1973-present.

Cendata
Contains full text and selected numeric data from Census Bureau economic and demographic reports, press releases, and new product announcements.

Child Abuse and Neglect
Contains citations, with abstracts, to materials concerned with the definition, identification, prevention, and treatment of child abuse and neglect.

CINCH-The Australian Criminology Database
Contains over 20,000 citations, with some abstracts, to the Australian literature on criminology.

CIS (CIS/Index)
Contains citations, with abstracts, to publications produced by the committees and subcommittees of the U.S. Congress.

CJ Data
Provides information on over 750 computer-readable data collections in the criminal justice area held by the ICPSR and other organizations in the U.S.

Combined Health Information Database
Contains 12 files of information on health education and health promotion topics for health professionals and the general public.

Computer ASAP
January 1988-present, with some titles going back to 1883. The most comprehensive full-text data base covering the computer industry, providing a wide range of information on computers, electronics, and telecommunications.

Computer Database
1983-present. Provides wide range of information on computers, telecommunications, and electronics. Contains abstracts to articles from 140 business and technical periodicals.

Computer Data Security
Contains full text of *Computer Data Security*, a special report covering security measures for prevention of computer theft, fraud, and viruses.

Computer Fraud & Security Bulletin
Contains full text of *Computer Fraud & Security Bulletin*, a monthly newsletter on computer crime and on prevention methods and related commercial products.

Conference Papers Index
Contains over 1.3 million citations to scientific and technical papers presented at regional, national, and international meetings.

Congressional Record Abstracts
Contains about 340,000 citations, with abstracts, to the Congressional Record (House, Senate, Extension of Remarks, and Digest sections), the official diary of the activities of the U.S. Congress.

Consumer Drug Information
Contains information on over 270 generic drugs that comprise over 4000 brand name products marketed in the U.S.

Crime Bytes
Contains public safety and crime information of interest to the general public and the law enforcement community. Includes hints on child safety, crime prevention, earthquake safety, "wanted" notices, and changes and additions to national and local laws.

Criminal Justice Abstracts
Contains full text of *Criminal Justice Abstracts* (Formerly *Crime and Delinquency Literature*), providing citations, with abstracts, to journals, reports, books, dissertations, magazines, and newspapers covering criminal justice topics. 1968-present.

Criminal Justice Periodical Index
Contains about 160,000 citations to articles in 120 magazines, journals, newsletters, and law reporting publications on the administration of justice and law enforcement. 1975-present.

Current Contents Search
Contains approximately 400,000 citations to articles listed in the tables of contents of about 6500 leading journals in the sciences, social sciences, and arts and humanities.

D&B Dun's Electronic Yellow Pages
Contains mailing and descriptive information on approximately 8 million U.S. businesses.

DHSS-Data
Contains approximately 57,000 citations, some with abstracts, to the holdings of the DHSS library, covering health services, social welfare, and social security. 1983-present.

Dialog Information Retrieval Service (Dialog)
Dialog now offers more than 290 data bases (soon to be 320). Dialog contains in excess of 80 million records, including references and abstracts of published literature, statistical tables, full text of selected articles, and directory, business, and financial data.

Dissertation Abstracts Online
Contains citations, with abstracts (since 1980), to dissertations accepted for doctoral degrees by accredited North American educational institutions and over 200 institutions elsewhere. 1861-present.

DrugDex
Contains about 775 monographs on drugs. Drug Consults. Contains over 5300 patient-based consultations, case histories, and documents from drug information centers and clinical pharmacology services worldwide.

DrugInfo and Alcohol Use and Abuse
Contains two files on alcohol and drug use/abuse that may be searched together or separately.
• *DrugInfo.* 1968-present. Contains citations, with abstracts, to monographs, journals, conference papers, instructional guides, and other materials that deal with the educational, sociological, medical, and psychological aspects of alcohol use and drug use/abuse.
• *Alcohol Use and Abuse.* 1968-1978. Contains citations to journal articles, reprints, unpublished papers, and chapters from books that deal with research in the area of chemical dependency.

Drug Information Fulltext
Contains full text of about 1400 monographs covering about 50,000 commercially available and experimental drugs in the U.S.

DrugLine
Contains over 4000 questions received and answers prepared by clinical pharmacologists and pharmacists at the Drug Information Center. 1982-present.

DrugNews
Contains citations, with evaluative summaries, to the worldwide literature on current developments in therapeutic drug research, including reports of significant adverse side effects. 1983-present.

Educational Resources Information Center (ERIC)
Objective is to make current educational research and related information available swiftly and inexpensively to researchers, teachers, administrators, and other users. Coverage is not limited to information on criminal justice education, but encompasses references on law enforcement issues, technologies, strategies, and legal responsibilities.

Embase
Contains over 4 million citations, with abstracts, from over 3500 journals representing the worldwide biomedical literature on human medicine and areas of biological sciences related to human medicine.

Emforensic
Contains citations, with abstracts, to the worldwide literature on forensic sciences. 1974-present.

Encyclopedia of Associations
Provides information on over 75,000 worldwide, non-profit associations and organizations.

The Expert and the Law
Contains full text of *The Expert and the Law*, a newsletter covering the application of scientific, medical, and technical knowledge to litigation. 1981-present.

Expernet
Contains references to about 1300 physicians who can serve as expert witnesses or consultants to attorneys.

Facts on File World News Digest
Contains full text of *Facts on File World News Digest*, providing news summaries of current events worldwide. 1975-present.

Family Resources
Provides more than 120,000 citations to journal and non-journal literature and references to other resources on marriage and family. 1970-present.

FBI's 10 Most Wanted Fugitives
Contains descriptions of individuals named on the FBI's 10 Most Wanted Fugitives List.

Federal Index
Contains citations to the *Congressional Record, Federal Register, and Weekly Compilation of Presidential Documents.* 1976-1980.

Federal Procurement Data Center
The Federal Procurement Data Center maintains a computerized compendium of the Federal Acquisition Regulations (FAR), many agencies' supplements to the FAR, and information relative to all active (and some completed) government contracts. It is accessible through DIALOG.

Federal Register Abstracts
Contains abstracts of each document published in the *Federal Register* (FR). 1986-present.

Federal Research In Progress
Contains descriptions of and references to research in progress and recently completed research sponsored primarily by federal government agencies.

Federal Sentencing Law and Practice
Contains full text of *Federal Sentencing Law and Practice*, including supplemental appendices. 1989-present.

Forensic Science Database
Contains about 35,000 citations, with some abstracts, to the worldwide literature on forensic sciences. 1976-present.

Forensic Services Directory
Contains the names of thousands of scientific, medical, and technical experts available to serve as expert trial witnesses or consultants to attorneys, corporations, and the government.

Foundation Directory
Contains descriptions of over 26,000 currently active grantmaking foundations.

Foundation Grants Index and Grants Database
Includes currently available grants and grant programs offered by federal, state, and local governments, commercial organizations, associations, and private foundations.

General Accounting Office Documents Retrieval System (GAODOCS)
GAODOCS contains experts from GAO reports and is searchable by subject, GAO division, and report name or number.

General Services Administration Consolidated List
The GSA Consolidated List is a computerized list of suspended and debarred bidders.

GPO Monthly Catalog
Contains approximately 305,000 citations to the publications of U.S. government agencies, including the U.S. Congress. 1976-present.

GPO Publications Reference File
Contains citations to about 21,000 public documents published by the executive, judicial, and legislative branches of the U.S. federal government and currently sold by the Superintendent of Documents. 1971-present.

Grants
Contains references to grants offered by federal, state, and local governments; commercial organizations; associations; and private foundations.

Handsnet
Contains news and information on hunger, health care, housing, legal aid, and other poverty-related issues. 1987-present.

Historical Abstracts
Contains citations, with abstracts, of the worldwide literature from approximately 2000 journals and since 1980, books and dissertations on political, diplomatic, economic, social, cultural, and intellectual history and related areas of the social sciences and humanities. 1973-present.

House Member Information Network (MIN)
MIN is a group of on-line information-retrieval systems, which include the following: government statistics; the substance and present status of bills and resolutions; floor amendments; floor proceedings; pre-award grants; post-award grants; and available contracts and awarded contracts, listing every civilian contract of $10,000 or more and every defense contract of $25,000 entered into by the federal government over the last four quarters. MIN also provides full text of the Congressional Record since the 99th Congress.

Industry Data Sources
1979-present. Provides access to sources of marketing, financial, and statistical data on 65 major industries, both American and foreign.

Information and Technology Transfer Database
Contains over 3 million citations, with some abstracts, to materials covering a wide variety of subjects; energy, law enforcement and justice, waste management, fiber optics and lasers, transportation, medicine, health, earth sciences, construction, civil engineering, and agriculture. 1892-present.

The Information Bank Abstracts
Contains abstracts of all news and editorial matter from the final Late Edition of *The New York Times* newspaper, the Eastern Edition of *The Wall Street Journal* newspaper, and selected material from approximately 40 other sources published in the U.S., Canada, and Europe.

Judicial Conduct Reporter
Contains full text of *Judicial Conduct Reporter*, a quarterly publication covering commentary and analysis of matters relating to judicial conduct. 1979-present.

JURIS (Justice Retrieval and Inquiry System)
Contains a family of files providing full text of U.S. federal court decisions, statutes, regulations, treaties, and other primary and secondary legal materials.

Labor and Employment Law in Review
Contains full text of articles summarizing developments in labor and employment law.

Labor Law I
Contains about 242,000 citations, with summaries, indexing, and other locator information, to federal and state court decisions, administrative agency rulings, and labor arbitration decisions published in 7 BNA printed information services.

Labor Law II
Contains about 3300 citations, with summaries, indexing, and other locator information, to federal and state court decisions, administrative agency rulings, and labor arbitration decisions published in seven BNA printed information services.

Law Enforcement and Criminal Justice Information Database
Contains citations, with some abstracts, to the literature on law enforcement and criminal justice. 1954-present.

Legal Resource Index
Contains over 325,000 citations to legal and law-related periodical literature. 1980-present.

LEXIS Federal Sentencing Library
Contains sentencing-related decisions from the Supreme Court since 1970, the Court of Appeals since 1789, and the District Courts since 1789.

LEXIS Public Health and Welfare Library
Contains selected social security case decisions from the Supreme Court, Courts of Appeals, District Courts, Claims Court, Bankruptcy Courts, and the Federal Tax Courts since 1790, *United States Code Service* Titles 26, 28, 29, 30, 42, and 45, sections of the Code of Federal Regulations related to the Social Security Administration, and Social Security Rulings since 1966.

National Newspaper Index
Contains citations to articles, news reports, editorials, letters to the editor, obituaries, product evaluation, biographical pieces, poetry, recipes, columns, cartoons, illustrations, and reviews from *The Christian Science Monitor, Lost Angeles Times, The New York Times, The Wall Street Journal, The Washington Post.* 1970-present.

NCJRS (National Criminal Justice Reference Service)
Contains over 92,000 citations, with abstracts, to both print and non-print information on all aspects of law enforcement, crime prevention and security, criminal justice, and juvenile justice. 1972-present.

The National Law Journal
1983-present. Contains full text of *The National Law Journal,* a weekly newspaper for the legal profession.

The National Report on Substance Abuse
Contains full text of *The National Report on Substance Abuse,* a newsletter on corporate policies toward drug abuse in the workplace. 1987-present.

National Texts and Periodicals (NTP)
NTP consists of selected articles from over 200 law reviews and bar journals.

New York Times Index
This source is published semimonthly. It is an index giving exact reference to date, page, and column where articles will be found. It contains cross references to names and related topics and answers questions without having to reread the article.

Newssearch
Contains citations to the current month's magazine, journal, and newspaper literature.

Newswire ASAP
Kyodo's, July 1987-present, PR Newswire, January 1985-present and Reuters June 1987-present. Database offering the complete text and comprehensive subject indexing of news from Kyodo's Japan Economic Newswire, PR Newswire, and Reuters Financial Report.

NEXIS
NEXIS is a full-text data base consisting of general news, business and financial information from more than 150 newspapers, magazines, wire services, etc. Magazine data dates from January 1975; newspaper data dates from January 1977.

NTIS (National Technical Information Service)
Contains about 1.4 million citations, most with abstracts, to unrestricted technical reports from U.S. and non-U.S. government-sponsored research, development, and engineering analysis. 1964-present.

On-Line Retrieval of Bibliographic Information, Timeshared (ORBIT)
ORBIT is an on-line, interactive retrieval system designed and implemented by the SDC Search Service Division Development Corporation, Santa Monica, California. The ORBIT user interacts directly with the retrieval program via a terminal and telecommunication line.

Readers Guide to Periodical Literature
This source is a reference guide to articles in over 125 popular magazines. It is published semimonthly, with a cumulative index every two years. This contains a full dictionary cataloging of all articles.

Register of Stolen Art and Artifacts
Contains information on 15,000 stolen art works. 1966-present.

Scorpio
This research service contains several different data bases, to include abstracts of the following: The Library of Congress Computerized Catalog, the Bibliographic Citation File, Congressional Statute Files, and the National Referral Center Master File.

Securities Information Center (SIC)
The SIC is operated by Itel Corporation under contract with the Securities and Exchange Commission. Banks and brokerage houses that receive bad securities are required to report this information to the SIC. 1977-present.

Sentencing
Contains full text of all reported and unreported British Columbia Court of Appeals sentencing decisions, full text of selected cases throughout Canada covering the law on sentencing, and about 120,000 citations, with abstracts, to British Columbia trial-level sentencing decisions.

Social Sciences Index
Contains over 240,000 citations to articles and book reviews in about 350 English-language periodicals in the social sciences. 1983-present.

Social Scisearch
Contains over 2.2 million citations to significant articles from the 1400 most important social sciences journals worldwide and social sciences articles from 4500 journals in the natural, physical, and biomedical sciences. 1969-present.

Social Work Abstracts
Contains about 19,000 citations, with abstracts, to journal articles, doctoral dissertations, and other materials on social work and related fields.

SSIE Current Research
Contains descriptions of and references to research in progress and recently completed research sponsored primarily by federal government agencies. 1978-1982.

Sociological Abstracts
Coverage includes literature in sociology and related areas in the social and behavioral sciences from 1963-present. Abstracts included in addition to the citations. The social, political, and even economic aspects of criminal justice can be successfully searched through the *Social Scisearch and Sociological Abstracts* data bases.

Standard & Poor's (S&P)
S&P has several data bases regarding corporations. These data bases are available through DIALOG, including information on 36,000 corporations and 340,000 "key executives," with 74,000 profile biographies. S&P can provide substantial information on financial institutions, including a list of the corporate officers and directors, mailing addresses, total deposits, primary bank, and primary law firm.

Substance Abuse in the Workplace: An Employer's Prospective
Contains information on employee substance abuse in the workplace. 1987 only.

Technical Advisory Service for Attorneys
Contains references to about 14,000 individuals in a variety of occupations available to serve as expert witnesses or as consultants to attorneys.

United States Government Publications
Reports, studies, fact sheets, maps, handbooks, and conference proceedings from various government agencies as well as congressional documents from 1976 to present.

Westlaw Criminal Justice Data Base
Contains full text of articles and documents selected from a variety of law-related monographs and periodicals relating to federal criminal justice.

Westlaw Criminal Justice Topical Highlights Data Base
Contains summaries of significant recent state and federal cases covering criminal justice, including the nature, investigation, prosecution, and punishment of crimes.

Westlaw Federal and Multistate Criminal Justice Data Bases
Contains full text of case law and other documents related to U.S. state and federal law covering criminal acts and the investigation, prosecution, and punishment of crimes.

Westlaw Federal Data Base
Contains full text of U.S. federal laws, regulations, executive documents, and court decisions.

10

Government Documents

Many people think that government publications are limited to huge piles of statutes and laws. But the truth is, government documents provide a wealth of information in almost every field, and criminal justice is no exception. Government documents include not only those published by the federal government, although it is the major source, but documents published by state and local governments as well. These publications serve as a means of keeping the public informed so that it can make better use of the governmental services provided. The contents of government publications vary, but usually consist of results of government research, annual reports, statistical information, congressional hearings, bibliographies, directories, special and irregular publications, audiovisual materials, maps, and charts. Federal publications are printed by the United States Government Printing Office (GPO), Washington, D.C., an independent body in the legislative branch of government. Distribution of the documents is the responsibility of the Superintendent of Documents, an office created within the GPO.

Publications currently offered for sale by the Superintendent of Documents are listed in the *GPO Sales Publications Reference File (PRF)*. Anyone wishing to purchase a particular document need only look in this catalog to determine availability and ordering information. The *PRF* will also be very useful to researchers desiring to locate a specific government publication.

The contents of the *PRF* are arranged in three ways: (1) by GPO stock numbers, (2) by Superintendent of Documents classification numbers, and (3) by alphabetical arrangement of subjects, titles, agency series and report numbers, key words and phrases, and authors. *PRF* is issued six times yearly, with monthly updates.

Most federal government documents published will be available through libraries that are Federal Depository Libraries. For a complete list of these, see the section of this book titled *Specialized Libraries*.

LOCATING GOVERNMENT DOCUMENTS

Government documents will usually be located as a separate collection in a designated section of the library. Many documents collections will also include international, state, and local government documents as well. Most libraries organize government documents by a Superintendent of Documents number assigned to each publication. The *Monthly Catalog of United States Government Publications*, (described in greater detail later in this section) identifies the Superintendent of Documents number of each government document. It is accessible by author, title, subject, and key word indexes. Once the Superintendent of Documents number has been identified for a particular document, the researcher can look it up in the government documents section of the library in much the same way that the researcher uses a card catalog number to look up a book.

The governmental agency producing the majority of documents relating to criminal justice is the Department of Justice and its affiliated agencies, such as the FBI, Federal Bureau of Prisons, National Institute of Justice, Bureau of Justice Statistics, Immigration and Naturalization Service, and Drug Enforcement Administration.

Several different guides to government publications and government publications themselves are alphabetically annotated below.

American Statistics Index. A comprehensive index to statistical publications published by the federal government. (Washington, DC: Congressional Information Service, Inc.) (For additional information on this reference see Chapter 11, "Statistical Data").

Bibliographic Guide to Government Publications. An annual publication with an alphabetized subject index. The work consists of two volumes, A through N, and O through Z. The main subject heading for government publications relating to criminal justice is Crime and Criminals. (Boston: G.K. Hall and Company).

City and County Data Book. Devoted to statistical analyses of many different characteristics of each county in the United States. (Washington, DC: U.S. Bureau of the Census). (For more information regarding this publication, see Chapter 11, "Statistical Data").

Comprehensive Index to the Publications of the United States Government 1881-1893, John G. Ames. Mainly comprised of listings of congressional publications during the designated period. (Washington, DC: U.S. Department of Interior, 1905). (See also Chapter 15, "Historical Research Sources").

Congressional Directory. This publication has appeared in every session of Congress since 1809 and contains brief biographical information on every member of both houses. It also lists the membership of each congressional committee and outlines committee assignments given to each member. (Washington, DC: Congress).

Congressional District Data Book and Congressional District Data Book Supplement, Redistricted States. A biennial publication since 1961 which makes it possible to examine congressional voting records in regard to district characteristics. It includes information on vital statistics, bank deposits, retail trade, local governments, housing, and so forth. (Washington, DC: U.S. Department of Commerce).

Congressional Index. Designed to provide assistance to researchers regarding the status of legislation pending in Congress. Public bills and resolutions are indexed, and subject and author indexes are included, as well as a Headline Legislation Index for bills which have received widespread publicity. Members of the House and Senate are listed in separate divisions with biographical data and

committee assignments provided. Also included is a list of all permanent committees and their subcommittees, public hearings held by all committees, subjects not identified by their bill numbers, and reports of investigations and studies by committees as they are submitted to Congress. Progress of public bills and resolutions are reported from their introduction to their final resolution. (Chicago, IL: Commerce Clearing House, Inc.).

Congressional Information Service Index (CIS) Annual. A basic index to information contained in the working papers of Congress. It includes information on almost every important area of public policy. Hearings, committee prints, House and Senate Reports and Documents, Executive Reports and Documents, and public laws are covered. Monthly indexes, cumulated annually, are provided. (Washington, DC: Congressional Information Service, Inc.).

Congressional Quarterly Weekly Reports. This is a weekly report of news relating to Congress, including tabulations of votes on bills. Quarterly and annual cumulative indexes are provided. (Washington, DC: Congressional Quarterly, Inc.).

Congressional Record. Published Monday through Friday while Congress is in session, this source contains primary sources of information on topics discussed on the Congressional floor. Indexes include an alphabetical listing of subjects and names and a history of bills and resolutions arranged by their numbers. (Washington, DC: Congress).

Consumer's Guide to Federal Publications. A pamphlet which describes subject bibliographies of government publications that are available to the public free of charge from the Superintendent of Documents. Publications listed in the bibliographies are for sale. Subject bibliographies and their ordering numbers of interest to criminal justice students include: Accidents and Accident Prevention; Alcohol, Tobacco and Firearms; Courts and Correctional Institutions; Crime and Criminal Justice; Criminal Justice Agencies; Drug Education; FBI Publications; Firefighting, Prevention and Forest Fires; Grants and Awards (See also Grants section, Appendix III.); Juvenile Delinquency; Law Enforcement; Subversive Activities; Supreme Court Reports; Violence. To request any of these bibliographies free of charge, include the title and subject bibliography number and write to: Superintendent of Documents, Washington, D.C. 20402, phone: (202) 783-3238.

Criminal Justice Research: Biennial Report of the National Institute of Justice, Fiscal Years 1980 and 1981. This report, required to be submitted every two years to Congress, describes and summarizes all Federal Government criminal justice research activities. (Washington, DC: U.S. Department of Justice, National Institute of Justice).

Cumulative Subject Index to the Monthly Catalog of U.S. Government Publications 1900-1971. This fifteen-volume work provides a single cumulative index to the majority of United States Government publications published from 1900 to 1971. Each subject citation contains at least two important numbers. The first number refers the researcher to the year of the *Monthly Catalog* (see below) in which the full bibliographic reference appeared, and the second number is the item number which refers the researcher to the exact page or individual entry number of the full reference. Criminal justice students should seek volume four of this set and turn to the heading of Crime and Criminals. (Washington, DC: Carrollton Press, Inc., 1975).

A Descriptive Catalog of the Government Publications of the United States September 5, 1774 — March 4, 1881. Benjamin P. Moore. Cited documents are listed by date of publication. There are no annotations but a subject index is included. (Washington, DC: GPO, 1881). (See also Chapter 15, "Historical Research Sources").

Digest of Public General Bills and Resolutions. Furnishes a summary of the essential characteristics and/or changes of public bills and resolutions made during sessions of Congress. It also shows the status of bills acted upon and enacted. Indexes include sponsor and co-sponsor, short title, and subject index. Supplements are issued irregularly and a final issue is published upon adjournment of Congress. (Washington, DC: Library of Congress).

Documents Catalog. (Washington, DC: U.S. Government Printing Office, 1893. Reprint. New York: Johnson Reprint, 1963).

Federal Regulatory Directory. Published biennially by Congressional Quarterly, this is a comprehensive guide to federal regulatory activities, describing developments in the regulatory process as well as the agencies and personnel and their functions. Includes addresses and phone numbers for regional and national offices.

Government Publications Index. An index to U.S. government publications by subject, title, author, and issuing agency. (Santa Monica, CA: Information Access Corp, 1980-present).

Government Reports Announcements and Index. This bi-weekly publication indexes government reports. Behavioral and social sciences, as well as physical and life sciences, are represented. (Springfield, VA: National Technical Information Service, 1959-date).

Guide to United States Government Serials and Periodicals. John Andriot. An annual publication that guides the reader to serials, periodicals, and irregular publications of the United States Government. Contents are arranged alphabetically by branch of government, department, and agency. Agency, subject, and title indexes are provided. (McLean, VA: Documents Index, 1969-date).

Index to Current Urban Documents. Issued quarterly, covers the publications of 272 of the largest cities and counties in the United States. These publications include annual reports, audit reports, budgets, community development programs, demographic profiles, conference transcripts, consultant's reports, directories, economic studies, environmental impact statements, evaluations and analyses, feasibility studies, inventories, planning reports, policy statements, plus many more. Access is through geographic and subject indexes. (Westport, CT: Greenwood Press).

Index to Government Periodicals. Issued quarterly. Indexes 147 selected United States Government periodicals, including *FBI Law Enforcement Bulletin, Drug Enforcement,* and *Federal Probation.* (Chicago, IL: Infordata International, Inc., 1973-date).

Introduction to United States Public Documents, Joe Movebead. Intended as a textbook for library science students but the chapters dealing with the publications of the various branches of government are exceptionally good for anyone researching public documents. (Littleton, CO: Libraries Unlimited, 1983).

Metropolitan Area Annual. Describes current developments in city governments, provides various city statistics, directories of city officials, and directories of state agencies functioning at the local level. (Albany, NY: State University at Albany, Graduate School of Public Affairs, 1966-date).

Monthly Catalog of United States Government Publications. Lists the publications issued by the Government Printing Office each month. Detailed author, title, subject, and other specialized indexes are provided each month and cumulated semi-annually and annually. (Washington, DC: GPO).

Monthly Checklist of State Publications. A record of state documents issued during the last five years which have been received by the Library of Congress. Citations include monographs, periodicals, publications of associations of state officials and regional organizations and library studies, manuals, and statistical reports. (Washington, DC: Library of Congress).

Municipal Yearbook. Describes activities in and provides statistical data on major American cities. (Chicago, IL: International City Managers Association, 1934-date). (See Chapter 11, "Statistical Sources of Data," for additional information on this reference).

National Directory of State Agencies. Biennial. (Arlington, VA: Information Resource Press).

The National Union Catalog of Manuscript Collections. Annual. Describes manuscript collections housed permanently in the Library of Congress. (Washington, DC: Library of Congress, 1959 to date).

Official Congressional Directory. Published for each Congress elected; this official directory is a manual of Congressional committees as well as a guide to executive departments and the judicial branch. (Washington, DC: U.S. Congress).

A Popular Guide to Government Publications. Lists many documents in a wide variety of subjects, mainly popular in nature. (New York: Columbia University Press, 1968-date).

Popular Names of U.S. Government Reports. Bernard A. Bernier. Many times "Popular Names" are given to government commissions, this book can be an excellent help in locating a specific government commission report. (Washington, DC: U.S. Library of Congress, 1984).

Recent Publications on Governmental Problems. Monthly. (Chicago, IL: Merriam Center Library, 1932-date).

A Reference List of Audiovisual Materials Produced by the United States Government. (Washington, DC: GPO).

State Government Research Checklist. Bimonthly. (Lexington, KY: Council of State Governments, 1947-date).

State Manuals, Blue Books, and Election Results, Charles Press and Oliver Williams. Explains what state government publications are available to the public. Each state is represented. (Berkeley, CA: Institute of Governmental Studies, University of California, 1962).

Statistical Reference Index. Monthly. (Washington, DC: Congressional Information Service, 1980-date).

Subject Guide to Major United States Government Publications. Ellen Jackson. Describes important United States Government publications from early periods to the present. (Chicago, IL: American Library Association, 1968-date).

Uniform Crime Reports for the United States. Generally published annually and analyzes crime in the United States. Statistical tables of offenses known, arrests, persons charged, and police employee data are included. This is a very important publication with a wide range of uses. (Washington, DC: Federal Bureau of Investigation).

United States Government Manual. Describes the objectives and activities of most government agencies and lists names of management personnel within each agency. (Washington, DC: Office of Federal Register, National Archives and Records Service, General Services Administration).

United States Government Publications, Anne Boyd and Rae E. Rips. Provides a description of important publications of the Departments of the United States Government with an explanation of indexes. (New York: H.W. Wilson, 1949-date).

U.S. Superintendent of Documents. *Monthly Catalog of United States Government Publications.* (Washington, DC: Government Printing Office, 1895-date).

Washington Information Directory 1990-1991. This publication gives information on the Executive Office of the President, Executive Offices, and federal agencies. Also included are chapters with information on specific departments. A ready reference list is also given. (Washington, DC: Congressional Quarterly, Inc.).

NATIONAL COMMISSION REPORTS

In addition to various government publications and sources concerned with government publications, the National Commission Reports are also very good sources of information. Most of these, however, are out of print at the NCJRS and the GPO, but NCJRS has produced a "SLIM" (Selected Library in Microfiche) of Commission reports. The Wickersham Reports (see Chapter 15) are included in the SLIM package. The full text of all reports are available for sale from the NCJRS (see Chapter 16).

A brief annotation of each report produced by the respective Commission is provided below.

National Advisory Commission on Criminal Justice Standards and Goals, Washington, D.C.

Community Crime Prevention. Discusses community support and involvement of citizens in the reduction of crime. The Commission has proposed almost 75 standards and recommendations that focus on citizen action, the delivery of public services, the reduction of criminal opportunities, and integrity in government. Actions by private citizens which should and could be done to reduce crime are spelled out. (GPO Stock #2700-00181, NCJ 10911, 1973).

Corrections. Recommends specific steps to improve the American correctional system. Recommendations for where, why, how, and what improvements should be made. Among them, the Commission urges that disparities in sentencing be removed, and that steps be taken to insure offender's rights during and after incarceration. It also recommends that juveniles and sociomedical cases (alcoholics, drug addicts, prostitutes, and the mentally disturbed) be diverted to non-correctional treatment programs. Another goal states that confinement should be used chiefly for dangerous offenders while a majority of offenders be referred to improved and extended community-based programs. (GPO Stock #2700-00175, NCJ 10865, 1973).

Courts. Contains almost 100 specific standards and recommendations to upgrade and reorganize the processing of criminal cases at state and local levels. It spells out in detail where, why, how, and what improvements should be made to improve the judicial segment of the criminal justice system. Priorities include devising standards for attaining speed and efficiency in the pretrial and trial processes and prompt finality in appellate proceedings, upgrading defense and prosecution functions, and to assure high quality in the judiciary. Among the Commission's recommendations are the elimination of all but the investigative function of the grand jury, elimination of formal arraignment, unification of all courts within each state, and the upgrading of criminal court personnel. (GPO Stock #2700-00173, NCJ 10859, 1973).

Criminal Justice System. Discusses standards for reform in the management and operation of the criminal justice system and focuses on planning, education, and information systems. The Commission stresses the need for additional planning at the metropolitan and regional levels, and indicates the necessity for qualifying performance objectives. Among recommendations are the development of state integrated multiyear planning and the establishment of criminal justice coordinating councils by all major cities and counties. Nearly 70 recommendations detail what the segments of the criminal justice system—police, courts, and correctional agencies—can do to upgrade and modernize many of their functions. (GPO Stock #2700-00176, NCJ 10864, 1973).

National Strategy to Reduce Crime. Presents an overview of the work of the National Advisory Commission on Criminal Justice Standards and Goals and the recommended strategies for reducing crime in the United States. It covers criminal justice planning, community crime prevention, police, courts, and corrections, and also addresses issues of criminal code reform and handgun control. The Commission proposed a 50 percent reduction in the rates of high-fear crimes such as homicide, forcible rape, aggravated assault, robbery and burglary by 1983. Juvenile delinquency prevention, improved delivery of social services, speedier trials and increased citizen participation in community crime control activities are specified for priority action. Also emphasized is the need for community support for the police, and the need to develop more effective correctional programs regarding the reintegration of offenders into the community. (GPO Stock #077-000-0204-8, NCJ 10697, 1973).

Police. Includes suggestions for overall improvements in police functions to increase protection against crime. Areas of working with the community, planning and organization, technology and support services, fiscal management, and coordination with other criminal justice agencies are areas targeted for improvement by the Commission. The Commission recommends that police departments establish a specialized unit in order to maintain communication with citizens, and that each police department encourage and participate in neighborhood security programs and establish procedures to facilitate processing of complaints. (GPO Stock #2700-00174, NCJ 10858, 1973).

Working Papers of the National Conference on Criminal Justice, January, 1973. Standards in each of the four areas of police, courts, corrections, and community crime prevention are presented along with a commentary providing the background and justification for the proposed changes. (GPO Stock #052-003-0030-0, NCJ 07993, 1973).

National Advisory Committee on Criminal Justice Standards and Goals, Washington, D.C.

Report of the Police Chief Executive Committee of the International Association of Chiefs of Police. Concerned with the process of selecting and retaining a qualified police chief executive. Also included are steps, based on due process, for removing an unqualified police chief from office. Standards included in this report were developed and reviewed by the Police Chief Executive Committee of the International Association of Chiefs of Police. (GPO Stock #052-003-00222-1, NCJ 38355, 1975).

Report of the Task Force on Criminal Justice Research and Development. Contains guidelines for improving the quality, relevance, and utilization of research results at all levels of government, but some topics are addressed at the federal level. Included is a detailed discussion of institutions supporting research in criminal justice, the federal role in supporting criminal justice research (agencies involved), and how principal agencies are organized to manage their research and development responsibilities. Issues such as research constraints, ethical issues, research design and methodologies, project selection, confidentiality of data, and ways of making data more accessible for research are discussed. Three general types of criminal justice research and development are discussed: technology research, research on problems of criminal justice organization (arrest, prosecution, sentencing, and parole), and research on new criminal justice problems. (GPO Stock #052-003-00221-3, NCJ 38328, 1976).

Report of the Task Force on Disorders and Terrorism. Contains standards and goals that pertain to almost every aspect of disorders and terrorism. Proposals for training police and law enforcement agencies in preventive measures that can be taken against mass violence, management of disorders, deterrence of terrorism, and evaluation of threats of disorder and terrorism are presented. Detailed plans to assist police during riots and other civil disorders are included. The role of the courts both during and after such occurrences, including recommendations on how to deal with trials of cases arising out of terroristic incidents is discussed. Institutional conditions and correctional objectives are considered due to the number of prison disorders in recent years. Overviews of international terrorism, terrorism and new weapons technology, and terrorism in Argentina, Canada, and West Germany are provided in the appendices. (GPO Stock #052-003-0024-8, NCJ 39469, 1976).

Report of the Task Force on Juvenile Justice and Delinquency Prevention. Centers on efforts to improve delinquency prevention programs and the juvenile justice system. Standards on delinquency prevention, organization and coordination of delinquency prevention programs, police roles and responsibilities in the juvenile justice system, jurisdiction and processes of the juvenile court and the adjudication process are included, as well as standards on endangered children, dispositions, prosecution and defense services, intake and correctional services, and planning and evaluation in the juvenile systems. (GPO #Stock 052-003-00223-0, NCJ 42399, 1976).

Report of the Task Force on Organized Crime. A comprehensive report containing standards for the prevention and reduction of organized crime. A brief history of organized crime in the United States, a description of the general characteristics of organized crime, and the results of a study of various methods of dealing with the problem by state and local governments is presented. Programs based on successful models to help state and local governments and private citizens combat organized crime are outlined. Specific policies, law enforcement procedures, prosecutorial tools, and legal procedures for adoption by the criminal justice system are presented as well as recommendations for training programs to combat organized crime. (GPO Stock #052-003-00220-5, NCJ 38354, 1976).

Report of the Task Force on Private Security. Presents recommendations for upgrading the personnel, equipment, interagency cooperation, and regulation of private security.

These recommendations are based on maximizing the ability, competency, and effectiveness of the private security industry for its role in the prevention and reduction of crime. Consideration is given to government licensing and registration of private security, incorporation of private security crime prevention techniques in building design and construction, improvement of private security industry salaries to reflect the responsibilities of private security, upgrading of training and education for private security personnel, improvement of alarm systems to decrease false alarms, inclusion of private security input in government planning and development, and improvement of the working relationships of police and private security. Specific topics include personnel selection, training, and ethics, standards and goals on the use of alarm systems and environmental security, the relation of private security to law enforcement, consumers and higher education, and licensing and regulation of private security personnel. (GPO Stock #052-003-00225-6, NCJ 40543, 1976).

National Commission on Marijuana and Drug Abuse, Washington, D.C.

Drug Use in America: Problems in Perspective. Examines the origins of the drug problem and recommends ways to reduce its impact. Societal attitudes regarding drug usage are explored, recent trends in the incidence, prevalence, pattern, conditions and circumstances of drug use are described, and major classes of drug usage behavior are identified. (GPO Stock #052-066-00003-4, NCJ 09518, 1973).

Drug Use in America: Problems in Perspective, Volume 1 — Patterns and Consequences of Drug Use Appendix. Describes drug use, drug-induced behavior, drug dependence, and establishes a process for assessing the impact on society. Contains 27 papers on the patterns and consequences of drug use, covering specific areas of drugs and their effects, drugs and antisocial behavior, and drug use in general. (GPO Stock #5266-00004, NCJ 37696, 1973).

Drug Use in America: Problems in Perspective, Volume 2 — Social Response to Drug Use Appendix. Contains 23 papers on the social responses to drug use, covering specific areas of managing the governmental response, drug education and the response of the educational system, the impact of broadcast media on drug use and influences in American life. (GPO Stock #5266-00005, NCJ 37697, 1973).

Drug Use in America: Problems in Perspective, Volume 3 — The Legal System and Drug Control Appendix. Contains 20 papers on the legal system and drug control, covering areas of the statutory framework of the drug/narcotics control system, legal controls on the availability of psychoactive substances, and the response of the criminal justice system to drug use. (GPO Stock #5266-00006, NCJ 36082, 1973).

Drug Use in America: Problems in Perspective, Volume 4 — Treatment and Rehabilitation Appendix. Contains 17 papers on the treatment and rehabilitation of drug addicts, covering specific areas of crisis intervention and emergency treatment, the treatment of drug dependence, drug dependence and the legal system, and the statutory framework of drug treatment laws. (GPO Stock #5266-00007, NCJ 37698, 1973).

Marihuana: A Signal of Misunderstanding, First Report.
Discusses the nature and scope of marihuana use, the
effects of the drug, the relationship of marihuana use to
other behavior, the existing law, and ideas for future
policies. It includes a review of the incidence of marihuana
use according to age, grade, frequency of use, duration of
use, and personality types of users. It also evaluates the
pharmacological effects of the drug on human behavior and
the social impact of marihuana use. (GPO Stock #5266-
0001, NCJ 09449, 1972).

Marihuana: A Signal of Misunderstanding, Appendix.
Addresses major issues and concerns regarding marihuana
use. Considers biosocial aspects relating to the drug's effect

on individuals and society in general, medicinal and
intoxicant use of marihuana, relationship of marihuana use
to violent and nonviolent crime, and explores the
hypothesis that marihuana use leads to use of other drugs,
especially heroin. Marihuana laws at the international,
federal, and state levels are reviewed and law enforcement
behavior with respect to marihuana use is analyzed. Public
attitude and behavior toward marihuana and other drug use
is also presented. The final section of this report deals with
policies and programs on a state-by-state basis of
marihuana education, as well as future research
recommendations for agencies engaged in research
activities on marihuana. (GPO Stock #052-066-00002-6,
NCJ 45382, 1972).

National Commission on the Causes and Prevention of Violence, Washington, D.C.

*Final Report: To Establish Justice, To Insure Domestic
Tranquility.* Presents a historical overview of violence in
America and an examination of various forms of violence.
Recommendations for the control and prevention of violent
crime, group violence, civil disobedience, assassination,
and campus disorders. Relationships between violence and
law enforcement, firearms, and violence on the media are
analyzed. The role of religion in decreasing violence is also
considered. (NCJ 00275, 1969).

*Volumes 1 and 2: Violence in America — Historical and
Comparative Perspectives.* These volumes present an
overview of violence in Europe and America. Elements
considered are immigrant societies, the frontier tradition,
and the history of working class protest and violence. (NCJ
00763, 1969).

*Volume 3: Politics and Protest — Violent Aspects of Protest
and Confrontation.* Analyzes the nature and causes of
protest and confrontation in the United States and
associated incidents of violence. Specifics include anti-war
protests, black and white militancy, racial attitudes of white
Americans, the police in protest, judicial response in crisis,
and social responses to group behavior. (NCJ 00765, 1969).

*Volume 4: Rights in Concord — The Response to the
Counterinaugural Protest Activities in Washington, D.C.
January 18-20, 1969.* Presents an account of the
confrontations between government officials, police, and
demonstrators. Preparations for the anti-war protest and
preparations by law enforcement agencies are outlined.
(NCJ 00766, 1969).

*Volume 5: Shoot-Out in Cleveland — Black Militants and the
Police.* Centers around a description of the 1968 gun battle
between Cleveland police and black snipers, and the arson
and rioting that followed. Techniques for quieting the
violence are outlined. (NCJ 00767, 1969).

*Volume 6: Shut It Down — A College in Crisis — San
Francisco State College, October 1968 — April 1969.*
Identifies major reasons for violent campus disorders
including demands for a black studies program and an open
admissions policy for minority students. Peaceful protests
are traced through to the stage of violent confrontation.
(NCJ 00768, 1969).

Volume 7: Firearms and Violence in American Life. Firearm
ownership, trends in sales control laws, and the relationship
of firearms ownership to suicide, accidents, crime, and
group violence are discussed. (NCJ 00769, 1969).

Volume 8: Assassination and Political Violence. Consequences of assassination and the environmental factors
that encourage groups or individuals to attack political
leaders are identified and presented. Also included are
appendixes covering political assassinations in other
countries, and a survey of attitudes toward political
violence in the United States. (NCJ 00770, 1969).

Volume 9: Mass Media and Violence. Explores issues of
whether freedom of the press condones indiscriminate
broadcasting of violence and whether there is a causal
relation between violence in media and violence in society.
(NCJ 00771, 1969).

Volume 9A: Mass Media Hearings — A Report to the National Commission on the Causes and Prevention of Violence. Presents testimony from network executives, reporters, and scholars regarding the contributions of mass media to the incidence of violence in America. (NCJ 09969, 1969).

Volume 10: Law and Order Reconsidered. Examines the extent to which weaknesses in American institutions (federal and local governments, families, churches, schools) and laws have contributed to violence. (NCJ 00772, 1969).

Volume 11: Crimes of Violence. Looks at the causes and means of preventing violence. Topics considered are acts of violence, criminal statistics, levels and trends of individual violence, organized crime and violence, the offender and his victim, and the costs of crime. (NCJ 00569, 1969).

Volume 12: Crimes of Violence. Examines individual violence, the offender and the correctional system, research guidelines, and the relationship of violence to youth, drugs, and the urban environment. (NCJ 005700, 1969).

Volume 13: Crimes of Violence. Examines crimes of violence by women, the relationship of violence to juvenile gangs, drugs, accidents, and organized crime as well as various theories of violence. (NCJ 00571, 1969).

President's Commission on Law Enforcement and Administration of Justice, Washington, D.C.

Challenge of Crime in a Free Society. A comprehensive work which discusses crime and criminals in America, as well as victims and what preventive measures can be taken to reduce crime. Contains more than 200 specific recommendations which call for a greatly increased effort on the part of the federal government, states, counties, cities, civic, religious, and business organizations, and individual citizens. (GPO Stock #040-000-00100-0, NCJ 00042, 1967).

Task Force Report: Corrections. Discusses aspects of new directions that the corrections system must take, such as greater emphasis on rehabilitation, community supervision, and better qualified staff, as well as parole, probation, legal status of the convict, and creating change in the correctional system. (GPO Stock #040-000-00095-0, NCJ 00179, 1967).

Task Force Report: Courts. Concerned with upgrading the court system. Plea negotiations, legal rights to counsel, education of all officers of the court, the court process, and law reform are considered. This report stresses the need for lower court reform in particular. (GPO Stock #040-000-00096-8, NCJ 00176, 1967).

Task Force Report: Crime and Its Impact — An Assessment. An overview of the urban crime problem. Factors considered include the problem of unreported crime, public attitudes toward crime and law enforcement, the characteristics of victims and victim-offender relationships, among other crime problems. (NCJ 00494, 1967).

Task Force Report: Drunkenness. An examination of treating drunken offenders as well as alternatives. Recommends that drunkenness not be treated as a criminal offense but that civil detoxification procedures be established. (NCJ 00178, 1967).

Task Force Report: Juvenile Delinquency and Youth Crime. Analyzes socioeconomic aspects of juvenile delinquency and includes recommendations for change, including the modernization of the juvenile court and involving the youthful offender in community life by encouraging society to respond to the needs of youth. (GPO Stock #040-000-00102-6, NCJ 00172, 1967).

Task Force Report: Narcotics and Drug Abuse. Contains recommendations to improve research and education in drug enforcement and to improve drug enforcement. Among the recommendations are to increase staffs of bureaus of customs and narcotics, adoption of drug abuse control legislation, and to undertake research projects and develop educational materials. (GPO Stock #040-000-00103, NCJ 00175, 1967).

Task Force Report: Organized Crime. Examines why organized crime has increased despite control efforts and strategies. Efforts to control it are presented. Appendices include articles on the function and structure of criminal syndicates, the politics of corruption, aspects of the evidence-gathering process and an economic analysis of organized crime. (NCJ 00173, 1967).

Task Force Report: Police. Presents a complete study of police in the United States. Examines policies, organization, management, police standards, personnel, integrity and relationship to the community. (NCJ 00177, 1967).

Task Force Report: Science and Technology. Encourages directing attention to the police apprehension process,

police communications, court management, corrections, criminal justice information systems, and the role of science and technology in all areas of criminal justice. Appendices include information on police apprehension, nonlethal weapons, delays in courts, and information flow. (NCJ 00174, 1967).

National Planning Association

National Manpower Survey of the Criminal Justice System, Volume 1: Summary Report, August, 1978. The first of a series resulting from a national manpower survey which assesses present and future manpower needs of the criminal justice system, and includes recommendations concerning training and management. (GPO Stock #027-000-00650-7, NCJ 43739, 1978). Related volumes to specific areas are as follows: Volume 2: Law Enforcement (NCJ 43760), Volume 3: Corrections (NCJ 43740), Volume 4: Courts (NCJ 43741), Volume 5: Criminal Justice Education and Training (NCJ 43742), Volume 6: Criminal Justice Manpower Planning (NCJ 43743).

National Manpower Survey of the Criminal Justice System: Executive Summary. Summarizes results of the national survey of personnel resources, training and educational needs in the field of law enforcement and criminal justice, as presented in Volumes 1-6 listed above. (GPO Stock #027-000-00642-6, NCJ 45597, 1978).

National Institute of Justice

The National Institute of Justice (NIJ), United States Department of Justice, publishes many government documents, most of which are accessible through the varied services of NIJ/NCJRS. For example, the NIJ sponsored the National Evaluation Program to assess the vast number of Law Enforcement Assistance Administration (LEAA) block grant programs. The full text of 501 documents published by the NIJ between 1968 and 1979 is available for purchase in microfiche from the NCJRS under the SLIM (Selected Libraries in Microfiche) Program.

See Chapter 12, titled *NCJRS,* for a complete list.

Freedom of Information Act (FOIA)

The Freedom of Information Act was signed into law during Lyndon Johnson's administration. Essentially, this law provides that unclassified government information is available, and if it is not made available to a requesting individual, the burden of proof lies with the government agency to show why it should not be made available. Directions and rules on where and how to obtain information must be published by each government agency in the *Federal Register.* Types of information that must be made available are as follows:

The results of administrative court cases and rulings.

Policy statements not appearing in the *Federal Register.*

Administrative staff manuals affecting the public.

Types of information *exempt* under the Freedom of Information Act are as follows:

Documents classified as secret, top secret, or confidential.

Rules and procedures concerning the internal workings of the government.

Information designated as exempted by statute.

Trade secrets.

Internal communications.

Personal and medical files.

Certain investigatory records.

Regulatory records of a financial institution.

Specific geological information.

If you find it necessary to request government information under the Freedom of Information Act, you will need to determine the appropriate agency from which to request the information, and then describe what you want as specifically as possible. Information held by various federal, state, and local agencies is often extensive and covers a broad spectrum. Some of the materials these agencies possess is not generally known to the public but most is accessible upon request, due to the new FOIA laws. Most persons in charge of a particular agency will be glad to assist you in locating your requested information.

The following publications are excellent sources of additional information on how to obtain government materials under this act:

Legally Available U.S. Government Information as a Result of the Public Information Act, Matthew J. Kerbee. (Arlington, Virginia: Output Systems Corporation, 1970.)

Your Right to Government Information: How to Use the FOIA. (New York: American Civil Liberties Union, 22 East 40th Street, New York, New York 10016.)

In addition to the above-described sources, there are many government agencies that are good sources of criminal justice information. These are described below. In addition to the printed matter that these agencies have to offer, don't forget the people you meet. They, too, are very good sources of information.

Federal Field-Based Information

There are several federal agencies that may be visited or written to for various types of information. In addition, do not forget that some of these agencies, such as the FBI, also have regional offices throughout the country that may be easily accessible to you. Also, do not overlook federal courts as a source of information because one may be in close proximity to you.

State Field-Based Government Information

The Attorney General's Office in most states is thought of as the top law enforcement agency and will maintain statewide records regarding criminal justice matters, including statistics on crime by city, county, type of crime, and so on. Information concerning new or proposed legislation or reforms to the judicial process may also be found here.

The State Department of Corrections will maintain records on the number of persons in state prisons, on probation, or released on parole. Information can also be obtained regarding expenditures, number of staff, types of services, recidivism rate, and other types of information. This agency is also a good source through which original data from interviewing prisoners can be collected. This is usually possible but permission should first be obtained in writing from the director of the department.

Other state agencies that will have information pertaining to criminal justice include the offices of the state highway patrol, and the state's bureau of investigation.

Local Field-Based Government Information

Police Departments and Sheriffs' Departments keep records of the different crimes that are reported to them as well as data on the time of day, location, crimes cleared by arrest, unsolved cases, patterns or trends, traffic accidents, local manpower, and so forth.

The *County Court House* maintains records relating to trials, including transcripts of trials, court appearances, dispositions, bail, divorce and probate, land ownership, civil suits and other information relating to criminal justice and law.

Other sources of local records include such community service organizations as rape crisis centers, mental health centers, welfare departments, the coroner's office, various courts, probation and parole offices, local correctional departments, juvenile detention centers, and museums.

Addresses of local criminal justice agencies can be found in the following publication:

Criminal Justice Agencies. (Washington, DC: United States Department of Justice, LEAA, National Criminal Justice Information Statistics Service, 1975.) Consists of ten volumes, as described below. Each volume is probably among the holdings of any library, but can also be purchased from the Government Printing Office on microfiche only. Include the GPO Stock Number when requesting these directories from the GPO.

This publication is divided according to region. Each region contains addresses of local criminal justice agencies in the states listed.

> *Region 1:* Connecticut, Maine, Massachusetts, New Hampshire, Rhode Island, Vermont. (GPO Stock #027-000-00301-0.)
>
> *Region 2:* New Jersey, New York. (GPO Stock #027-000-00302-8.)
>
> *Region 3:* Delaware, District of Columbia, Maryland, Pennsylvania, Virginia, West Virginia. (GPO Stock #027-000-00315-0.)
>
> *Region 4:* Alabama, Florida, Georgia, Kentucky, Mississippi, North Carolina, South Carolina, Tennessee. (GPO Stock #027-000-00314-1.)
>
> *Region 5:* Illinois, Indiana, Michigan, Minnesota, Ohio, Wisconsin. (GPO Stock #027-000-00308-7.)
>
> *Region 6:* Arkansas, Louisiana, New Mexico, Oklahoma, Texas. (GPO Stock #027-000-00307-9.)
>
> *Region 7:* Iowa, Kansas, Missouri, Nebraska. (GPO Stock #027-000-00297-8.)

Region 8: Colorado, Montana, North Dakota, South Dakota, Utah, Wyoming. (GPO Stock #027-000-00303-6.)

Region 9: Arizona, California, Hawaii, Nevada. (GPO Stock #027-000-00271-4.)

Region 10: Alaska, Idaho, Oregon, Washington. (GPO Stock #027-000-00304-4.)

Information for each state is listed in the following sequence: enforcement, courts, prosecution and legal services, defender agencies, adult correctional institutions, juvenile correctional institutions, other correctional institutions, probation and parole agencies, and "other," which includes drug programs and administrative or planning agencies.

11

Statistical Data

FEDERAL JUSTICE STATISTICS
(Excerpted from U.S. Dept. of Justice, Bureau of Justice Statistics, Bulletin.)

Fifty years ago the Wickersham Commission (see Chapter 15 of this book, titled *Historical Research Sources*), this country's first national crime commission, published a report on criminal justice statistics, noting as a basic principle that accurate statistics are a key to understanding and improving the administration of justice. The 1931 report, which bears the name of a former Attorney General, noted also that such statistics did not exist: "Accurate data are the beginning of wisdom in such a subject, and no such data can be had for the country as a whole, nor have they even been available hitherto with respect to many of the activities of the Federal government in the enforcement of Federal laws."

A comprehensive federal transaction data base would reflect all transactions occurring in the investigative, prosecutorial, judicial, and correctional segments of the criminal justice system that describe successive actions taken with respect to the same criminal event. Ironically, while the federal government has, over the past decade, encouraged and assisted the states in developing comprehensive state-level transaction data, the federal justice system itself has not experienced comparable progress toward that end. There exists no body of comprehensive statistics about federal offenders and little information about the flow of cases from federal investigators to U.S. Attorneys to the federal court and corrections systems.

Comprehensive Criminal Justice Statistics: Uses, Barriers, and Methods. Statistics describing the components of state criminal justice systems are now routinely maintained at the state level. Although the systems vary in comprehensiveness and data quality from state to state, they have become increasingly important in every jurisdiction as the needs have increased for improved criminal justice planning, fiscal control, policy assessment, and response to legislative requests for information (for example, to analyze the impact of determinate sentencing systems).

The needs to plan, to support the fiscal process, to assess policy, and to respond to legislative inquiry exist as well at the federal level. The data to meet these needs, however, have not been maintained at the Federal level as they have at the State level.

Improved justice statistics for the federal system are needed for more than planning, control, and policy assessment at the federal level. They are also essential to enable federal authorities to respond to Attorney General's directive to balance coordination between the federal and state and local criminal justice systems by establishing Law Enforcement Coordinating Committees. A prerequisite to effective coordination is a basic understanding of the relative magnitudes of case flow from one stage of federal criminal case processing to adjacent stages.

Barriers to developing comprehensive justice statistics that have been confronted at the state level exist at the federal level as well. Independent data systems have been developed and maintained by federal investigative agencies, the Executive Office for U.S. Attorneys, the Administrative Office of the U.S. Courts, the Federal Prison

System, and ancillary federal agencies. As a result, data definitions vary from agency to agency, as do reporting periods and crime classification schemes. These barriers make the prospect of developing a comprehensive federal transaction data base incorporating the various data sets maintained by federal agencies fairly difficult, at least for the near future. They also limit the inferences to be drawn from comparing the reports of different justice agencies.

Specific uses of available data to assess federal criminal justice policy are numerous, even prior to data linkage. Simple numeric descriptions of federal case flow and events can reveal the frequency with which specific problems, such as crimes committed while on bail, and bail jumping, actually occur. The data can also be used to assess a host of other issues: case referral policies and rates of case flow between federal and local agencies; the quality of evidence and investigations; rates of pretrial misconduct and the criteria used in making pretrial release decisions; rates of recidivism and chronic-offender case-targeting decisions; delays in case processing at each stage of the system; and consistency in case processing and sentencing practices. Although the case record can serve as the basis for many of these analyses, the data could be reorganized to allow other issues to be addressed. For example, studying recidivism and its predictors requires that the data be reorganized to describe offenders rather than current cases. Likewise, a study of arrest quality might require that the data be restructured to focus on federal investigative functions rather than individual cases. Similarly, studying case backlogs may require a reorganization of the data by unit of time.

Analyses such as these require a thorough understanding of the structure of the system, of the issues relevant to system operation, and of the data as they relate to those issues.

The accompanying chart and discussion describe the fundamental stages of federal case processing. The schematic has simplified what is in fact an extremely complicated set of interactions among individuals, cases, and organizations. Accordingly, it does not provide an inclusive description of the many processing options available at the various decision points in the system, nor does it in all cases draw the distinction between the movement of the offender and his case record. The chart is intended to identify, however, those processing stages that should be reflected in a comprehensive federal statistics data base.

The Federal System. The federal criminal justice system is divided into 94 judicial districts. Each has a Federal District Court and a U.S. Attorney. According to the Administrative Office of the U.S. Courts, approximately 50,000 criminal cases enter this system each year. Basic similarities exist between the way these cases are processed and the way cases are usually handled at the state and local levels. At the federal level, as at the state and local levels, criminal justice responsibilities are divided into the components of law enforcement, prosecution, adjudication and sentencing, and corrections.

There are also some fundamental differences between the federal and state systems. The federal system is perhaps most readily distinguishable from state and local systems in terms of the kinds of crimes unique to federal jurisdictions, including major crimes (e.g., major drug offenses and crimes of serious fraud and corruption), crimes that cross state boundaries (e.g., interstate transport of stolen property, cargo theft), crimes involving federal money (e.g. counterfeiting, forgery of U.S. checks), and crimes committed on U.S. Government property.

Criminal offenses that are investigated and prosecuted at the federal level typically do not involve crimes of violence. These are commonly handled at state or local levels. Federal criminal cases usually result from long-term investigations of crimes such as embezzlement, fraud, drug dealing, or forgery. These cases may involve offenders who have committed many offenses over several months or years, or have stolen large sums of money.

Five investigative agencies conduct a substantial majority of the investigative work done at the federal level: the Federal Bureau of Investigation, the Drug Enforcement Administration, the Secret Service, the Postal Inspection Service, and the Bureau of Alcohol, Tobacco, and Firearms. Other federal agencies, including the Customs Service, the Internal Revenue Service, the Food and Drug Administration, the Immigration and Naturalization Service, the Securities and Exchange Commission, and individual executive departments also employ investigators to monitor infractions that are the responsibility of those agencies. Investigative activities include crime detection, evidence collection, making arrests, presenting cases to federal prosecutors, and conducting follow-up investigations.

Prosecuting federal cases is the responsibility of the Department of Justice litigating divisions and the Office of the U.S. Attorney in each district. U.S. Attorneys are appointed by the President but generally have long-standing familiarity with the concerns of their districts. They are supported in Washington, D.C., by the Executive Office for the U.S. Attorneys.

Many, if not most, federal crimes are "dual jurisdiction" offenses that may be prosecuted either federally or locally. The decision by a U.S. Attorney to prosecute a bank robbery, for example, may rest on such factors as the seriousness of the offense, the prior record of the offender, policies of the agencies involved, and the degree of involvement of local law enforcement officials in investigating the offense. Generally, the federal government will prosecute cases brought by federal agents when the cases meet the U.S. Attorney's standards of seriousness and have enough evidence to merit prosecution.

In addition to the 94 U.S. Attorneys and the 94 Federal District Courts, there are 13 Circuit Courts of Appeal, and the Supreme Court of the United States. Statistical information about case processing in the judicial branch of the federal system is maintained by the Administrative Office of the U.S. Courts.

After receiving sentences, convicted offenders in the federal system may be turned over to the Division of Probation in the Administrative Office of the U.S. Courts or the Bureau of Prisons. Offenders sentenced to incarceration are confined in one of the 42 federal correctional facilities located throughout the country.

Eligibility for parole is determined by using guidelines developed by the Federal Parole Commission. These guidelines permit evaluating each federal inmate on the basis of offense seriousness and relevant aspects of the inmate's criminal history.

Federal Data Sources. The agencies that make up the federal criminal justice system maintain a variety of data that document the processing of cases and defendants within each agency and describe the criminal record of individual offenders. At the investigation stage there are several automated data bases, including the FBI's Computerized Criminal History File (CCH); the Criminal Automated Reporting System of the Bureau of Alcohol, Tobacco, and Firearms; and the automated files maintained by the Drug Enforcement Administration and the Secret Service. Also, manual files are maintained by other agencies that engage in investigative work.

Information about the cases processed by U.S. Attorneys is maintained by the Executive Office for the U.S. Attorneys in its Docket and Reporting System. The system provides data about criminal (and civil) case rejections, filings, and dispositions.

Court data maintained by the Administrative Office of the U.S. Courts in the Automated Docket System provide information about criminal case filings and terminations in the federal courts. The "termination" file contains offense, disposition, and sentencing information.

Finally, the Federal Bureau of Prisons uses automated prison records to monitor the confinement and release of federal offenders.

In addition to the data bases listed above, special-purpose data sets provide a variety of information about federal defendants, cases and practitioners. These include: the U.S. Parole Commission longitudinal recidivism files; pretrial release data maintained by the Federal Pretrial Services Agency; COURTRAN files designed by the Federal Judicial Center, that provide automated court records for 13 federal districts; Prosecutor's Management Information System (PROMIS) currently in two U.S. Attorney's offices, with plans to extend it to other offices; other data developed as part of specific studies sponsored by federal agencies (e.g., coded presentence investigation reports).

Conclusion. Maintaining statistical information about the federal criminal justice system is not an easy task. It is one that at present is done primarily within each district and aggregated nationally by the numerous agencies operating separately within the federal executive and judicial branches.

Movement toward a comprehensive system of federal criminal justice statistics would certainly help to improve understanding of federal case processing and enable the various agencies of the federal justice network to conduct analyses that are needed to enable them to carry out their mandates. It would also foster better coordination both within the federal government and between the federal and local systems.

The Bureau of Justice Statistics has undertaken to build toward these ends. Currently, efforts are being directed toward a comprehensive review of federal data sources to determine feasibility of developing an integrated data base. BJS will also release a major Compendium of federal Criminal Justice Statistics, which will provide a single-source reference to criminal justice statistics describing the federal criminal justice system. Additionally, reports will be issued that analyze statistical data relevant to particular priority issues associated with the federal offender and the federal criminal justice system.

BUREAU OF JUSTICE STATISTICS

The Bureau of Justice Statistics (BJS) is an agency of the U.S. Department of Justice. It is mandated by Congress to collect, analyze, publish, and disseminate statistics on crime, victims of crime, criminal offenders, and operations of justice systems at all levels of government throughout the United States. It also is a source of financial and technical support to state and local statistical and operating agencies throughout the Nation. It develops national policy on such issues as the privacy, confidentiality, and security of data and the interstate exchange of criminal records.

BJS began its work in 1969 as the National Criminal Justice Information and Statistics Service (NCJISS) of the Law Enforcement Assistance Administration, consolidating existing justice statistical programs throughout the federal government in a single agency and developing new programs to meet data needs. In 1979, the Justice System Improvement Act (JSIA) established the Bureau of Justice Statistics and mandated that it continue the NCJISS statistical programs. The act also created the Office of Justice Assistance, Research, and Statistics (OJARS), which coordinates the work of BJS, the National Institute of Justice, and the Office of Juvenile Justice and Delinquency Prevention. Collectively, these agencies are sometimes referred to as JSIA agencies or OJARS agencies.

More information about any BJS program can be obtained from BJS at 633 Indiana Avenue, N.W., Washington, D.C. 20531, (202) 724-7765.

The BJS Data Collection Programs

BJS collects data about criminal justice agencies, victims of crime, and criminal offenders. Most of these data are collected for BJS by another organization, such as the Bureau of the Census, professional associations, or research organizations, under contract to BJS.

BJS National Statistical Program

The largest part of the BJS program is national data collection, which includes—

- the National Crime Survey (NCS), which interviews a sample of households to determine the incidence and characteristics of criminal victimization

- the new Law Enforcement Management and Administrative Statistics (LEMAS) program

- the prosecution and adjudication program, which includes
  —two annual series, the National Judicial Reporting and the Prosecution of Felony Arrests Programs
  —periodic collection of data on public defense
  —a new statistical series being developed to cover the pretrial stage of criminal justice processing

- the corrections statistics program, which
  —periodically surveys persons held in local jails, state prisons, and juvenile facilities
  —enumerates correctional populations annually, including persons in prisons and jails, on probation and parole, and under sentence of death
  —conducts censuses of state prisons and local jails

- the justice expenditure and employment program, which produces annual data for the federal, state, and local justice systems.

Major BJS Surveys

National Crime Survey. Begun in 1973, produces annual national estimates of the amount of crime against persons and households; victimization rates; the characteristics of victims, criminal events, and offenders; reporting of crime to the police; and the reasons for not reporting.

State Court Caseloads. Begun in 1975, produces annual national and state-level data on state and local filings and dispositions of civil, criminal, juvenile, and traffic cases.

Prosecution Statistics. Compiles data for selected jurisdictions on felony case processing. The data cover case attrition, reasons for case rejection, pretrial release decisions, continuances, trial rates, time from arrest to disposition, guilty pleas, conviction rates, and sentences.

National Indigent Criminal Defense Survey. Begun in 1983, produces national and State-level data on public defender systems. The data cover costs, employment, organization, fees paid, caseloads, types of cases (felony, misdemeanor, juvenile, mental commitments, appeals), and disposition of cases.

National Prisoner Statistics. Produces annual and semiannual national and state-level data on the numbers of prisoners in state and federal facilities. Every 5 years, data are collected on detailed characteristics of state prisons, such as age of facility, security level, programs offered, confinement space, employment, and operating costs. Also at 5-year intervals, data are collected from a survey of state prisoners; data collected include criminal histories, incarceration offense, drug and alcohol use, and demographic characteristics. Much of the information dates to the early 1900s.

National Jail Statistics. First conducted in 1970. It now produces annual national estimates of the number of jail inmates. Every 5 years, it produces detailed national and state-level data on the characteristics of inmates and jails similar to those produced by the National Prisoner Statistics program.

Capital Punishment. Yields annual national and state-level data on the numbers and characteristics of persons sentenced to death and those executed. Some of the information dates to 1930.

Uniform Parole Reports. Begun in 1965, produces annual national and state-level data on the number of persons on parole, the number released to parole during the year, and the number who were returned to prison while on parole. The characteristics of persons placed on parole and of persons who leave parole each year are also collected.

National Probation Reports. Begun in 1980, produces annual national and state-level data on the number of persons on probation, the number placed on probation, and the number leaving probation. Collection of data on the characteristics of probationers is planned.

National Corrections Reporting Program. Begun in 1983, collects annual data from all states on all offender movements from prison admission through parole release, including demographic, offense, and sentencing data.

Directory of Justice Agencies. Begun in 1970 and updated periodically, produces national and state-level data on the numbers of justice agencies, by type of agency and selected characteristics (for example, jurisdiction, employment, and various workload measures). The directory was developed for statistical purposes but it is also used as a list from which users can purchase printouts or mailing labels.

Justice Expenditure and Employment Survey. Begun in 1967, produces annual national and state-level data on the costs of the justice system and the numbers of persons employed by justice agencies. Its geographic and substantive details vary over the years because of changes in survey methodology.

Federal Criminal Justice Statistics. Produces annual data on the processing of federal criminal cases from arrest through incarceration; special topics being analyzed include bank robbery and drug offenses. Data relate to 1978 through 1981, with more recent data being added to the data base.

White Collar Crime. Begun in 1983, collects data from selected financial institutions on electronic-funds-transfer crime.

Computer Crime. Begun in 1983, collects data on prosecutions and prosecutorial experience under State computer crime statues.

Victim and Witness Assistance. Summarizes recent federal and state laws. The report discusses the impact that proposed victim/witness programs may have on demands for criminal justice data and the extent to which such programs may require modifications of current information management policies.

The BJS Data Analysis and Publication Programs

BJS has an extensive data analysis and publication program that produces different types of reports aimed at different audiences. Sometimes the organizations that collect data for BJS also analyze the data for BJS publication, but most frequently BJS personnel analyze the data from the BJS statistical series and author reports for BJS publication.

BJS also has an External Analysis Program, in which researchers analyze data of current topical interest for BJS publication. Analyses now under way address such topics as: career criminals; processing habeas corpus petitions; repeated victimization; recidivism; the deterrent effect of the criminal justice system; plea bargaining; causality in crime statistics; school crime; outcomes of state parole and incapacitation policies; civil and criminal dockets; the alternatives of rehabilitation, deterrence, incapacitation, and retribution.

Report series published by BJS include:

BJS Bulletins. Initiated in 1981, summarize data from the various statistical series. The bulletins are published monthly in a four-page, nontechnical format, suitable for a broad audience. Each bulletin addresses a topic on crime or the administration of justice.

BJS Special Reports. Written in nontechnical language and are aimed at a broad audience. Each Special Report focuses on a topic of current public interest and policy debate. It addresses the selected topics in a comprehensive, but nontechnical, manner.

BJS Technical Reports. Present findings of BJS statistical series and technical research programs, and they address issues of statistical methodology and special topics in a more detailed and technical format than in the Bulletin and Special Reports series. These reports are aimed at a technical audience.

BJS Report to the Nation on Crime and Justice. Comprehensive presentation of statistical information concerning crime and the administration of justice. In addition to BJS data series, the report draws on data from other federal, state, and local agencies as well as a variety of other research and reference materials. The report uses nontechnical language and graphic presentation suitable for a general audience.

BJS Detailed Findings Reports. Detailed data collected through the various BJS statistical series. Extensive tabular material is presented along with technical details on the sample design, survey methodology, and statistical definitions used. The reports are suitable for users who desire more detailed and technical information than is available in the shorter bulletins and special reports.

BJS Sourcebook of Criminal Justice Statistics. Begun in 1972, it is compiled annually from more than 100 separate sources, presented with minimal text and extensive tables. An index and a list of sources guides users to data not published in the Sourcebook because of space considerations.

BJS Compendium of Federal Justice Statistics. First issued in 1984, compiles data from agencies and courts that have federal jurisdiction. The report presents data on eight federal offenses for the whole federal system and for each district. Topics include investigations, arrests, prosecutions, trials, sentencing, and incarcerations.

BJS Privacy and Security Series. Describes state legislative activity relating to the privacy and security of criminal justice systems and analyze emerging issues in the area of criminal justice information policy. A compendium of state privacy legislation is issued every 2 years.

BJS Computer Crime Series. Discuss subjects such as recent legislation, expert witness procedures, computer security techniques, and the prosecution of computer crime; a document describing the nature of electronic-fund-transfer crime is also available.

BJS Directory of Automated Criminal Justice Information Systems. Serves as a current reference for data processors and criminal justice planners in developing new information systems and in enhancing present systems. It is intended to foster communication among developers and users of criminal justice information systems, to facilitate the transfer or adaptation of exemplary systems, and to minimize duplication of effort. The directory is issued periodically.

How to Obtain Data and Reports From BJS

BJS distributes its reports through the National Criminal Justice Reference Service (NCJRS). The Reference Service notifies its mailing list of forthcoming publications, and users return a form requesting copies of desired publications. To get a registration form for the Reference Service mailing list or to order a BJS report, write to NCJRS, Box 6000, Rockville, MD 20850, or call (301) 251-5500.

BJS sponsors the National Criminal Justice Data Archive at the Inter-University Consortium for Political and Social Research at the University of Michigan. The archive assists users whose needs are not satisfied by published statistics. All BJS data tapes (covering most of the BJS data series) and much other high-quality data are stored at the archive and are disseminated via magnetic tapes compatible with the user's computing facility. The archive also disseminates microfilmed National Crime Survey data for users who desire more detail than is contained in BJS publications, but who lack access to computing facilities. For more information, contact the Criminal Justice Data Archive, P.O. Box 1248, Ann Arbor, MI 48106, (303) 763-5010.

BJS State Statistical and Systems Program

Statistical analysis centers have been established in about 40 states. The centers: provide statistical information services and policy guidance to the Governors, executive branch agencies, state and local agencies, the judiciary, the press, and the public; are clearinghouses for statistical information among criminal justice agencies within the state; investigate specific issues in criminal justice and develop analytic methods and techniques; provide the data they collect to BJS for compilation into multi-state reports.

Users desiring data specific to single states contact Criminal Justice Statistics Association at (202) 347-4608.

Through BJS funding, a catalog and library of statistical reports produced by the centers is maintained by the Criminal Justice Statistics Association, 444 North Capitol Street, N.W., Suite 122, Washington, D.C. 20001, (202) 347-4608.

BJS supports the development and operation of state uniform crime reporting systems in more than 40 states to facilitate the submission and improve the validity and reliability of data submitted by local police agencies to the FBI's Uniform Crime Reporting Program. These data include offenses known to the police, arrests, offenses cleared, and employment data.

BJS supports the National Clearinghouse for Criminal Justice Information Systems, 925 Secret River Drive, Suite H, Sacramento, CA 95831, (916) 392-2550. The clearinghouse: operates an automated index of criminal justice information systems maintained by state and local governments throughout the Nation; issues technical publications; provides technical assistance and training for state and local government officials.

Bureau of Justice Statistics Reports

Single copies are available at no charge from the National Criminal Justice Reference Service, Box 6000, Rockville, MD 20850. Multiple copies are for sale by the Superintendent of Documents, U.S. Government Printing Office, Washington, D.C. 20402.

NATIONAL CRIME SURVEY

Criminal Victimization in the United States (annual)
  Summary Findings of 1973-79 Changes in Crime and of Trends Since 1973, NCJ-62993
  A Description of Trends from 1973 to 1978, NCJ-66716
  1978 (final report), NCJ-66480
  1977, NCJ-58725

1976, NCJ-49543
1975, NCJ-44593
1974, NCJ-39467
1973, NCJ-34732

Intimate Victims: A Study of Violence Among Friends and Relatives, NCJ-62319

Crime and Seasonality, NCJ-64818

Criminal Victimization of New York State Residents, 1974-77, NCJ-66481

Criminal Victimization of California Residents, 1974-77, NCJ-70944

Indicators of Crime and Criminal Justice: Quantitative Studies, NCJ-62349

Criminal Victimization Surveys in 13 American Cities (summary report, 1 vol.), NCJ-18471
    Boston, NCJ-34818
    Buffalo, NCJ-34820
    Cincinnati, NCJ-34819
    Houston, NCJ-34821
    Miami, NCJ-34822
    Milwaukee, NCJ-34823
    Minneapolis, NCJ-34824
    New Orleans, NCJ-34825
    Oakland, NCJ-34826
    Pittsburgh, NCJ-34827
    San Diego, NCJ-34828
    San Francisco, NCJ-34829
    Washington, D.C., NCJ-34830

Public Attitudes About Crime (13 vols.):
    Boston, NCJ-46235
    Buffalo, NCJ-46236
    Cincinnati, NCJ-46237
    Houston, NCJ-46238
    Miami, NCJ-46239
    Milwaukee, NCJ-46240
    Minneapolis, NCJ-46241
    New Orleans, NCJ-46242
    Oakland, NCJ-46243
    Pittsburgh, NCJ-46244
    San Diego, NCJ-46245
    San Francisco, NCJ-46246
    Washington, D.C., NCJ-46247

Criminal Victimization Surveys in Chicago, Detroit, Los Angeles, New York, and Philadelphia: A Comparison of 1972 and 1974 Findings, NCJ-36360

Criminal Victimization Surveys in Eight American Cities: A Comparison of 1971/72 and 1974/75 Findings-National Crime Surveys in Atlanta, Baltimore, Cleveland, Dallas, Denver, Newark, Portland, and St. Louis, NCJ-36361

Criminal Victimization Surveys in the Nation's Five Largest Cities: National Crime Panel Surveys in Chicago, Detroit, Los Angeles, New York, and Philadelphia, 1972, NCJ-16909

Crimes and Victims: A Report on the Dayton/San Jose Pilot Survey of Victimization, NCJ-013314

Applications of the National Crime Survey Victimization and Attitude Data:

Public Opinion About Crime: The Attitudes of Victims and Nonvictims in Selected Cities, NCJ-41336

Local Victim Surveys: A Review of the Issues, NCJ-39173

The Police and Public Opinion: An Analysis of Victimization and Attitude Data from 13 American Cities, NCJ-42018

An Introduction to the National Crime Survey, NCJ-43732

Compensating Victims of Violent Crime: Potential Costs and Coverage of a National Program, NCJ-43387

Rape Victimization in 26 American Cities, NCJ-55878

Crime Against Persons in Urban, Suburban, and Rural Areas: A Comparative Analysis of Victimization Rates, NCJ-53551

Criminal Victimization in Urban Schools, NCJ-56396

Restitution to Victims of Personal and Household Crimes, NCJ-72770

Myths and Realities About Crime: A Nontechnical Presentation of Selected Information from the National Prisoner Statistics Program and the National Crime Survey, NCJ-46249

NATIONAL PRISONER STATISTICS

Capital Punishment (annual) 1982, NCJ-70945

Prisoners in State and Federal Institutions on December 31, 1979, NCJ-73719

Census of State Correctional Facilities, 1974 advance report, NCJ-25642

Profile of State Prison Inmates: Sociodemographic Findings from the 1974 Survey of Inmates of State Correctional Facilities, NCJ-58257.

Census of Prisoners in State Correctional Facilities, 1973, NCJ-34729.

Census of Jails and Survey of Jail Inmates, 1978, preliminary report, NCJ-55172.

Census of Jails and Survey of Jail Inmates, 1978, preliminary report, NCJ-55172

Profile of Inmates of Local Jails: Sociodemographic Findings from the 1978 Survey of Inmates of Local Jails, NCJ-65412

The Nation's Jails: A report on the census of jails from the 1972 Survey of Inmates of Local Jails, NCJ-19067

Uniform Parole Reports:

Parole in the United States (annual):
    1979, NCJ-69562
    1978, NCJ-58722
    1976 and 1977, NCJ-49702

A National Survey of Parole-Related Legislation. Enacted
    During the 1979 Legislative Session, NCJ-64218

Characteristics of the Parole Population. 1978, NCJ-66479

Children in Custody: Juvenile Detention and Correctional
    Facility Census 1977 advance report:
        Census of Public Juvenile Facilities, NCJ-60967
        Census of Private Juvenile Facilities, NCJ-60968
        1975 (final report), NCJ-58139
        1974, NCJ-57946
        1973, NCJ-44777
        1971, NCJ-13403

State and Local Probation and Parole Systems, NCJ-41335

State and Local Prosecution and Civil Attorney Systems,
    NCJ-41334

National Survey of Court Organization:
    1977 Supplement to State Judicial Systems, NCJ-
        40022
    1975 Supplement to State Judicial Systems, NCJ-
        29433
    1971 (full report), NCJ-11427

State Court Model Statistical Dictionary, NCJ-62320

State Court Caseload Statistics:
    The State of the Art, NCJ-46934
    Annual Report, 1975, NCJ-51885
    Annual Report, 1976, NCJ-56599

A Cross-City Comparison of Felony Case Processing, NCJ-
    55171

*Trends in Expenditure and Employment Data for the
    Criminal Justice System, 1971-77,* (annual), NCJ-
    57463

*Expenditure and Employment Data for the Criminal Justice
    System* (annual)

1979 Advance Report, NCJ-73288
1978 Summary Report, NCJ-66483
1978 Final Report, NCJ-66482
1977 Final Report, NCJ-53206

Justice Agencies in the U.S.: Summary Report of the
    National Justice Agency List, NCJ-65560

Dictionary of Criminal Justice Data Terminology: Terms and
    Definitions Proposed for Interstate and National Data
    Collection and Exchange, NCJ-36747

UTILIZATION OF CRIMINAL JUSTICE STATISTICS PROJECT

Sourcebook of Criminal Justice Statistics 1980 (annual),
    NCJ-71096

Offender-Based Transaction Statistics: New Directions in
    Data Collection and Reporting, NCJ-29645

Sentencing of California Felony Offenders, NCJ-29646

Crime-Specific Analysis:
    The Characteristics of Burglary Incidents. NCJ-42093
        An Empirical Examination of Burglary Offender
            Characteristics, NCJ-43131
        An Empirical Examination of Burglary Offenders and
            Offense Characteristics, NCJ-42476

Sources of National Criminal Justice Statistics: An
    Annotated Bibliography, NCJ-45006

Federal Criminal Sentencing: Perspectives of Analysis and a
    Design for Research, NCJ-33683

Variations in Federal Criminal Sentences: A Statistical
    Assessment at the National Level, NCJ-33684

Federal Sentencing Patterns: A Study of Geographical
    Variations, NCJ-33685

Predicting Sentences in Federal Courts: The Feasibility of a
    National Sentencing Policy, NCJ-33686

OTHER SOURCES OF STATISTICAL DATA

Statistics are an important form of information to any field of knowledge. Statistics can also help determine the relevance of a problem or issue. There are many sources of statistics, such as public opinion polls, journals, books, pamphlets, government reports, and newspapers, and sometimes the task of finding a source with mention of desired statistical data is easier said than done. However, there are several publications that now provide statistical information. But the researcher must be aware of these publications before he can locate and use them. To help you develop this awareness, the following annotations of statistical reference sources are offered. These represent only a sample of the sources that are likely to be available in most libraries. Your library may possess additional sources.

American Statistics Index (ASI). A comprehensive guide and index to the statistical publications of the United States Government. Includes indexes by subject and name, category, title, and agency report number, and an index which tells the reader what publications have been abstracted in the *ASI Abstracts Volume*. Monthly. (Washington, DC: Congressional Information Service, 1974-date). (This is also available as a computerized database. See American Statistics Index in Chapter 9, "Computerized Literature Searches").

American Statistics Index: Abstracts Volume. Abstracts many of the citations that appear in the *ASI Index Volume*. Broken down into categories of Executive Office of the President, Department of Agriculture, Department of Commerce, Department of Defense, Department of Health, Education, and Welfare, Department of Housing and Urban Development, Department of the Interior, Department of Justice, Department of Labor, Department of State, Department of Transportation, Department of Treasury, Independent Agencies, Special Boards, Committees, and Commissions, United States Courts and United States Congress. Each of these departments is further subdivided and publications of each agency are abstracted. To date.

Book of the States. A very good source covering all aspects of state governments. It includes information on police administration activities on the state level, and chapters on law enforcement and public protection, and highway safety. Biennial. (Chicago, IL: Council of State Governments, 1935 to date).

Bureau of the Census Catalog. This is the current listing of publications available from the Bureau. A subject index leads to abstracts of subject content with ordering information. Annual.

California Statistical Abstract. This annual covers all types of statistics for California, including those related to crime, prisons, and law enforcement. Index in back. The 1970 *Abstract* is a historical volume, incorporating data "as far back as availability or space limitations permitted." (Sacramento, CA: Department of Finance, 1970-date).

City and County Data Book. Regarded as a complement to the Statistical Abstracts of the United States (see below), and covers 144 items for each county in the United States and 148 items for each of the 683 cities having 25,000 or more population. Items include population, dwelling units, retail and wholesale trade, vital statistics, and so forth. 1988. (Washington, DC: United States Bureau of the Census, GPO).

Compendium of Social Statistics. Contains statistics relating to the environmental conditions of life and work in the nations of the world, i.e., infant mortality, dwelling size, expenditure levels, work force, and employment conditions. (New York: United Nations, 1963-date).

Complaints and Arrests: Statistical Report. Monthly statistics by precinct. Monthly. (New York: Police Department, Office of Management Analysis, 1975-date).

1983-84 Congressional Directory. Lists all Members of Congress by state, alphabetically, and by term of office. A short biography is included for each Senator and Representative. In addition, you will find a complete listing of all federal agencies and commissions, including addresses, phone numbers, and names and titles of officials. Other features include a listing of diplomatic representatives to the U.S., maps of each state's congressional districts, and much more. (Washington, DC: U.S. Government Printing Office, 1983-date).

Congressional District Data Book and Congressional District Data Book Supplement: Redistricted States. A variety of statistical data from a number of sources are presented in this biennial supplement to the *Statistical Abstract of the United States*. Information is organized by congressional district and concerns such topics as bank deposits, elections, housing, local governments, retail trade, non-white populations, vital statistics, and so forth. (Washington, DC: U.S. Government Printing Office, 1961-date).

Corrections Statistics in the United States. Presents summary tables and commentary for published national government reports on correction statistics from 1850 to 1984. Includes statistics on: capital punishment, state and federal prisons, jails, institutions for juvenile delinquents, parole and probation, and information on incarceration. 100s of charts, tables and graphs. (Upland, PA: DIANE Publishing Co.).

Crime and Delinquency in California. An annual statistical compilation covering the following topics: crimes, arrests, adult felony arrest dispositions, adult corrections, the juvenile justice system, and criminal justice agency expenditures and personnel. Charts and graphs show trends for both crime rates and criminal justice administration. (Sacramento, CA: Bureau of Criminal Statistics, 1972-date).

Crime, Courts, and Figures; An Introduction to Criminal Statistics, N. Walker. Provides an in-depth look at statistics and the criminal justice system. (New York: Peter Smith, 1973).

The Criminal Justice Data Directory. Describes Bureau of Justice Statistics sponsored data collections as well as a number of other relevant datasets. This 152-page directory is a must for any serious criminal justice researcher. (Ann Arbor, MI: Criminal Justice Archive and Inter-University Consortium for Political and Social Research, 1982).

The Criminal Justice System in the City of New York — An Overview. (Albany, NY: Commission of Investigation, 1974).

Criminal Victimization in the United States. In addition to information about the nature of the crime, and about the victim and perpetrator, these studies include the relationship between the victim and the perpetrator, income and the place of residence of victim, and whether or not the crime was reported to officials. Annual. (Washington, DC: U.S. Census Bureau, 1973-date).

Demographic Yearbook. Offers detailed world figures on population, projected trends, births, deaths, marriages, life expectancy, and so forth. (New York: Statistical Office, United Nations, 1949-date).

Directory of Criminal Justice Issues in the States, Volume 1. H. Saizow and J. Boneta (eds.) Summarizes all activities of the state statistical analysis centers (SAC's) conducted during 1983. The directory is designed to inform national policymakers on critical criminal justice issues under debate in the states, inform state policymakers on the activities of other states, and strengthen awareness of the work of the SAC's. Included for each of 259 activities performed in 1983 is the title, brief description, data sources used, date of completion, and contact person. Activities are indexed by substantive area. Appendix. (Washington, DC: Criminal Justice Statistics Association, 1984).

Directory of Federal Statistics for Local Areas: A Guide to Sources, 1976. Contains an excellent summary of federal statistics sources and is apt to be available in every library. Arrangement is by topical chapters: Agriculture, Banking and Finance, Commerce and Trade, Communication and Transportation, Crime and Law Enforcement, Education, Environment and Climate, Government and Revenue Sharing, Housing and Construction, Income and Earnings, Labor and Employment, Manufacturing, Mineral Industries, Population, Prices, Vital Statistics and Health. (Washington, DC: Bureau of the Census, 1978).

Expanding the Perspective of Crime Data: Performance Implications for Policymakers. K.M. Williams, et al. Examines apprehension, conviction, and incarceration performance measures for various crimes. Data from approximately 100,000 "street crime" cases, handled through normal prosecution and court operation in the District of Columbia over a six-year period, gathered by Prosecutor's Management Information System (PROMIS). This data was then analyzed by the Institute for Law and Social Research, and results provided the basis for this publication. (Washington, DC: Law Enforcement Assistance Administration, GPO Stock #027-000-00575-6, NCJ 40230, 1977).

Expenditure and Employment Data for the Criminal Justice System. Published annually. Documents expenditure data for criminal justice activities in the United States. Data concerns the federal government, each of the 50 states, and the aggregate local level of government within each state. Annual. (Washington, DC: United States Department of Justice, Bureau of Justice Statistics).

Guide to United States Government Statistics. John L. Androit. An annotated guide to over 1200 United States Government publications relating to statistics. (McLean, VA: Documents Index, 1973).

Handbook of Resources for Criminal Justice Evaluators. Designed to provide evaluators, planners, and decision-makers with information about techniques that could improve the handling of problems encountered in criminal justice evaluation. Four problems are addressed: 1) technical and research problems, 2) types of evaluations to be done and what questions should be answered, 3) insuring privacy and confidentiality of data collected and protection of human subjects, and 4) providing documentation to newly hired evaluators about local resources, organizational structure of the office, administrative procedures, and sources of data. (Washington, DC: United States Department of Justice, Law Enforcement Assistance Administration, National Institute of Law Enforcement and Criminal Justice, 1978).

Historical Statistics of the United States, Colonial Times to 1957. Summarizes social and economic developments of the United States from 1610 through 1957. A subject index is provided as are notations of access to originally published sources. (Washington, DC: United States Bureau of Statistics, GPO, 1960). (See Chapter 15, "Historical Research Sources," for additional sources).

Index to International Statistics. (IIS). An index to statistical publications of international organizations, including the United Nations System. (Bethesda, MD: Congressional Information Service, 1983-date).

International Crime Statistics. A biannual publication which provides crime statistics on an international basis. (Saint-Cloud, France: International Criminal Police Organization, INTERPOL). (See Chapter 14, "Sources of International Data," for additional suggestions on obtaining data with international relevance.)

Inter-University Consortium for Political Research. An academic data source which includes results of current research projects, academic surveys, and similar information. Surveys reflect motivation and attitudes of the individuals surveyed. A nominal fee is charged for data. (Ann Arbor, MI: The University of Michigan Press).

An Inventory of Surveys of the Public on Crime, Justice, and Related Topics. Addressed to the studies of crime, delinquency, criminal justice, law enforcement, and closely related areas by means of the sample interview survey method. Studies included for review had to involve interviews or a questionnaire given to a study population not preselected on the basis of roles within criminal justice institutions. (Washington, DC: United States Department of Justice, National Institute on Law Enforcement and Criminal Justice, Law Enforcement Assistance Administration, 1972).

Judicial Criminal Statistics, 1933-1945. (U.S. Bureau of the Census: Dependent and Delinquent Classes, microfiche #1502).

Juvenile Court Statistics. Contains estimates and analyses of juvenile delinquency cases and dependency and neglect cases disposed of by juvenile courts in 1974. (Washington, DC: United States Department of Justice, Law Enforcement Assistance Administration, 1974).

Municipal Yearbook. Primarily a statistical almanac, published annually since 1934. Provides information on most United States cities with populations in excess of 10,000, although some towns with populations in the 5-10,000 range are also included. (Chicago, IL: International City Managers Association).

National Crime Surveys: Criminal Victimization in the U.S. Bureau of Justice Statistics. (Washington, DC: U.S. Government Printing Office, 1973-date).

National Prisoner Statistics. Bureau of Justice Statistics. (Washington, DC: U.S. Government Printing Office, 1926-date).

National Statistical Compendiums. Microfiche. (Washington, DC: CIS).

New York State Felony Processing Quarterly Report: Indictment through Disposition. Provides detailed statistics on felony arrests, indictments, dispositions, and processing times. (Albany, NY: Division of Criminal Justice Services, 1974-date).

New York State Statistical Yearbook. Section K, "Public Safety," making use of figures from the Department of Criminal Justice Services and the Department of Correctional Services, supplies tables dealing with arrests, offenses, and correctional institutions. Most tables separate New York City from upstate; some also provide breakdowns into large urban areas, small urban areas and suburbs. Annual. (Albany, NY: Division of the Budget, 1967-date).

Office of Justice Assistance, Research, and Statistics (OJARS). This office is a result of the Justice System Improvement Act of 1979, signed by President Carter 12/27/79. This Act will reorganize the way in which the federal government provides financial and technical aid to the nation's criminal justice system. Under this legislation OJARS will provide staff support and coordinate administrative activities of the Law Enforcement Assistance Administration, the National Institute of Justice, and Bureau of Justice Statistics. OJARS will undoubtedly become a major source of criminal justice information in the near future.

Periodicals and Sources. A 20-page guide which lists almost 900 United States Government statistical publications. Periodicals listed contain facts and figures on topics such as business, crime, natural resources, foreign trade, health, and demography. (Washington, DC: Congressional Information Service).

Police Practices: The General Administrative Survey, John F. Heaphy (ed.) A general survey report of police administrative practices of 56 police departments which serve cities of more than 250,000. (Kansas City, MO: The Police Foundation with the Assistance of the Police Executive Research Forum, 1978).

Police Source Book. B. Swainton, G. Hannigan, and D. Biles. This overview provides descriptive and statistical material on the status and organization of the police in Australia. The authors discuss the history and background of the Australian police, the principal law enforcement establishments and expenditures, police structure and organization, legal powers, and the typical police officer. Other topics of discussion include discipline and accountability; working conditions, uniforms, and weapons; ranks and salary; recruitment; and education and training. The report also describes police transport, communications, internal security, traffic control, and criminal investigation. International participation, major police organizations, and improvements in police capabilities are outlined. Tables, bibliography. (Phillip, ACT, Australia: Australian Institute of Criminology, 1983).

Prisoners in State and Federal Institutions. Annual. (Washington, DC: U.S. Government Printing Office, 1967-date).

Quantitative Studies in Criminology: 1978. Charles Wellford (ed.) Discusses advanced statistical techniques used in criminology and compares recent research to demonstrate the value of a rigorous methodology and the areas to be considered for the application of advanced statistical techniques. Emphasis is given to the measurement of crime, deterrence, the use of longitudinal analyses, and empirical studies of police. (Beverly Hills, CA: Sage Research Progress Series in Criminology, Volume 8, 1978).

Report to the Nation on Crime and Justice: The Data. Comprehensive picture of crime and criminal justice in the U.S. represented in graphs and simple-to-understand graphs and charts. (Washington, DC: U.S. Government Printing Office, 1983).

Social Indicators III: Selected Data on Social Conditions and Trends in the United States. Combines colorful graphs and charts with authoritative statistics to give you a comprehensive picture of American life and society. Includes facts and figures on population and the family, our health and nutrition, the housing situation and our environment, income and productivity trends, and social security and welfare programs. (Washington, DC: U.S. Government Printing Office, 1980).

Sourcebook of Criminal Justice Statistics. U.S. Department of Justice, Bureau of Justice Statistics. Annual. (Washington, DC: U.S. Government Printing Office, 1973-date).

Criminal Justice Abstracts. 11:122-147. "Sources of Basic Criminal Justice Statistics: A Brief Annotated Guide with Commentaries." Eugene Doleschal. March, 1979.

Sources of National Criminal Justice Statistics: An Annotated Bibliography. Annotates sources of criminal justice statistics including public opinion, literature pertaining to crime, drugs, law enforcement, diversion, courts, juveniles, corrections, furloughs, probation and parole, and general sources. Alphabetically lists sources, addresses of publishers, and subject index. (Washington, DC: United States Department of Justice, Law Enforcement Assistance Administration, National Criminal Justice Information and Statistics Service, GPO Stock #027-000-00681-7, 1977).

State Court Caseload Statistics, Annual Report. Provides data regarding the number and types of cases handled through state courts. (Washington, DC: United States Department of Justice.)

State and Local Probation and Parole Systems. Included in this volume are lists of state and local probation agencies, their functions, government affiliations, case loads, number of employees, activities, and funding sources. A separate section discusses the organization of each state's probation and parole system, and presents full descriptive profiles of the system. (Washington, DC: U.S. Government Printing Office, 1978).

State and Metropolitan Area Data Book, 1986. Gives variety of information for states and metropolitan areas of the U.S., derived mainly from the latest available censuses. Provides facts and figures on births and deaths, marriages and divorces, households and families, health, education, employment, personal wealth, crime, housing, banking, elections, land ownership, energy, wholesale trade. (Washington, DC: U.S. Government Printing Office).

Statesman's Year Book; Statistical and Historical Annual of the States of the World. Provides statistics and other information on international organizations and every country during the preceding year. Data covering each nation's constitution, political and governmental structure, financial basis, gross national product, court system, and so forth is included. (London and New York: Macmillan, 1864-date).

Statistical Abstracts of the United States. Published annually. Includes a comprehensive selection of data from several significant statistical sources. Reliable summary of statistics on the social, political, and economic organization of the United States. Also serves as a reference to other sources of statistical information, and is very good for locating statistics on just about any current problem. This publication is the most reliable source for data regarding births, deaths, marriages, divorces, number of physicians, dentists, nurses, immigration and naturalization, law enforcement, courts and prisons, geography and climates, public lands and parks, recreation and travel, elections, and incomes. Annual. (Washington, DC: United States Bureau of the Census, 1979).

Statistical Reference Index (SRI). Aims to provide current access to selected statistical reference material on a wide spectrum of subject matter, representative of all types of data available from American sources. Provides access to over 2,000 publications, representing over 6,000 individual issuances from more than 1,000 associations and institutes, business organizations, commercial publishers, independent research organizations, state government agencies, and university research centers...all of the leading sources of published statistical information outside of the U.S. government, 1980-date. SRI covers:

National data — production, costs, and earnings in major industries and business sectors, operating ratios and market characteristics of business and commerce, data related to key areas of social or public interest; public opinion and salary surveys; demographic data; and national economic trends.

State-wide data — statistical compendiums and 20-40 additional selected basic reports for each state on areas such as vital statistics, health, agriculture, business conditions and economic indicators, employment, education, state taxation and finance, elections, construction, insurance, tourism, motor vehicles and accidents, and judicial systems.

Data on foreign countries — world economic or demographic trends, and foreign country studies; international finance, investment, and trade data; foreign country social and economic indicators.

Local or otherwise narrowly focused data — detail by county and municipality, provided in many state reports if the subject matter is judged to have research value beyond the limited area of coverage.

Locating information — Brief annotations in SRI's multiple-access index section direct users to full publication descriptions in a separately bound abstracts section. To facilitate diverse research approaches, several indexes contained in the index section are Index by subjects and names, Index by categories, Supplementary indexes.

Statistical Services Directory: A Guide to the Organizations, Corporations, Professional and Trade Associations, Research Centers, Universities, Publishers, Foundations and Government Agencies That Provide Statistical Services, Second Edition. (Detroit, MI: Gale Research, 1984).

Statistics Sources. Paul Wasserman (ed.) Provides data on industrial, business, social, educational, financial, and other topics for the United States and selected foreign countries and also directs the user to other sources of statistical data. (Detroit, MI: Gale Research Company, 1971).

Uniform Crime Reports for the United States. Offers an annual assessment of crime across the nation, based on police statistics since 1930. Seven offenses comprise the crime index: murder, forcible rape, robbery, aggravated assault, burglary, larceny-theft, and motor vehicle theft. Data consisting of narrative comments, charts, and tables on crime index offenses reported, crime index offenses cleared by arrest, persons arrested, and persons charged are offered. (Washington, DC: Federal Bureau of Investigation, 1930-date).

United Nations Statistical Year Book. Contains a summary of statistics for world population, manpower, agriculture, consumption, productivity, external trade, education, social statistics, etc. Subject and nation indexes, written in French and English, are included. (New York: United Nations, 1948-date). (See also Chapter 14, "Sources of International Data").

The United States Government Manual 1983/84. Pinpoints the exact official you need to contact. It provides comprehensive information on the agencies of the legislative, executive, and judicial branches, as well as the quasi-official agencies, boards, commissions, and committees in the federal sphere. A typical agency entry includes a list of principal officers, a summary of the agency's mission and history, a description of its programs and activities, and a list of addresses and telephone numbers. (Washington, DC: U.S. Government Printing Office).

Vital Statistics in Corrections, 1989 Edition. The latest numbers on corrections budgets, salaries, staff demographics, fringe benefits, incarceration rates, correctional unions and employee groups, and more will be at your fingertips in this updated edition. (Laurel, MD: American Correctional Association, 1989).

VICTIMIZATION REPORTS

Another major source of criminal justice statistics are victimization reports, presented by the Bureau of Justice Statistics, National Crime Survey. These victimization surveys differ from the FBI's *Uniform Crime Reports (UCR)* in that the *UCR* compiles crimes reported to local police, sheriffs' departments, and state police, which are in turn reported to the FBI. Also reported in the *UCR* are the number of crimes cleared by arrest. Therefore, the amount of crime committed each year is actually much greater than that reported in the *UCR*. The victimization surveys contain a wealth of information relating to characteristics of victims as well as crime rates. The following reports, available from the NCJRS (Box 6000, Rockville, Maryland 20850), or for purchase from the Superintendent of Documents (United States Government Printing Office, Washington, D.C. 20402), should be consulted for additional statistical information.

The Cost of Negligence: Losses from Preventable Household Burglaries (NCJ 53527).

Crimes Against Persons in Urban, Suburban and Rural Areas: A Comparative Analysis of Victimization Rates (NCJ 53551).

Crimes and Victims: A Report on the Dayton-San Jose Pilot Survey of Victimization (NCJ 013314).

Criminal Victimization in the United States. Summary Findings of 1977-78, Changes in Crime and of Trends Since 1973 (NCJ 61368); A Description of Trends from 1973 to 1977 (NCJ 59898); 1977 (Final Report) (NCJ 58725); 1976 (NCJ 49543); 1975 (NCJ 44593); 1974 (NCJ 39467); 1973 (NCJ 34732).

Criminal Victimization Surveys in 13 American Cities, Summary Report, 1 Volume (NCJ 18471). Boston (NCJ 34818; Buffalo (NCJ 34820); Cincinnati (NCJ 34819); Houston (NCJ 34821); Miami (NCJ 34822); Milwaukee (NCJ 34823); Minneapolis (NCJ 34824); New Orleans (NCJ 34825); Oakland (NCJ 34826); Pittsburgh (NCJ 34827); San Diego (NCJ 34828); San Francisco (NCJ 34829); Washington, D.C. (NCJ 34830).

Criminal Victimization Surveys in Chicago, Detroit, Los Angeles, New York, and Philadelphia: A Comparison of 1972 and 1974 Findings (NCJ 36360).

Criminal Victimization Surveys in Eight American Cities: A Comparison of 1971/72 and 1974/75 Findings (National Crime Surveys in Atlanta, Baltimore, Cleveland, Dallas, Denver, Newark, Portland, and St. Louis) (NCJ 36361).

Intimate Victims: A Study of Violence Among Friends and Relatives (NCJ 62319).

An Introduction to the National Crime Survey (NCJ 43732).

Additional Statistical Reports

Capital Punishment, (annual) 1978, (NCJ 59897).

Census of Jails and Survey of Jail Inmates, 1978, Preliminary Report (NCJ 55172).

Census of Prisoners in State Correctional Facilities, 1973 (NCJ 34729).

Census of State Correctional Facilities, 1974, Advanced Report (NCJ 25642).

Children in Custody: Juvenile Detention and Correctional Facility, 1977, Advance Report: Census of Public Juvenile Facilities (NCJ 60967); Census of Private Juvenile Facilities (NCJ 60968); 1975 (Final Report) (NCJ 58139); 1974 (NCJ 57946); 1973 (NCJ 44777); 1971 (NCJ 13403).

Crime Specific Analysis: The Characteristics of Burglary Incidents (NCJ 42093); An Empirical Examination of Burglary Offender Characteristics (NCJ 43131); An Empirical Examination of Burglary Offenders and Offense Characteristics (NCJ 42476).

A Cross-City Comparison of Felony Case Processing (NCJ 55171).

Delinquency Dispositions: An Empirical Analysis of Processing Decisions in Three Juvenile Courts (NCJ 34734).

Federal Criminal Sentencing: Perspectives of Analysis and a Design for Research (NCJ 33683).

Federal Sentencing Patterns: A Study of Geographical Variations (NCJ 33685).

The Judicial Processing of Assault and Burglary Offenders in Selected California Counties (NCJ 29644).

Juvenile Dispositions: Social and Legal Factors Related to the Processing of Denver Delinquency Cases (NCJ 17418).

Myths and Realities about Crime: A Non-technical Presentation of Selected Information from the National Prisoner Statistics Program and the National Crime Survey (NCJ 46249).

The Nation's Jails: A Report on the Census of Jails from the 1972 Survey of Inmates of Local Jails (NCJ 19067).

Offender-Based Transaction Statistics: New Directions in Data Collection and Reporting (NCJ 29645).

Parole in the United States, 1978 (NCJ 58722); 1977 and 1976 (NCJ 49702).

The Patterns and Distribution of Assault Incident Characteristics Among Social Areas (NCJ 40025).

Patterns of Robbery Characteristics and Their Occurrence Among Social Areas (NCJ 40026).

Pre-Adjudicatory Detention in Three Juvenile Courts (NCJ 34730).

Prisoners in State and Federal Institutions, 1978. Advanced Report (NCJ 58324); 1977 Final Report (NCJ 52701).

Profile of State Prison Inmates: Sociodemographic Findings from the 1974 Survey of Inmates of State Correctional Facilities (NCJ 58257).

Program Plan for Statistics 1977-81 (NCJ 37811).

Sentencing of California Felony Offenders (NCJ 29646).

State Court Caseload Statistics: The State of the Art (NCJ 46934); Annual Report, 1975 (NCJ 51885); Annual Report, 1976 (NCJ 56599).

State Court Model Statistical Dictionary (NCJ 62320).

Survey of Inmates of Local Jails, 1972, Advance Report (NCJ 13313).

Variations in Federal Criminal Sentences. A Statistical Assessment at the National Level (NCJ 33684).

Who Gets Detained? An Empirical Analysis of the Pre-Adjudicatory Detention of Juveniles in Denver (NCJ 17417).

PUBLIC OPINION POLLS

Each year thousands of polls are taken by private research companies that specialize in determining public opinion. For example, the Nielsen Ratings are used to determine the popularity of various television shows, and politicians regularly use polls to determine what issues are most important to the public. The pollsters also conduct a number of inquiries to determine public opinion regarding a variety of criminal justice issues. The findings from these polls are recorded and kept for future reference.

Polls, particularly the Gallup, Harris, and Roper Opinion Polls, are fairly well known, and their findings are published regularly in many newspapers. Even so, polls as a source of data are still often overlooked or neglected by many researchers. This may, in part, be due to the fact that there is difficulty in locating results of a particular poll in an unindexed newspaper, or because their importance as a form of data is not recognized. However, there are simple means of locating results of public opinion surveys, at least some of which will be available in most libraries for the asking, or by writing to the pollster requesting the desired information. Sources providing information on polls include the following:

Index to International Public Opinion. (Prepared by Survey Research Consultants International, Inc. Annual.) See Chapter 14, "Sources of International Data," for a complete description.

The ABC/Washington Post Poll. (New York: ABC News Polling Unit).

American Association for Public Opinion Research. (Princeton, NJ).

American Enterprise Institute for Public Policy Research. (Washington, DC).

American Public Opinion Index. Annual. (Louisville, KY: Opinion Research Service, 1981-date).

California Poll. Public opinion poll concentrated within the state and questions Californians on the hottest issues at any particular time. The results, which often indicate future trends for the nation, are published approximately forty times a year. To date. (San Francisco: Survey Research Services).

CBS News/New York Times Poll. (New York: CBS News).

Current Opinion. A monthly publication that includes results of recent, selected surveys conducted by leading opinion research organizations in the United States and abroad. Topics vary from issue to issue. Criminal justice topics include the death penalty, legalization of marihuana, and gun control. (Williamstown, MA: Roper Public Opinion Research Center).

Gallup Opinion Index. (Formerly *Gallup Political Index*.) Includes monthly surveys, covering a wide range of topics such as the Presidency, capital punishment, crime rates, and so forth. (Princeton, NJ: Gallup International, 1965-date).

The Harris Survey. A frequent press release appearing in newspapers across the country and includes results of public opinion research conducted by Louis Harris and Associates. (Chicago, IL: The Chicago Tribune).

Index to International Public Opinion. See Chapter 14, "Sources of International Data," for a complete description. Annual. (Survey Research Consultants International, Inc.).

Minnesota Poll. Published weekly in the Sunday edition of the *Minnesota Star and Tribune*. Weekly. (Minneapolis: Minneapolis Star Tribune, 1964-date).

Public Attitudes About Crime. Boston (NCJ 46235); Buffalo (NCJ 46236); Cincinnati (NCJ 46237); Houston (NCJ 46238); Miami (NCJ 46239); Milwaukee (NCJ 46240); Minneapolis (NCJ 46241); New Orleans (NCJ 46242); Oakland (NCJ 46243); Pittsburgh (NCJ 46244); San Diego (NCJ 46245); San Francisco (NCJ 46246); Washington, D.C. (NCJ 46247). These publications represent results of crime surveys conducted in the designated cities. (Washington, DC: United States Department of Justice).

Public Opinion About Crime. Composed of three sections: (1) The Attitudes of Victims and Non-Victims in Selected Cities (NCJ 41336), (2) The Police and Public Opinion: An Analysis of Victimization and Attitude Data from 13 American Cities (NCJ 42018), and (3) Public Opinion Regarding Crime, Criminal Justice, and Related Topics (NCJ 17419). Available. (Washington, DC: United States Department of Justice).

Roper Public Opinion Poll. Contains a massive amount of poll data, concentrating on all academic and professional poll and survey groups worldwide. The surveys and studies are available to students on cards or tapes at reasonable rates. Currently available. (Williamstown, MA: Williams College).

Newspaper and Magazine Indexes and Abstracts

Public Opinion. Bimonthly. (Washington, DC: American Enterprise Institute for Public Policy Research, 1978-date).

Public Opinion Quarterly. Quarterly. (New York: Elsevier Science Publishing, 1937-date).

Roper Center for Public Opinion Research. (Storrs, CT: University of Connecticut).

ORGANIZATIONS THAT PRODUCE CRIMINAL JUSTICE STATISTICS

American Correctional Association (ACA), 4321 Hartwick Rd., Suite L208, College Park, MD 20740.

Association for Correctional Research and Information Management (ACRIM), c/o Tom Johnson, 600 J St., Division of Criminal Justice, California State University, Sacramento, CA 95819.

CJAIN: The Criminal Justice Archive and Information Network, PO Box 1248, Ann Arbor, MI 48106.

Criminal Justice Statistics Association (CJSA), 444 N. Capitol Street, NW, Suite 122, Washington, DC 20001.

National Center for Juvenile Justice (NCJJ), 701 Forbes Avenue, Pittsburgh, PA 15219.

National Center for State Courts (NCSC), 300 Newport Avenue, Williamsburg, VA 23185.

Administrative Office of the United States Courts, Washington, DC 20544.

U.S. Bureau of the Census, Fourteenth Street between Constitution Avenue and E Street, NW, Washington, DC 20230.

U.S. Bureau of Justice Statistics (BJS), 633 Indiana Avenue, NW, Washington, DC 20531.

U.S. Federal Bureau of Investigation, Ninth and Pennsylvania Avenues, NW, Washington, DC 20535.

U.S. Office of Justice Assistance, Research and Statistics, 633 Indiana Avenue, NW, Washington, DC 20531.

Statistical Analysis Centers

Most states now have Statistical Analysis Centers for criminal justice data. The following are state centers.

Alabama Criminal Justice Information Center
858 South Court Street
Montgomery, AL 36104
(205) 832-4930

University of Alaska
3211 Providence Drive
Anchorage, AK 99508
(907) 786-1815

Information Analysis Section
Department of Public Safety
PO Box 6638
Phoenix, AZ 85005
(602) 223-2232

Special Services Section
Arkansas Crime Information Center
One Capitol Mall
Little Rock, AR 72201
(501) 682-2232

Bureau of Criminal Statistics and Special Services
PO Box 903427
Sacramento, CA 94203-4270
(916) 739-5568

Division of Criminal Justice
Department of Public Safety
700 Kipling Street
Suite 3000
Denver, CO 80215
(303) 239-4442

Justice Planning Division
Office of Policy and Management
80 Washington Street
Hartford, CT 06106
(203) 566-3522

Office of Criminal Justice Plans and Analysis
1111 E Street, NW
Suite 500C
Washington, DC 20004
(202) 727-6554

Division of Criminal Justice
Information Systems
Florida Department of Law Enforcement
PO Box 1489
Tallahassee, FL 32302
(904) 487-4808

Georgia Crime Information Center
PO Box 370748
Decatur, GA 30037
(404) 244-2601

Hawaii Criminal Justice Data Center
Department of the Attorney General
465 South King Street
Honolulu, HI 96813
(808) 548-2090

Support Services Bureau
Department of Law Enforcement
6111 Clinton Street
Boise, ID 83704
(208) 334-2162

Information Resource Center
Criminal Justice Information Authority
120 South Riverside Plaza
Chicago, IL 60606
(312) 793-8550

Indiana Criminal Justice Institute
150 West Market Street
Suite 200
Indianapolis, IN 46204
(317) 232-1619

Division of Criminal Justice and Juvenile Planning
Executive Hills East
Des Moines, IA 50319
(515) 242-5816

Kansas Bureau of Investigation
1620 Southwest Tyler
Topeka, KS 66612
(913) 232-6000

Office of the Attorney General
Capitol Building
Frankfort, KY 40601
(502) 564-4002

Louisiana Commission on Law Enforcement
2121 Wooddale Boulevard
Baton Rouge, LA 70806
(504) 925-4440

Maine Criminal Justice Data Center
Department of Corrections
State House
Station 111
Augusta, ME 04333
(207) 289-2711

Maryland Justice Analysis Center
Institute of Criminal Justice and Criminology
University of Maryland
College Park, MD 20742
(301) 454-4538

Massachusetts Committee on Criminal Justice
100 Cambridge Street
Room 2100
Boston, MA 02202
(617) 727-0237

Office of Criminal Justice
Lewis Cass Building
PO Box 30026
Lansing, MI 48909
(517) 373-6510

Criminal Justice
State Planning Agency
658 Cedar Street
St. Paul, MN 55155
(612) 296-7819

Department of Criminal Justice Planning
301 West Pearl Street
Jackson, MS 39203
(601) 949-2006

Department of Public Safety
Missouri Highway Patrol
1510 East Elm
Jefferson City, MO 65101
(314) 751-4026

Research Planning Bureau
Board of Crime Control
303 North Roberts Street
Helena, MT 59620
(406) 444-3604

Commission on Law Enforcement and Criminal Justice
PO Box 94946
Lincoln, NE 68509
(402) 471-2194

Crime Information Services Bureau
Nevada Highway Patrol
555 Wright Way
Carson City, NV 89701
(702) 885-5713

Office of the Attorney General
State House Annex
Concord, NH 03301
(603) 271-3658

Research and Evaluation
Department of Law and Public Safety
Hughes Justice Complex CN-085
Trenton, NJ 08625
(609) 984-2814

Institute for Criminal Justice Studies
Onate Hall
University of New Mexico
Albuquerque, NM 87131
(505) 277-4257

Bureau of Statistical Services
Division of Criminal Justice Services
Executive Park Tower
Stuyvesant Plaza
Albany, NY 12203
(518) 457-8393

Criminal Justice Analysis Center
Governor's Crime Commission
Department of Crime Control
PO Box 27687
Raleigh, NC 27611
(919) 733-5013

Criminal Justice Research
Office of the Attorney General
State Capitol
Bismarck, ND 58505
(701) 221-6108

Office of Criminal Justice Services
Ohio Department of Development
65 East State Street
Suite 312
Columbus, OH 43216
(614) 466-0310

Planning and Research
Oklahoma Department of Corrections
PO Box 11400
Oklahoma City, OK 73136
(405) 425-2590

Crime Analysis Center
Department of Justice
Justice Building
Salem, OR 97310
(503) 378-8056

Bureau of Statistics and Policy Research
Pennsylvania Commission on Crime and Delinquency
PO Box 1167
Harrisburg, PA 17108
(717) 787-5152

Governor's Commission on Justice
222 Quaker Lane
Suite 100
West Warwick, RI 02893
(401) 277-2620

Office of Criminal Justice Programs
Office of the Governor
1205 Pendleton Street
Columbia, SC 29201
(803) 734-0423

State Statistical Center
Criminal Justice Training Center
Division of the Attorney General
Pierre, SD 57501
(605) 773-3331

State Planning Office
307 John Sevier Building
500 Charlotte Avenue
Nashville, TN 37219
(615) 741-1676

Criminal Justice Policy Council
PO Box 13332
Capitol Station
Austin, TX 78711
(512) 463-1810

Commission on Criminal and Juvenile Justice
Room 101
Utah State Capitol
Salt Lake City, UT 84114
(801) 538-1031

Vermont Criminal Justice Center
State Office Building
Montpelier, VT 05602
(802) 828-3897

Department of Criminal Justice Services
805 East Broad Street
Richmond, VA 23219
(804) 786-4000

Office of Financial Management
Forecasting and Estimation Division
Insurance Building
MS AQ-44
Olympia, WA 98504
(206) 586-2501

West Virginia State Police
725 Jefferson Road
South Charleston, WV 25309
(304) 746-2124

Office of Justice Assistance
30 West Mifflin Street
Suite 330
Madison, WI 53702
(608) 266-7646

Identification Unit
Division of the Attorney General
316 West 22nd Street
Cheyenne, WY 82002
(307) 777-7523

Office of the Attorney General
PO Box 192
San Juan, PR 00902
(809) 783-3382
Office of Justice Research Services

Law Enforcement Planning Commission
Office of the Governor
8 Crown Bay
Sub Base
St. Thomas, VI 00801
(809) 774-6400

National Criminal Justice Reference Service (NCJRS)

THE NATIONAL INSTITUTE OF JUSTICE (NIJ)

NCJRS—the National Criminal Justice Reference Service—is sponsored by the National Institute of Justice, the research branch of the U.S. Department of Justice. The Institute's mission is to develop knowledge about crime, its causes, and control. In carrying out this mandate, the National Institute of Justice established NCJRS in 1972 to disseminate information from research, demonstrations, evaluations, and special programs to federal, state, and local governments, and serve as an international clearinghouse of justice information. NCJRS maintains the Juvenile Justice Clearinghouse for the National Institute for Juvenile Justice and Delinquency Prevention, operates the Dispute Resolution Information Center for the Federal Justice Research Program, and distributes publications and statistical information for the Bureau of Justice Statistics through the Justice Statistics Clearinghouse. The NCJRS Customer Service Number is: 800-851-3420; 301-251-5500.

This chapter will be your fingertip reference to the many ways in which NCJRS can provide you with professional information, that is both quick and comprehensive—and attuned to your everyday needs as a criminal justice practitioner, policymaker, or scholar. To become a registered NCJRS user and receive the bimonthly *NIJ Reports*, special product announcements and notifications of new NCJRS services, contact NCJRS for a registration form.

You do not have to be a registered user to take advantage of NCJRS products and services—but the few minutes' time you'll invest to become one can bring you real dividends. Here are a few tips for using their services effectively:

Read *NIJ Reports*. The bimonthly journal of the National Institute of Justice offers a regular column by the Director of the National Institute, a Research in Action section, a Selective Notification of Information section (abstracts of significant new publications in criminal justice with information on how to obtain them), a Calendar of Events (meetings, conferences, and seminars on the national and regional scenes), and announcement pages (information on new ways to use NCJRS services).

The following description of the services of NCJRS was provided to the author by Kris Rose and is excerpted from that information.

NCJRS Clearinghouses for Specific Information

NCJRS offers toll-free access to highly trained criminal justice reference specialists who can help you find answers to specific questions. The NCJRS Customer Service Center is staffed from 8:30 a.m. until 7:00 p.m. eastern standard time, Monday through Friday. After hours, you may leave a message on the telephone answering machine, and a specialist will return your call. If you are seeking criminal justice information or want to learn about NCJRS services, call the customer service number.

NCJRS also maintains clearinghouses that respond to specialized information needs:

NIJ AIDS Clearinghouse (301-251-5500). Sponsored by the National Institute of Justice, this clearinghouse is the only centralized source of information on how AIDS affects criminal justice professionals and their work. Staff specialists with a broad knowledge of AIDS issues are available to answer questions, make referrals, and suggest publications pertaining to AIDS as it relates to the criminal justice system.

Construction Information Exchange (800-851-3420). NIJ created the Construction Information Exchange to exchange data and information about prison and jail construction. The exchange has three components: the construction data base of facilities built since 1978, the *National Directory of Corrections Construction*, and the *Construction Bulletin* series.

Juvenile Justice Clearinghouse (800-638-8736). The Juvenile Justice Clearinghouse is the Office of Juvenile Justice and Delinquency Prevention's link to juvenile justice practitioners and policymakers. The clearinghouse produces and disseminates the agency's publications and prepares customized responses to information requests.

Justice Statistics Clearinghouse (800-732-3277). The Bureau of Justice Statistics supports this clearinghouse for those seeking crime and criminal justice data. In addition to distributing BJS publications, the clearinghouse responds to statistics requests by offering document data base searches, statistics information packages, referrals, and other related products and services.

National Victims Resource Center (800-627-NVRC). Sponsored by the Office for Victims of Crime, the National Victims Resource Center (NVRC) responds to requests from researchers, practitioners, and individual victims for victim-related information. It has more than 7,000 victim-related books and articles covering child physical and sexual abuse, victims services, domestic violence, victim-witness programs, and violent crime. NVRC also maintains a legislation data base containing state crime victim compensation statutes categorized by common search elements.

Bureau of Justice Assistance Clearinghouse (1-800-688-4252). The Bureau of Justice Assistance Clearinghouse informs state and local criminal justice practitioners about BJA products and programs. It disseminates BJA program briefs and reports to help criminal justice practitioners in their daily work.

NCJRS reference specialists are prepared to respond to your criminal justice information needs. Drawing on their subject expertise and NCJRS resources, the reference specialists can answer questions about a whole range of criminal justice issues, such as—

- AIDS information.
- Law enforcement.
- Drugs and crime.
- Courts.
- Corrections.
- Juvenile justice.
- Statistics.
- Criminology.
- Victims.
- Corrections construction.
- Other criminal justice topics.
- Asset forfeiture.
- Drug control.
- Drug testing.
- Treatment Alternatives to Street Crimes (TASC).
- Drug recognition programs.
- Drug Education Programs.
- Intensive probation/parole supervision programs.
- Electronic monitoring programs.
- Information sharing and outreach systems.
- Court delay reduction.
- Jail capacity programs.

THE BUREAU OF JUSTICE ASSISTANCE

Under the Anti-Drug Abuse Act of 1988, the Bureau of Justice Assistance (BJA) provides funds and technical assistance to state and local units of government to control crime and drug abuse and to improve the criminal justice system.

In support of these activities, BJA has created the *Bureau of Justice Assistance Clearinghouse*, now a component of the National Criminal Justice Reference Service. The clearinghouse informs state and local criminal justice practitioners about BJA products and programs.

The following BJA publications may now be obtained from the *Bureau of Justice Assistance Clearinghouse*. They provide useful information on some of the most critical issues of the day related to criminal justice, and will be valuable additions to your criminal justice library.

The following is a selected list of publications from the Bureau of Justice Assistance Clearinghouse.

Adjudication, Brochure. BC000114

An Invitation to Project DARE: Drug Abuse Resistance Education, Program Brief, June 1988. 10 pp. DD114802

Building Integrity and Reducing Drug Corruption in Police Departments, September 1989. 126 pp. DD120652

Drug Recognition Program, Monograph, April 1989. 24pp. DD117432

Electronic Monitoring in Intensive Probation and Parole Programs, Monograph, February 1989. 24 pp. DD116319

Estimating the Costs of Drug Testing for a Pretrial Service Program, Monograph, June 1989. 34 pp. DD118317

FY 1988 Report on Drug Control, 1989. 136 pp. $6.50. Call for ordering information. DD117435

FY 1988 Report on Drug Control, Executive Summary, 1989. 9 pp. DD118277

Intensive Supervision Probation and Parole (ISP), Program Brief, November 1988. 28 pp. DD106663

Prosecution Management Support System, Program Brief, March 1989. 25 pp. DD117093

Reducing Crime by Reducing Drug Abuse: A Manual for Police Chiefs and Sheriffs, January 1989. 166 pp. DD113110

Treatment Alternatives to Street Crime (TASC), Brochure. BC000113

Treatment Alternatives to Street Crime (TASC), Resource Catalog, October 1989. 161 pp. DD119847

Treatment Alternatives to Street Crime (TASC): Implementing the Model, Implementation Manual, September 1988. 322 pp. DD116322

Treatment Alternatives to Street Crime (TASC): Participant's Manual, Training Manual, September 1988. 108 pp. DD116321

Treatment Alternatives to Street Crime—TASC Programs, Program Brief, January 1988. 31 pp. DD116323

Urinalysis as Part of a Treatment Alternative to Street Crime (TASC) Program, Monograph, July 1988. 22 pp. DD115416

Drugs & Crime Data Center and Clearinghouse

This service was begun in 1987 and is funded by the Bureau of Justice Assistance (BJA) and managed by the Bureau of Justice Statistics (BJS).

Drugs & Crime Clearinghouse
Box 6000
Aspen Systems Corporation
Rockville, MD 20850
(800) 732-3277

This service responds to policymakers' urgent need for the most current data about:

- illegal drugs
- drug law violations
- drug-related crime
- drug-using offenders in the criminal justice system
- the impact of drugs on criminal justice administration.

The Data Center & Clearinghouse serves the drugs-and-crime information needs of:

- federal, state, and local policymakers
- criminal justice and public health practitioners
- researchers and universities

- private corporations
- the media
- the public

with special attention to the needs of state and local government agencies, especially those seeking data to meet the statistical requirements of the Anti-Drug Abuse Grant Program of the Bureau of Justice Assistance (BJA).

1-800-666-3332 toll-free

Following is a selected list of publications available from the Drugs and Crime Data Center and Clearinghouse. Call them directly for specific information or a complete catalog of their products.

The Drugs and Crime Resource Package

Drugs and Crime Resource Package (NCJ 107589-04). In one convenient, durable package you get a topical bibliography and more than two dozen NIJ, BJA, BJS, and OJJDP publications. $38.00. Order no. 42.

Prepackaged Topical Searches

Each topical search of the NCJRS data base contains 30 abstracts and citations and costs $5.00. Order nos. 43-52.

AIDS and IV Drug Use (TS011647)
Asset Forfeiture and Seizure (TS011652)
Cocaine and Crack (TS011648)
Drinking and Driving (TS011619)
Drug Abuse Programs for Offenders (TS011636)
Drug Law Enforcement (TS011642)
Drug Legalization (TS011653)
Drug Testing (TS011640)
Drug Trafficking (TS011641)
Drugs in the Workplace (TS011645)

Note: Topical searches are free to federal, state, and local criminal justice agencies. To obtain free topical searches, do not use the order form. Call NCJRS at 800-851-3420 (or 301-251-5500 from Maryland and Metropolitan Washington, D.C.), or write on your agency's letterhead to NIJ/NCJRS, Box 6000, Rockville, MD 20850.

Prepackaged Topical Bibliographies

Each topical bibliography provides up to 200 abstracts and citations and costs $17.50. Order nos. 53-55.

Drug Law Enforcement (TB010616)
Drug Treatment in Criminal Justice Settings (TB010623)
Drugs in the Workplace (TB010620)

Custom Searches

Your topic not shown above? Call NCJRS and ask for a *custom* search containing up to 400 citations on your chosen topic. Custom searches on paper cost $48.00, and on diskettes $65.00.

International Summaries

Learn from drug-related research in other countries. See the order form for six *International Summaries*—four-page summaries of foreign documents from Australia, Finland, Sweden, Switzerland, and West Germany. They cost just $4.00 each. Order nos. 56-61.

Issues and Practices Reports

Arresting the Demand for Drugs: Police and School Partnerships To Prevent Drug Abuse NCJ 105199. November 1987, 131 pp. Free. Call or write NCJRS.

Assessment of Pretrial Urine Testing in the District of Columbia NCJ 119968. December 1989, 34 pp. Free. Order no. 08

Characteristics of Different Types of Drug-Involved Offenders NCJ 108560. February 1988, 35 pp. Free. Call or write NCJRS.

A Criminal Justice System Strategy for Treating Cocaine-Heroin Abusing Offenders in Custody NCJ 113915. March 1988, 33 pp. Free. Call or write NCJRS.

Identifying Drug Users and Monitoring Them During Conditional Release NCJ 114730. February 1988, 25 pp. Free. Call or write NCJRS.

Police Drug Testing NCJ 105191. May 1987, 109 pp. $9.15. Order no. 41.

State and Local Experience With Drug Paraphernalia Laws NCJ 109977. February 1988, 139 pp. Free. Call or write NCJRS.

Street Level Drug Enforcement: Examining the Issues NCJ 115403. September 1988, 55 pp. Free. Call or write NCJRS.

Research in Brief/Research in Action

Controlling Drug Abuse and Crime: A Research Update NCJ 104865. March/April 1987, 6 pp. Free. Order no. 09.

1989 Drug Use Forecasting Annual Report NCJ 123941. June 1990, 16 pp. Free. Order no. 02. (See p. 36)

1988 Drug Use Forecasting Annual Report NCJ 122225. March 1990, 28 pp. Free. Order no. 10.

Drug Use Forecasting: January to March 1990 NCJ 124550. July 1990, 8 pp. Free. Order no. 03. (See p. 36.)

Drug Use Forecasting: October to December 1989 NCJ 123265. May 1990, 8 pp. Free. Order no. 04. (See p. 36.)

Drug Use Forecasting: July to September 1989 NCJ 122564, March 1990, 8 pp. Free. Order no. 11.

Drug Use Forecasting: April to June 1989 NCJ 120742. December 1989, 8 pp. Free. Order no. 12.

Drug Use Forecasting: January to March 1989 NCJ 119517. September 1989, 8 pp. Free. Order no. 13.

Drug Use Forecasting: Fourth Quarter 1988 NCJ 118275. June 1989, 12 pp. Free. Order no. 14.

Drugs & Crime: Controlling Use and Reducing Risk Through Testing NCJ 102668. September/ October 1986, 8 pp. Free. Order no. 15.

Employee Drug-Testing Policies in Prison Systems NCJ 112824. August 1980, 4 pp. Free. Order no. 16.

Local-Level Drug Enforcement: New Strategies NCJ 116751. March/April 1989, 6 pp. Free. Order no. 17.

Mandatory and Random Drug Testing in the Honolulu Police Department NCJ 117718. October 1989, 8 pp. Free. Order no. 18.

Prison Programs for Drug-Involved Offenders NCJ 118316. October 1989, 6 pp. Free. Order no. 19.

Project DARE: Teaching Kids To Say "No" to Drugs and Alcohol NCJ 100756. March 1986, 4 pp. Free. Order no. 20.

Urine Testing of Detained Juveniles To Identify High-Risk Youth NCJ 119965. May 1990, 8 pp. Free. Order no. 05.

Other Publications

AIDS and Intravenous Drug Use (NIJ AIDS Bulletin) NCJ 108620. February 1988, 4 pp. Free. Order no. 21.

The Police and Drugs (Perspectives on Policing) NCJ 117447. September 1989, 16 pp. Free. Order no. 22.

The National Archive
of Criminal Justice Data

A large source of data, in fact the world's largest single source of quantitative data on criminal justice, criminology, and general social science, is to be found at the National Archive of Criminal Justice Data. The following information about the archive was provided by Victoria W. Scheider, Archival Assistant Director of NACJD.

Sponsored by the Bureau of Justice Statistics (BJS) within the U.S. Department of Justice, the National Archive of Criminal Justice Data was established in 1978 under the auspices of the Inter-university Consortium for Political and Social Research (ICPSR). Headquarters of the Criminal Justice Archive are located, along with the central staff of the ICPSR, in the Institute for Social Research at the University of Michigan.

The central mission of the Criminal Justice Archive is to facilitate and encourage research in the field of criminal justice through the sharing of data resources. Specific goals include:

- Providing computer-readable data for the quantitative study of crime and the criminal justice system through the development of a central data archive that disseminates computer-readable social science data

- Supplying technical assistance in selecting data collections and the computer hardware and software for analyzing data efficiently and effectively

- Offering training in quantitative methods of social science research to facilitate secondary analysis of criminal justice data

13

ICPSR: MEMBERSHIP AND ACCESS TO DATA

Since 1962, ICPSR has served the academic community by acquiring, processing, and distributing data relevant to a broad spectrum of academic disciplines including criminology, law, political science, sociology, history, economics, gerontology, public health, and education. The Consortium maintains the world's largest repository of computer-based research and instructional data for the social sciences.

ICPSR is a membership-based organization with over 350 member colleges and universities in the United States and abroad. Payment of an annual institutional fee entitles faculty, staff and students at member schools to take advantage of the full range of ICPSR services. Because ICPSR is structured as a "partnership" with its member institutions, it is able to provide facilities and services to researchers and scholars that no single college or university could offer independently. Most ICPSR services are provided at no charge to the individual user.

To Order Data

Individuals at member institutions can order data through their campus representative. Individuals at nonmember institutions may obtain ICPSR data by paying an access fee. The Bureau of Justice Statistics supports the utilization of criminal justice data by individuals working in government or under grants from the Department of Justice.

Users at nonmember institutions or in government agencies wishing to order criminal justice-related data collections should contact Criminal Justice Archive staff members directly. Individuals at member schools can also contact staff regarding substantive and technical issues. Call or write to:

> National Archive of Criminal Justice Data
> Inter-university Consortium for Political and Social Research
> Institute for Social Research
> P.O. Box 1248
> Ann Arbor, Michigan 48106
> 800-999-0960
> 313-763-5010

ARCHIVAL DEVELOPMENT

The National Archive of Criminal Justice Data routinely receives data from four agencies within the U.S. Department of Justice:

- Bureau of Justice Statistics

- National Institute of Justice

- Office of Juvenile Justice and Delinquency Prevention

- Federal Bureau of Investigation

Many of the data files sent by these agencies are made available for public release in their original form. For other collections, additional data processing and documentation work is completed by Archive staff. Additional processing may include:

- Generating machine-readable documentation with full question text and code explanations

- Producing printed documentation that includes a copy of the original data collection instrument

- Providing SPSS, SAS, or OSIRIS control cards in machine-readable form

- Removing blanks and nonnumeric codes in the data file

- Performing consistency checks on variables in skip patterns within the original questionnaire

- Making univariate frequencies and other descriptive statistics available in either printed or machine-readable form

- Performing recodes to preserve the confidentiality of survey respondents or to facilitate use of the data for analysis

The National Archive of Criminal Justice Data releases several major serial data collections sponsored by agencies within the U.S. Department of Justice. For example, the Archive routinely distributes data from the *Juvenile Detention and Correctional Facility Censuses,* sponsored by the Office of Juvenile Justice and Delinquency Prevention. The Federal Bureau of Investigation provides *Uniform Crime Reporting Program Data* which are then processed and released by the Archive. Collections from the Bureau of Justice Statistics include:

- National Crime Surveys

- Capital Punishment in the United States

- Censuses of State Adult Correctional Facilities and Local Jails

- National Corrections Reporting Program

- National Surveys of Jails

- Surveys of Inmates of State Adult Correctional Facilities and Local Jails

- Offender Based Transaction Statistics (OBTS)

- Censuses of State Felony Courts

- National Judicial Reporting Program

- Expenditure and Employment Data for the Criminal Justice System

- National Surveys of Law Enforcement Agencies

Individual scholars and researchers also deposit data with the Archive. For more information about depositing data or about any of the specific collections listed above, contact the National Archive of Criminal Justice Data.

14

Sources of International Data

Researchers may often need to locate international data on a topic. The following sources can be good starting points for this endeavor.

Bibliography on Afghanistan, The Sudan and Tunisia. John J. Vidergar. (Monticello, IL: Vance Bibliographies, December 1978).

Bibliography of Canadian Bibliographies. Updated periodically. (Toronto, ON: Bibliographical Society of Canada).

Bibliography on Crime and Juvenile Delinquency in Africa. National Council on Crime and Delinquency. (New York: NCCD, 1963).

Canadian Government Publications. (Ottawa, ON: Department of Public Printing and Stationery, 1953-date).

Crime in Foreign Countries: A Selected List of Recent Selections. U.S. Library of Congress, Division of Bibliography. (Washington, DC: Library of Congress, 1935).

Criminology and Forensic Sciences: An International Bibliography, 1950-1980. Rudolf Vom Ende. (Detroit, MI: Gale Research, 1982).

Government Publications. (London: Stationery Office, H.M.S.P., 1936-date).

Index to International Public Opinion, 1982-1983. Elizabeth Hann Hastings and Philip K. Hastings (eds.) The fifth volume of the annual Index to International Public Opinion, 1982-1983 contains data drawn from surveys conducted and/or referenced in most parts of the world. All major regions are represented, with more than 125 individual nation states covered. The materials are selected on the basis of their widespread present and continuing interest to researchers and the public at large in their persistent quest

for understanding the peoples of the world. Much of the data herein are not only of topical, present day interest, but also deal with problems and issues that are of sustaining concern over time and transcend geographical boundaries.

With the publication of Volume V, the Index to International Public Opinion now covers the highlights of world events over a five-year period in relation to over 12,000 questions asked in more than 100 countries. The 1982-83 edition covers public reaction to events such as the Iranian hostage crisis, the Russian invasion of Afghanistan, and the Israeli invasion of Lebanon.

Over 700 pages in length, Volume V contains a wider range of substantive content. It contains a significantly greater number of tables than previous volumes, presenting breakdowns by such demographics as age, sex, race, religion, education, and economic level, among others. Almost 30 new topical subcategories have been added. The section on "Multinational Surveys" contains an extraordinary study, "Fundamental Values: A Global Perspective," including close to 100 tables. The subject index has been enhanced to provide greater access to the contents of the volume. (Survey Research Consultants International, Inc.).

Index to International Public Opinion, 1981-1982. 684 pages. Includes bibliographies.

Index to International Public Opinion, 1980-1981. 548 pages. Includes bibliographies.

Index to International Public Opinion, 1979-1980. 484 pages. Bibliog.

Index to International Public Opinion, 1978-1979. 386 pages. Bibliog.

International Bibliography on Crime and Delinquency. P.G. Van der Watt. "Six Decades of Crime Research in South Africa, 1900-1962," 2: 481-94 January, 1965.

International Bibliography of Police Literature. F. Andreotti. (London: M. & W. Publications, 1963).

International Bibliography of Selected Police Literature, Second edition. International Police Association. Contains bibliographical data and list of periodicals from a number of foreign police agencies. In English and foreign languages. (Liverpool: M. & W. Publications Ltd., 1968).

International Bibliography of the Social Sciences: Sociology. (Chicago, IL: Aldine, 1951-date).

International Exchange of Information on Current Criminological Research Projects in Member States. (Strasbourg, France: European Committee on Crime Problems, Directorate of Legal Affairs, Division of Crime Problems, Council of Europe).

International Criminology and Criminal Justice: A Selected Bibliography. Thomas R. Lagergreen and Kathleen A. Pitt. Abstracts 75 books and articles from other countries. All are in English. (Washington, DC: National Criminal Justice Reference Service, 1976).

International Handbook of Contemporary Developments in Criminology. Elmer H. Johnson (ed.) Volume 1. General issues and the Americas, Volume 2. Europe, Africa, the Middle East and Asia. In his introductory chapter, Johnson establishes a conceptual scheme for integrating the contributions of resident experts who analyze the crime patterns, socio-political system and criminological enterprise of their respective countries. The first part of volume I includes articles on transnational trends, international organizations, radical criminology, the feminist movement and crime, white collar crime, and other general issues. Country studies of the Americas follow. Country studies of Europe, Africa, the Middle East, and Asia continue in volume II. Bibliographies, with many annotated entries, accompany virtually every chapter. The product is a reference work essential to criminologists, criminal justice practitioners, social and economic planners, and students in universities and colleges throughout the English speaking world. (Westport, CT: Greenwood Press, 1983).

International Organizations, 1918-1945: A Guide to Research and Research Materials. George W. Baer (ed.) (Guides to European Diplomatic History Research and Research Materials.) Part I of this book provides a general introduction to international organizations and the international system. Part II presents a section on the archives of the League of Nations, United Nations Organization, Permanent Court of International Justice and Permanent Court of Arbitration, International Labor Organization, Unesco, and some of the other international organizations, conferences, and institutes. The details include a description of the main units of the archives, its holdings, and its publications; information on regulations and procedures for admission is sometimes included. Part III treats pertinent archival material in Great Britain, France, and the United States. For each of these countries there is a short summary of materials available of published and documentary series, and a selected list of significant private papers and their locations. Records in Germany, Italy, and Belgium are also noted. The remaining chapters are bibliographies. (Wilmington, DE: Scholarly Resources, 1981).

International Policing: A Selected Bibliography. Mark Shanley and Marjorie Kravitz. 168 annotated entries. (Washington, DC: NCJRS, February, 1978).

International Security Directory. (Henley-on-Thames, UK: 1979).

A London Bibliography of the Social Sciences. Eighteenth Supplement, 1983, Volume 41. Compiled and edited at the British Library of Political and Economic Science under the direction of D.A. Clarke. "The most extensive subject bibliography in the field....An essential addition to any major collection in the social sciences." - American Reference Books Annual. This annual publication catalogs the holdings of the British Library of Political and Economic Science (BLPES) and the Edward Fry Library of International Law. (BLPES is a depository for the publications of many governmental and international bodies throughout the world.) International in scope, the holdings encompass the whole range of the social sciences and are especially rich in economics; commerce and business administration; transport; statistics; political science and public administration; law; and the social and economic aspects of history. (Bronx, NY: H.W. Wilson Co., 1984).

National Bibliography of Chinese Publications, National Central Library Taipei (ed.) (New York: International Publication Service).

The Okhrana: The Russian Department of Police: A Bibliography, Edward E. Smith. (Stanford, CA: Hoover Institution on War, Revolution and Peace, 1967).

Parole in Foreign Countries: Bibliography. (Hackensack, NJ: National Council on Crime and Delinquency, 1969).

Police Studies: The International Review of Police Development. (New York: The John Jay Press).

Regency International Directory of Enquiry Agents, Private Detectives and Debt Collecting Agencies. Annual. (Folkestone, UK: Regency International Publications).

Selected and Annotated Guide to the Government and Politics of Egypt, Robert B. Harmon. (Monticello, IL: Vance Bibliographies, 1978).

A Selected International Bibliography on Capital Punishment. (Chicago, IL: University of Chicago Law School, 1968).

Social Control and Deviance in Cuba, Luis Salas Calero. (New York: Praeger Publishers, 1979).

Sociology. An International Bibliography of Serial Literature 1880-1980, Jan Wepsiec. This bibliography lists 2,300 current and ceased serial publications in sociology and the related areas of deviance and crime, social geography and psychology, social work, and community development. It includes periodicals, numbered research reports, and monographs, as well as abstracting, indexing, and bibliographic publications. (Bronx, NY: H.W. Wilson Co., 1983).

Soviet Intelligence and Security Services, 1964-1970: A Selected Bibliography of Soviet Publications with Some Additional Titles from Other Sources. (Washington, DC: Library of Congress, 1972).

The Soviet Secret Police, Simon Wolin and Robert M. Slusser (eds.) (Studies of the Research Program on the U.S.S.R., No. 14.) The most detailed picture yet publicly available of the history of the Soviet secret police, of its founder, the late Feliks Dzerzhinski and of the organization and operation of the secret police and associated agencies. This very useful work was financed by the Research Program on the USSR which has many other useful collections and distillations of emigré knowledge to its credit. (Westport, CT: Greenwood Press).

Statesman's Year Book: Statistical and Historical Annual of the States of the World. (London and New York: Macmillan, 1864-date). (See Chapter 11, "Statistical Data," for additional information on this source.)

UNITED NATIONS PUBLICATIONS

In addition to the above publications, the United Nations and United Nations Social Defence Research Institute have been very active in the criminal justice area, and have published many sources pertaining to the field.

Alternatives to Imprisonment: An Annotated Bibliography. (1977.)

Bibliography on Capital Punishment. (1971, mimeo.)

Bibliography on Dangerousness: Its Prediction and Treatment. (1975.)

Bibliography on Police Administration in Europe. (1975.)

Bibliography on Pre-Trial Detention. (1975.)

Capital Punishment. (1973.)

International Bibliography on Juvenile Delinquency. (1975.)

Additional United Nations publications:

A Guide to the Use of United Nations Documents, Including Reference to the Specialized Agencies and Special UN Bodies, Brenda Brimmer. Provides the reader with a detailed description of the documents classification system, information on research projects in general, and lists the publications of the United Nations. (Dobbs Ferry, NY: Oceana, 1962-date).

International Review of Criminal Policy. Deals with different topics each year. Each issue presents articles and summaries of meetings and programs which pertain to the specific criminal justice topic. (New York: United Nations, 1953 - present, annual).

Publications of the United Nations System: A Reference Guide. Coverage of specific publications, such as year books, bibliographies, and compilations of statistics. (New York: R.R. Bowker, 1972).

Report of the Secretary-General on Capital Punishment. United Nations. E/1980/9, United Nations, 1980.

Report of the Secretary-General on Crime Prevention and Control. United Nations. World Crime Survey, A/32/199, United Nations, 1977.

Report of the Sixth United Nations Congress on the Prevention of Crime and the Treatment of Offenders. United Nations.

Treatment of Offenders in Custody or in the Community with Special Reference to the Implementation of the Standard Minimum Rules for the Treatment of Prisoners Adopted by the United Nations. United Nations. Working paper prepared for the Secretariat.

United Nations Crime Prevention and Criminal Justice Newsletter. (Crime Prevention and Criminal Justice Branch, published semi-annually, since 1976).

United Nations Document Index (UNDEX). (New York: United Nations, 1950- present.) Issued monthly, includes resolutions, reports, verbatim records and other documents from the various departments of the U.N. A subject index, a list of documents issued, and a country index compose the three part index.

A World Directory of Criminological Institutes. (Rome, Italy: United Nations Social Defence Research Institute, VIA Giulia, 52, 00186, Publication #7, 1974).

Yearbook of the United Nations. Presents a yearly record of the activities of the United Nations and its related organizations. Specific documents dealing with these activities are listed. (New York: United Nations, 1946-present).

Other Related Titles

Canada's System of Justice. Brief text with references. (Ottawa, ON: Department of Justice, 1978).

Cities with Little Crime: The Case of Switzerland, Marshall B. Clinard. (London, UK: Cambridge University Press, 1978).

Comparative Analysis of the Statistical Dimensions of the Justice Systems of Seven Industrial Democracies, S.A. Bloch and others. (Los Angeles: University of Southern California, 1977).

Crime Control in Japan. William Clifford. Text with bibliography. (Lexington, MA: Lexington Books, 1976).

Crime in Developing Countries: A Comparative Perspective, Marshall B. Clinard and D.J. Abbott. (New York: John Wiley, 1973).

Crime, the Police and Criminal Statistics: An Analysis of Official Statistics for England and Wales Using Econometric Methods, Roy Carr Hill and N.H. Stern. (New York: Academic Press, Inc., 1979).

The Criminal Justice System of the USSR, Cherif M. Bassiouni and V.M. Savitski (eds.) (Springfield, IL: Charles C Thomas, 1979).

Criminal Statistics: England and Wales, 1978, Home Office. (London, UK: HMSO, 1979).

The Incidence of Female Criminality in the Contemporary World, Freda Adler. (New York: New York University Press, 1981).

Indian Police: A Developmental Approach. Text with bibliography. Prabhu D. Sharma. (Delhi: Research, 1977).

Inequality, Crime, and Public Policy, John Braithwaite. (Boston: Routledge and Kegan Paul, 1979).

Innovations in Criminal Justice in Asia and the Pacific, William Clifford. "Criminal Justice Adaptations and Innovations in Japan." William Clifford. (Canberra: Australian Institute of Criminology, 1979).

International Crime Statistics. International Criminal Police Organization. Annual. (Paris: Interpol).

International Security Directory. A world directory of police forces, fire departments, industrial security officers, and commercial security services and supplies. Annual. (Henley-on-Thames, UK: Security Gazette Ltd.).

The Islamic Criminal Justice System, M. Cherif Bassiouni (ed.) (New York: Oceana Publications, Inc., 1982).

Justice in Jerusalem, Gideon Hausner. (New York: Schocken Books, 1979).

Justice in Modern Sweden, Harold K. Becker and Einar O. Hjellemo. Text with bibliography. (Springfield, IL: Charles C Thomas, 1976).

Nations Not Obsessed with Crime. Freda Adler. (Littleton, CO: Fred B. Rothman & Co., 1983).

Police of the World. Roy D. Ingleton. (New York: Charles Scribner's Sons, 1979).

Russian Secret Police; Muscovite, Imperial Russian and Soviet Political Security Operations. Ronald Hingley. Text with bibliography. (New York: Simon & Schuster, 1971).

Secret World of Interpol. Omar V. Garrison. Text with bibliography. (Glasgow: William MacLellan, 1977).

Standard Minimum Rules for the Treatment of Prisoners and Effective Implementation of the Rules. (New York: United Nations Department of Public Information, 1984).

A Treatise on International Criminal Law, G.O.W. Mueller and D. Besharov. "The Existence of International Criminal Law and Its Evolution to the Point of Its Enforcement Crisis." M. Cherif Bassiouni and Ved Nanda (eds.). (Springfield, IL: Charles C Thomas, 1973).

SELECTED LIST OF INTERNATIONAL CRIMINAL JUSTICE PERIODICALS

British Columbia Police Journal. (Vancouver, BC: British Columbia Federation of Peace Officers).

British Journal of Criminology. (Littleton, CO: Fred B. Rothman & Co.).

Canadian Journal of Criminology. (Ottawa, ON: Canadian Association for the Prevention of Crime).

Canadian Police Chief. (Ottawa, ON: Canadian Association of Chiefs of Police, Inc.).

Canadian Police College Journal. (Ottawa, ON: Canadian Police College).

Criminologie. (Montreal, QUE: Universite de Montreal).

International Annals of Criminology. (Paris, FRA: Societe Internationale de Criminologie).

International Center for Comparative Criminology Annual Report. (Montreal, QUE: Universite de Montreal).

International Directory of Detective Agencies. (Neosho, MO: Inter State Service Co., Inc.).

International Drug Report. (Albany, NY: International Narcotic Enforcement Officers Association).

International Juvenile Officers' Assn. Conference Journal. (Holland, IL: International Juvenile Officers Association).

International Juvenile Officers' Assn. Reporter. (Holland, IL: International Juvenile Officers Association).

International Prisoners Aid Association Newsletter. (Louisville, KY: University of Louisville).

International Review of Criminal Policy. (New York: United Nations Department of Social Affairs).

Journal of the Canadian Society of Forensic Science. (Ottawa, ON: Canadian Society of Forensic Science).

RCMP Quarterly. (Ottawa, ON: Royal Canadian Mounted Police).

The following guides will direct the researcher to a number of periodicals relating to International Criminal Justice.

Guide to Foreign Legal Materials Series. (Dobbs Ferry, NY: Oceana Publications, Inc.).

Index to Foreign Legal Periodicals. (Chicago, IL: American Association of Law Libraries).

International Center for Comparative Criminology Annual Report. (Montreal, QUE: University of Montreal).

International Guide to Periodicals in Criminal Justice. (Greensboro, NC: Sandy Ridge Press).

The researchers interested in other International Periodicals that offer a broad general view of international events may wish to consult the following:

ASILS Newsletter. (Washington, DC: Association of Student International Law Societies).

Amnesty Action. (New York: Amnesty International, USA).

Annual Review of United National Affairs. (Dobbs Ferry, NY: Oceana).

Conflict Quarterly. (Fredericton, CAN: University of Brunswick).

Countries of the World and Their Leaders, Yearbook 1982. (Detroit, MI: Gale Research).

Department of State Bulletin. (Washington, DC: U.S. Government Printing Office).

Department of State Newsletter. (Washington, DC: U.S. Government Printing Office).

Facts on File Weekly World News Digest. (New York: Facts on File).

Foreign Affairs. (New York: Council on Foreign Relations).

Foreign Affairs Research. (Washington, DC: U.S. Department of State).

International Journal of Politics. (White Plains, NY: M.E. Sharpe, Inc.).

Police Studies: The International Review of Police Development. (Cincinnati, OH: Anderson Publishing Co.).

U.N. International Law Commission, Yearbook. (New York: United Nations Publications).

UN Monthly Chronicle. (New York: United Nations Department of Public Information.

15

Historical Research Sources

Historical research is the study of the past—the study of events that took place, what people said, wrote, and did, and the study of the trends that developed. As with other types of research, the main objective of a historical research project should be to make a contribution to knowledge on a particular subject of interest or significance. Historical research should be original. This does not mean that you have to study a subject or problem never before touched, but it does mean that you should handle the research in an original way. Remember that historical matters cannot be changed but the evidence of them is variable and their description and interpretations are often revised. Old ground can be covered again, and new evidence that will correct errors or improve interpretations can often be found. Facts overlooked by previous investigators, or new relationships between old facts, can be discovered by researchers re-examining the same material but with different perspectives and purposes in mind.

There are two types of sources that can be used to obtain historical data—primary and secondary. Both are important contributors to historical research. Primary sources are the actual materials, whether they be printed matter, rare items, photographs, etc., that were created in connection with the topic or event the researcher is studying. Thus the information that an investigator derives from these materials is obtained firsthand, or from the primary source. Primary sources allow for documentation of authenticity and for firsthand examination and interpretation.

Secondary sources are works of other researchers, although they may cite various primary sources. In other words, a secondary source is one that says "Someone said that someone said...." Secondary sources are important contributors to background and preparatory study of the primary sources.

PRIMARY SOURCES

Before setting out to examine primary sources, a historical researcher needs to do some preparatory work in the library that involves searching out secondary sources. As with other styles of research, a tentative bibliography needs to be developed and preliminary reading should be done. Learn as much as possible about the people, events, or developments you will be studying. Utilize the pertinent references in the library such as books, directories, journal articles, dissertations, newspapers, and encyclopedias. This process of information gathering from secondary sources will help identify names of persons, locations, significant events and dates for which you need more data, and may also lead you to various primary sources.

After doing some preliminary investigation of the appropriate secondary sources, you should be ready to examine any of the pertinent primary sources that might be accessible to you. These are found in a variety of places — private businesses, private organizations, government institutions, religious organizations, and private family collections. The Manuscript Division of the Library of Congress has the largest selection of primary sources, and a visit to this institution would almost certainly be an asset to any primary source search. However, not everyone undertaking historical research will be able to visit Washington, D.C. If this is the case for you, do not despair. Assistance in locating and using primary sources may be obtained from the following sources.

American Judicial Proceedings First Printed Before 1801: An Analytical Bibliography. Compiled by Wilfred J. Ritz. (Westport, CT: Greenwood Press). *American Judicial Proceedings First Printed Before 1801* is the first bibliography to list every law report, trial, or separate event of judicial significance occurring in or relating to what is now the United States, and for which there was material other than a newspaper account printed before 1801. It includes rules of court applicable to judicial proceedings, proceedings in England relating to the English colonies, and American reprints of reports and European trials. The volume fills a gap in legal and historical literature, which has virtually ignored the pre-1789 period — the first 182 years of American jurisprudence.

The bibliography is analytical in that the materials are arranged chronologically by jurisdiction — states and the United States — and by major subject. An *Index of Parallel Entries* gives cross references to sixty-six other bibliographic sources.

Researchers will find this an invaluable tool for identifying, for any year through 1801, all printed materials relating to American judicial proceedings: those of any state or the federal government. All common law judicial decisions, grand jury charges, confessions and dying speeches or convicted criminals, and sermons on their executions are included. The compilations show the status of American common law in 1776 when Independence was declared, in 1787 when the federal Constitution was drafted, and in 1789 when the federal government was organized.

Combined Retrospective Index to Book Reviews in Scholarly Journals, 1886-1974. This set provides author and title access to more than one million book reviews that appeared in complete backfiles of 459 scholarly journals in the social sciences. Most of the reviews were never included in any retrospective multi-title book review index. Review citations may be located in either of the separate author and title indexes.

Cumulated Magazine Subject Index, 1907-1949. An index to approximately 175 English, Canadian and American periodicals. Approximately one-half of the indexed journals are concerned with the national and local history of Anglo-American countries. Other major fields covered include travel, mountaineering, exploration, fine arts, and literature. Review references are entered under the subject of the book, with the exception of fiction which appears under the author's name. Reviews are distinguished from other entries by the word "review" enclosed in parentheses.

Directory of Historical Societies and Agencies in the United States and Canada. (Madison, WI: American Association for State and Local History, 1956-date).

Historical Statistics of the United States. Colonial times to 1970. (Washington DC: Government Printing Office, 1975). (See also Chapter 11, "Statistical Data").

Keepers of the Past. Clifford L. Lord (ed.) (Chapel Hill: University of North Carolina Press, 1965).

Materials and Methods for Historical Research. Carla Staffle. (New York: Libraryworks, 1979).

Nineteenth Century Reader's Guide to Periodical Literature, 1890-1899. An author and subject index to 51 general British and American journals. Review references are cited under the author of the book reviewed.

Poole's Index to Periodical Literature, 1802-1881. A subject index to 470 British and American periodicals. References to reviews of books with definite subjects appear under those subjects. Review references to works of fiction, poetry and drama appear under the author of the book reviewed.

Research in Archives: The Use of Unpublished Primary Sources, Philip Brooks. (Chicago, IL: University of Chicago Press, 1969).

Research on the Propensity for Crime at Different Ages, 1831. (Adophe Quetelet, translated by Sawyer F. Sylvester). This was the first scientific study of crime. Early in the 19th century Adolphe Quetelet began an empirical approach to the study of crime as a sociological phenomenon which was concerned with the use of present findings to predict future events.

Quetelet took from such sources as the Compte general de l'administration de la justice en France the number of crimes seen regularly for several years and uses these figures as the bases for prediction of the number of crimes in succeeding years. He then goes on to relate the rate of crime to certain other social factors. (Cincinnati, OH: Anderson Publishing Co.).

The Wellesley Index to Victorian Periodicals, 1824-1900. A listing of the contents of eight major British journals published during the years 1824-1900; one title, *The Edinburgh Review,* is indexed back to 1802. There is not an index to authors of books reviewed. To locate a review, ascertain the date of publication of the book in question and then consult the listing of each journal for that year and one or more additional years.

Where Are the Historical Manuscripts: A Symposium. (Sturbridge, Massachusetts: American Association for State and Local History).

SECONDARY SOURCES

For students undecided on a topic or merely contemplating historical research, several secondary sources on criminal justice topics have been listed below. This may assist you in choosing a topic or in locating additional secondary sources that may in turn cite primary sources. Also, following this list, the Wickersham Commission reports have been annotated and included. (For additional historical sources, see Chapter 9.)

Administration of Criminal Justice, 1949-1956. (Berkeley, CA: University of California, Institute of Government Studies, reprinted by Patterson Smith, Montclair, NJ, 1970).

Albions Fatal Tree. Douglas Hay. (New York: Pantheon Books, 1975).

The American Criminal: An Anthropological Study. Ernest A. Hooton. With the collaboration of the Statistical Laboratory of the Division of Anthropology, Harvard University. (Westport, CT: Greenwood Press, 1939).

American Newspapers 1821-1936: A Union List of Files Available in the United States and Canada. (New York: H.W. Wilson, 1937).

American Prisons: A History of Good Intentions. Blake McKelvey. Text with bibliography. (Montclair, NJ: Patterson Smith, 1977).

Anglo-American Legal Bibliographies: An Annotated Guide. William L. Friend. (Washington, DC: U.S. Library of Congress, 1944).

The Annals of Murder: A Bibliography of Books and Pamphlets on American Murders from Colonial Times to 1900. Thomas M. McDade. (Norman, OK: University of Oklahoma, 1961).

An Annotated Bibliography of Works on Juvenile Delinquency in America and Britain in the Nineteenth Century. Cecil P. Remick. (St. Paul, MN: West Publishing, 1978).

Bibliography of Crime and Criminal Justice. Dorothy C. Culver. (A) 1927-1931, and (B) 1932-1937. (New York: H.W. Wilson Company, (A) 1934 and (B) 1939).

Bibliography Manual for the Students of Criminology. Thorsten Sellin and J.P. Shaloo. (Philadelphia: The Authors, 1935).

Bibliography: Works on Criminal Law, Penology and Prison Discipline. Text with bibliography. (New York: Annual Report of The Prison Association of New York, 1870).

Bloodletters and Badmen: A Narrative Encyclopedia of American Criminals from the Pilgrims to the Present. Jay R. Nash. (Philadelphia: Lippincott, 1973).

The Blue and the Brass: American Policing 1890-1910. A unique collection of 64 articles, actually written by law enforcement officials before 1910, which provides the student of law enforcement with a vivid portrayal of policing at the turn of the century. (International Association of Chiefs of Police).

Brief Outline of the History and Organization of the R.C.M.P Musical Ride. Royal Canadian Mounted Police. Text with bibliography. (Ottawa: RCMP, 1978).

Broadmoor: A History of Criminal Lunacy and Its Problems. Ralph Partridge. (Westport, CT: Greenwood Press).

Catalog of Law Books Published Prior to 1894. G.E. Griswold. (New York: William S. Hein, 1977).

Catalog of the Public Documents of Congress and of All the Departments of the Government of the United States for the Period March 4, 1893 — December 31, 1940. (Washington, DC: Government Printing Office, 1896-1945). (See also Chapter 10, "Government Documents").

Comprehensive Index to the Publications of the United States Government, 1881-1893. John G. Ames. (Washington, DC: Government Printing Office, 1905). (See also Chapter 10, Government Documents").

The Concise Encyclopedia of Crime and Criminals. Sir Harold Richard Scott. (Englewood Cliffs, NJ: Prentice-Hall, 1961).

Conquest of Violence: Order and Liberty in Britain. Thomas A. Critchley. Text with bibliography. (New York: Schocken Books, 1970).

A Contribution Towards a Bibliography Dealing with Crime and Cognate Subjects. John Cumming. (Montclair, NJ: Patterson Smith, 1970, reprint of 1935 edition).

Cops and Bobbies: Police Authority in New York and London. Wilber R. Miller. Text with bibliography. (Chicago, IL: University of Chicago Press, 1973).

Crime and Authority in Victorian England: The Black Country, 1835-1860. David Phillips. Text with bibliography. (Totowa, NJ: Rowman and Littlefield, 1977).

Crime and Law Enforcement in the Colony of New York, 1691-1776. Douglas Greenberg. Text with bibliography. (Ithaca, NY: Cornell University Press, 1976).

Crime and Law in Nineteenth Century Britain. W.R. Cornish and others. Text with bibliography. (Dublin: Irish University Press, 1978).

Criminology. Arthur MacDonald. Text with bibliography. (New York: Funk & Wagnalls, 1893).

Criminology. M.F. Parmelee. Text with bibliography. (New York: Macmillan, 1918).

Criminology: A Bibliography of Research and Theory in the United States, 1945-1972. (Philadelphia: University of Pennsylvania, 1974).

Critical History of Police Reform: The Emergence of Professionalism. Samuel Walker. Text with bibliography. (Lexington, MA: Lexington Books, 1977).

In Defense of Whom? A Critique of Criminal Justice Reform. Gregg Barak. (Cincinnati, OH: Anderson Publishing Co., 1980).

A Descriptive Catalog of the Government Publications of the United States, September 5, 1774 — March 4, 1881. Benjamin P. Poore. (Washington, DC: Government Printing Office, 1881).

Discipline and Punish: The Birth of the Prison. Michel Foucault. Text with bibliography. (New York: Pantheon, 1977).

Doctoral Dissertations Accepted by American Universities, 1935-55. (New York: H.W. Wilson).

Encyclopedia of Criminology. Vernon Branham and Samuel Kutash (eds.) (New York: Philosophical Library, 1949).

The English Police: Its Origin and Development. E.H. Glover. Text with bibliography. (London: Police Chronicle, 1934).

The Evolution of Criminology. William V. Pelfrey. (Cincinnati, OH: Anderson Publishing Co., 1980).

The Foundation of Australia, 1786-1800: A Study in English Criminal Practice and Penal Colonization in the Eighteenth Century. Eris Michael O'Brien. (Westport, CT: Greenwood Press).

The Growth of Criminal Law in Ancient Greece. George Miller Calhoun. (Westport, CT: Greenwood Press).

To Guard My People: The History of the English Police. Percival Griffiths. Bibliography. (London: Benn, 1971).

A Guide to Material on Crime and Criminal Justice (through 1926). Augustus F. Kuhlman. (Montclair, NJ: Patterson Smith, 1969, orig. 1929).

Hatchet Men: The Story of the Tong Wars in San Francisco's Chinatown. Richard H. Dillon. Text with bibliography. (New York: Coward McCann, 1962).

Henry and Sir John Fielding: The Thief Catchers. Patrick Pringle. Text with bibliography. (London: Dobson, 1968).

Historical Approaches to Crime, Research Strategies and Issues. James A. Inciardi, et al. (Beverly Hills, CA: Sage Publications, 1977).

Historical Criminology: The Evolution of Criminological Ideas. Israel Drapkin. (Lexington, MA: Lexington Books, 1980).

Historical Statistics of the United States. (Washington, DC: United States Bureau of the Census, 1960). (See Chapter 11, "Statistical Data," for additional sources of statistical data.)

History and Bibliography of American Newspapers 1690-1820. Clarence S. Brigham. (Worcester, MA: American Antiquarian Society, 1947).

History of the British South Africa Police. Vol. 1, The First Line of Defence, 1899-1903. Peter Gibbs. Text with bibliography. (Salisbury, Rhodesia: BSAP, 1972).

A History of English Criminal Law and Its Administration from 1750. Vol. 3, Cross Currents in the Movements for the Reform of the Police. Leon Radzinowicz. Text with bibliography. (London: Stevens, 1956).

History of Police in England and Wales, 900-1966. Thomas A. Critchley. Bibliography. (London: Constable, 1967).

The Houston Police, 1878-1948. Louis J. Marchiafava. (Houston: Rice University Press, 1977).

Hue and Cry, The Story of Henry and John Fielding and Their Bow Street Runners. Patrick Pringle. (Bungay, Suffolk, Britain: William Morrow and Company, 1955).

Identification Wanted: Development of the American Criminal Identification System. Published by The International Association of Chiefs of Police. Using articles and correspondence written by police officials who were directly involved in events, this book tells the dual story of the development of identification technology and the little known 50-year struggle by the nation's police chiefs to organize a national identification system.

"I'm Frank Hamer": The Life of a Texas Peace Officer. Gordon Frost and John H. Jenkins. Text with bibliography. (New York: Pemberton Press, 1968).

Index to American Doctoral Dissertations 1956-1960. (Ann Arbor, MI: University Microfilms International).

Intemperance: The Lost War Against Liquor. Larry Engleman. (Riverside, NJ: The Free Press, 1979).

Iron Men: A Saga of the Deputy United States Marshals Who Rode the Indian Territory. C.H. McKennon. Text with bibliography. (Garden City, NY: Doubleday, 1967).

Issues in Criminology, 9:111-14, Spring, 1974, M.B. Miller. "At Hard Labor: Rediscovering the 19th Century Prison."

Just Measure of Pain: The Penitentiary in the Industrial Revolution, 1750-1850. Michael Ignatieff. Text with bibliography. (New York: Macmillan, 1978).

Juvenile Court Laws of the U.S.: Topical and State by State Summaries. Gilbert Cosulich. (New York: National Probation Association, 1939).

Juvenile Delinquency: A Critical Annotated Bibliography. Philippe S. Cabot. (New York: H.W. Wilson Company, 1946).

Law & Order in American History, Joseph Hawes (ed.) (Port Washington, NY: Kennikat Press, 1979).

Law and Order in the Capital City: A History of the Washington Police, 1800-1886. Kenneth G. Alfers. Text with bibliography. (Washington, DC: George Washington University, 1976).

Law-Finders and Law-Makers in Medieval England: Collected Studies in Legal and Constitutional History. Helen Maud. (Cambridge, UK: Merlin Press, 1962).

List of American Doctoral Dissertations Printed in 1912-38. (Washington, DC: United States Library of Congress).

List of Investigations into Police Conditions in New York City Made By State and City Authorities and Private Organizations, 1831-1948. James Katsaros. (New York: Municipal Reference Library, 1949).

List of References on Crime and Criminals in the U.S. with Special Reference to Statistics. U.S. Library of Congress, Division of Bibliography. (Washington, DC: USLC, 1922).

List of Works Relating to Criminology. New York Public Library. (New York: NY Public Library, 1911).

Lynch Law: An Investigation into the History of Lynching in the United States. James Elbert Cutler. (Westport, CT: Greenwood Press, 1905).

Mafia and Mafiosi. Henner Hess. A history of the Mafia. (Lexington, MA: Lexington Books, 1970).

Maintain the Right: The Early History of the Northwest Mounted Police, 1873-1900. Ronald Atkin. Text with bibliography. (New York: Stein & Day, 1973).

The Medieval Underworld, Andrew McCall. (North Pomfret, VT: Hamish Hamilton, 1979).

Memoirs of American Prisons: An Annotated Bibliography. D. Suvack. Lists almost 800 references to works published between the late 1700s and 1978. (Metuchen, NJ: Scarecrow Press, 1979).

Nineteenth Century Crime, Prevention, and Punishment. J.J. Tobias. (Newton Abbot, UK: David and Charles Publishers, 1972).

Peel. Norman Gash. Text with bibliography. (Harlow, UK: Longman, 1976).

Penology: The Evolution of Corrections in America. George C. Killinger, et al. (eds.) (St. Paul, MN: West Publishing, 1979).

Personality, Social Class, and Delinquency. John J. Conger and Wilbur Miller. (New York: Wiley, 1966).

Pioneering in Penology: The Amsterdam Houses of Correction in the Sixteenth and Seventeenth Centuries. J. Thorsten Sellin. Text with bibliography. (Philadelphia: University of Pennsylvania Press, 1944).

Pioneers in Criminology. Hermann Mannheim (ed.) Text with bibliography. (New York: Quadrangle, 1960).

Pioneers in Policing. Philip John Stead (ed.) Text with bibliographies. (London: McGraw-Hill, 1977).

The Police Encyclopedia. 8 vols., H.L. Adam. (London: Waverley, 1925).

Police and Prison Encyclopedia. G.W. Hale. (Boston: Richardson, 1894).

Poole's Index to Periodical Literature. Indexes by subject almost 600,000 articles from 470 American and British periodicals during 1802-1907. (Mongolia, MA: Peter Smith Publications).

Prison Books and Their Authors. John A. Langford. (Detroit, MI: Gale Research, 1970, reprint of 1861 edition).

Professional Criminals of America. (New York: Chelsea House, originally published in 1886, reprinted in 1969).

The Queen's Peace: The Origins and Development of the Metropolitan Police 1829-1979. David Ascoli. (London: Hamish Hamilton, 1979).

The Reformers: An Historical Survey of Pioneer Experiments in the Treatment of Criminals, Torsten Eriksson. (New York: Elsevier North Holland, 1976).

The Repression of Crime: Studies in Historical Penology, Harry E. Barnes. Text with bibliography. (New York: Doran, 1926).

The Rise of Scotland Yard: A History of The Metropolitan Police. Douglas G. Browne. Text with bibliography. (London: Harrap, 1956).

Rural Disorder and Police Reform in Ireland, 1812-1836. Galen Brocker. Text with bibliography. (Toronto, ON: University of Toronto Press, 1970).

The San Quentin Story, as Told to Dean Jennings. Clinton T. Duffy. (Westport, CT: Greenwood Press, 1950).

Secret Societies in China In the Nineteenth and Twentieth Century. Jean Chesneaux. (Ann Arbor, MI: University of Michigan Press, 1972).

A Selected Bibliography on Juvenile Delinquency. (Washington, DC: United States Department of Health, Education and Welfare, Social Security Administration, Children's Bureau, 1954).

A Short History of the British Police. Sir Charles Reith. (London: Oxford University Press, 1948).

Silent Witness: The Emergence of Scientific Criminal Investigations. Published by The International Association of Chiefs of Police. The story of crime laboratory development and various investigative aids is told through articles written by key participants in events. Covers ballistics, forensic sciences, the lie detector and similar technological advances in 62 articles.

Sources for the Study of the Administration of Criminal Justice 1938-1948, A Selected Bibliography. Dorothy C. Tompkins. (Montclair, NJ: Patterson-Smith, 1970, orig. 1949).

State Reports on Correction and Punishment, Poverty, and Public Welfare, Prior to 1930. In microform. (Westport, CT: Redgrave Information Resources, 1973).

Statesman's Year Book: Statistical and Historical Annual of the States of the World. (London and New York: Macmillan, 1864). (See Chapter 11, "Statistical Data," for further information on this reference.)

The Stranglers: The Cult of Thuggee and Its Overthrow in British India. George L. Bruce. Text with bibliography. (New York: Harcourt, Brace & World, 1969).

Studies in Juvenile Delinquency: A Selected Bibliography. (Washington, DC: United States Department of Health, Education and Welfare, Social Security Administration, Children's Bureau, 1956).

The Super Crooks. R.M. Williams. Short history, 1584-1973. (Chicago, IL: Playboy Press, 1973).

The Sutherland Papers. Albert Cohen, Alfred Lindesmith and Karl Schuessler (eds.) Selected bibliography of Sutherland's writing. (Bloomington: Indiana University Press, 1956).

A Systematic Source Book of Juvenile Delinquency. Walter A. Lunden. (Pittsburgh: University of Pittsburgh, 1938).

They Have No Rights: Dred Scott's Struggle for Freedom. Walter Ehrlich. (Westport, CT: Greenwood Press, Inc. 1979).

They Were in Prison: A History of the Pennsylvania Prison Society, 1787-1937, Formerly the Philadelphia Society for Alleviating the Miseries of Public Prison. Negley K. Teeters. Text with bibliography. (Philadelphia: Winston, 1937).

Thief Taker General: The Rise and Fall of Jonathan Wild, Gerald Howson. Text with bibliography. (New York: St. Martin's Press, 1971).

Thirty Years of Lynching in the United States, 1889-1918. (Westport, CT: Greenwood Press, 1919).

The Victorian Railway Murders. Arthur and Mary Sellwood. (North Pomfret, VT: David and Charles Publishers, 1979).

Violence in America: Historical and Comparative Perspectives. Hugh Davis Graham and Ted R. Gurr. (Beverly Hills, CA: Sage Publications, Inc., 1979).

Wayward Puritans: A Study In the Sociology of Deviance. Kai T. Erikson. (New York: John Wiley, 1966).

MISCELLANEOUS SOURCES

A valuable source of historical statistical data can be found in the early editions (1967 and later) of the Uniform Crime Reports (Washington, DC: United States Department of Justice, Federal Bureau of Investigation). However, there have been major problems relating to the methods used to collect data for the *Uniform Crime Reports* (see explanation under victimization surveys in Chapter 11, "Statistical Data").

Out-of-Print Books

Many older books that are desirable for historical research are also out of print and therefore no longer available from the publisher. There are, however, sources specifically designed to assist researchers in determining the availability of out-of-print books. Two of these sources are briefly described below.

Guide to Reprints. An annual cumulative guide, alphabetically arranged, to books, journals, and other materials which are available in reprint form. (Kent, CT: Guide to Reprints, Inc., 1987).

Books on Demand. Makes available approximately 84,000 selected books as on-demand reprints in the broad categories of General and Reference Works, Humanities, Social Sciences, Sciences, and Technology and Applied Science.

Wickersham Commission Reports

Another good source of historical information regarding criminal justice topics can be found in the Wickersham Commission Reports, formerly known as the National Commission on Law Observance and Enforcement. The Commission, under the leadership of George W. Wickersham, a former Attorney General, studied all aspects of law enforcement. The resultant fourteen reports each address a particular problem, and ways to improve the administration of justice are suggested. These reports, reprinted by Patterson-Smith of Montclair, New Jersey in 1968, are also available for sale in microfiche from the NCJRS. Each is briefly annotated below.

Report #1: Preliminary Report on Prohibition. Contains proposals for the improvement of enforcement of the prohibition laws. The scope of the problem as well as administrative and legal difficulties are outlined.

Report #2: Enforcement of the Prohibition Laws of the United States. A review of difficulties encountered in enforcing prohibition laws, along with proposals for more effective enforcement. Liquor control is traced from colonial times. Many sources of illegal liquor are described, as are corruption, negative public opinion, economic difficulties, and the strain on the courts and penal institutions.

Report #3: Criminal Statistics. Discusses the importance of statistics and provides a survey of criminal statistics of the United States.

Report #4: Prosecution. Examines the administration of criminal justice in the United States during 1931. Included are recommendations concerning organizations, methods, and basic principles as well as information on the public prosecutor, the public defender, and the grand jury.

Report #5: Enforcement of the Deportation Laws of the United States. Examines the 1931 laws concerning the deportation of aliens. Included are recommendations for improvement of the system.

Report #6: Child Offender in the Federal System of Justice. Examines methods used by police, courts, probation, and penal institutions in dealing with minors who have violated federal laws. Recommendations include that the federal government recognize the concept of juvenile delinquency and that youthful offenders be dealt with at the local level.

Report #7: Progress Report on the Study of the Federal Courts. Concerned with the efficiency of the administration of justice in federal courts. Data presented regards the daily business of the federal courts, including the kinds and numbers of cases coming before these courts, the various statutes bringing those cases into those courts, the kinds of parties involved in such cases, the various methods and devices which were employed in the courts to delay or expedite trials, and the various dispositions made of the cases.

Report #8: Criminal Procedure. Presents a 1931 investigation into criminal procedure and includes recommendations for reorganization of the administration of federal law and court procedure.

Report #9: Penal Institutions, Probation, and Parole. Concerned with three principal methods of penal treatment: imprisonment, probation, and parole. Brings to light the inadequacies and inefficiencies of the prison system and recommends wage incentives for prisoners, educational opportunities in prisons, and indeterminate sentences for the development of a proper institutional program and the establishment of an adequate system of parole.

Report #10: Crime and the Foreign-Born. Analyzes the extent of criminal involvement by foreign-born Americans, their relations with the criminal justice system in general, and public attitudes toward the immigrant population and crime. Statistics relating nationality to crime rate, type of crime, and number of arrests in various cities is presented. Various factors which could cause foreigners to violate the law, but which do not affect native Americans, such as language, foreign law and customs, are analyzed.

Report #11: Lawlessness in Law Enforcement. Illegal law enforcement practices such as the use of cruel treatment by police to force confessions of guilt from prisoners are examined. Other violations discussed include actions which jeopardize personal liberty, the right to bail, the presumption of innocence until conviction of guilt by due process, and the right to employ counsel. Actual cases of prisoner beatings and torture by police are documented, and actions taken by cities to eliminate unlawful treatment by police are describe.

Report #12: Cost of Crime. Presents data on economic loss as a result of crime, and analyzes the problem of determining the cost of crime.

Report #13: Causes of Crime, Volumes 1 and 2. Morphological, physiological, mental, social, economic, and political factors in crime are explored in the first volume. The second volume deals with the relationship between unemployment and crime, along with the special problems of the black population as it relates to both work and crime.

Report #14: Police: Conditions in the United States. Examines the state of police departments in 1931. Deficiencies in organization, recruitment, training, and performance are given special attention. Prevention of crime as a recently recognized responsibility of the police officer is discussed, as is the status of the woman police officer and her contribution to crime prevention.

Report #15: The Mooney Billings Report. Suppressed by the Wickersham Commission, New York: Gotham House, 1932.

John Jay College of Criminal Justice

The Library Special Collections. One of the finest sources of historical information on criminal justice is located at the special collections section of The Library of The John Jay College of Criminal Justice in New York City. The dedicated professionals at John Jay have collected and cataloged most of the important works ever researched in criminal justice. A partial annotated list of some of these special collections is as follows:

American Correctional Association, Annual Congress on Corrections. The papers and debates that make up the proceedings of this Association document the gradual evolution of the science of penology from the point of view of both the scholar and the practitioner. The first four indexes covering the period 1870-1946 have been reprinted in one volume. Discussions as well as formal presentations are indexed.

Anti-Saloon League of America, 1880, 1894-1938. "The Saloon Must Go" was the motto of this non-partisan pressure organization which sought to mobilize church forces against the liquor traffic. The collection includes correspondence, financial records, historical sketches, audits, news clippings and legal briefs. Records have been arranged according to provenance except with material in the Press Release, Book Reviews, and Press Statement subseries. *The Guide to the Microfilm Edition of Temperance and Prohibition Papers* contains background information on the League plus a general description of the Series and a detailed reel description.

Bureau of Social Hygiene: Project and Research Files — 1913-1940. The working papers of one of the earliest privately funded social science research institutions in the United States document the approach of experts to subjects of interest to the criminal justice researcher. Among the documented studies are Abraham Flexner's study of commercialized prostitution and Raymond Fosdick's study of police systems in the United States and Europe. A hidden treasure is Reel 9 which documents efforts during 1927-28 to establish a system of uniform crime reporting. The *Guide* provides a brief history of the Bureau and describes the organization and contents of the files.

Center for Knowledge in Criminal Justice Planning. Records. (1974-78) Spec. Coll. X 102. (Approximately 75 linear feet). The "Center" was established in 1975 to work on an LEAA funded follow-up to the provocative and controversial book, *The Effectiveness of Correctional Treatment* (1975) by Douglas Lipton, Robert Martinson and Judith Wilks. Martinson and Wilks were, respectively, Director and Associate Director of the follow-up project. The materials in the collection include scattered files from a 1974 project on deterrence in which Martinson was involved, files associated with *The Effectiveness of Correctional Treatment*, and the administrative and working files of the "Center" during the grant period. For additional information, and permission to use the material in this collection, see the Chief Librarian.

COINTELPRO: The Counterintelligence Program of the FBI. This FBI program was established to "expose, disrupt, and neutralize" extremist and radical groups perceived as threatening to the internal security of the U.S. The files contain intensive investigative reports made during the 1960s of the American Communist and Socialist Workers parties, the Ku Klux Klan, the Black Panthers, the SDS, plus many others. The material is arranged under such operational headings as Black Nationalist Hate Groups, White Hate Groups, New Left, etc. These files are revealing of both the organizations investigated and the FBI.

G. Tyler Mairs (fl. 1914-1951). In addition to correspondence between G.T. Mairs, Fingerprint examiner of the Magistrate's Court (Brooklyn), and students and specialists in dactyloscopy, this collection contains charts, photographs, and newspaper clippings which provide valuable information for the study of criminal identification by fingerprints. Finding aid in preparation.

International Penitentiary Congress, 1st-9th (1872-1925). International Penal and Prison Congress, 10th-12th (1930-1950). Transactions of the original congresses have been reprinted, including official documents, discussions, and papers presented. This material demonstrates on the international level an interchange of thought and experience similar to that found in the proceedings of the American Correctional Association. English summaries are provided where the presentation was not in English. Accompanied by subject and name indexes.

John Howard. Original works by and about this eighteenth century English prison reformer whose assiduous studies of British prisons and European lazarettos prompted significant reform legislation. The biographies are either by contemporaries or by close contemporaries. In addition to detailed descriptions of prison conditions, Howard's works contain exquisite plates of the facades and floor plans of institutions visited. Also included are tables indicating the number of prisoners by type of crime, punishments, executions, pardons, fees charged, and so on. Access is provided through the card catalog.

Lewis E. Lawes (1883-1947). Papers. Spec. Coll. X 101 (13 Boxes). Lawes was best known for his 21 years as Warden of Sing Sing, and for his ability to keep himself and his ideas in the public eye. The collection includes extensive correspondence with political and cultural figures, photographs, several volumes of Sing Sing publications, and over 1,000 pages of scrapbook material dealing with crime in general and Lawes' career in particular.

Contact the Chief Librarian for additional information, and permission to use this material.

Newgate Calendar of Malefactor's Bloody Register (5 volumes). An eighteenth century publication of illustrated true sagas of the "most notorious criminals (of both sexes)" from 1700 to 1773. It was designed, in part, to guide the young of eighteenth century England, Scotland, and Ireland. The name index includes a list of all the capital convictions at the Old Bailey for that time period.

New York City Court of General Sessions. Typewritten transcripts of the complete proceedings of some 2700 criminal trials from the 1880s through the 1920s. These transcripts contain primary material important not only in the study of the interaction between persons accused of crimes and the criminal justice system but in the study of immigration patterns and urban development during this period. A preliminary index has been prepared for each transcript indicating defendant's name, judge, prosecuting attorney, defense attorney, and charge. The library has received an NEH grant to preserve the transcripts on microfilm and produce and index. Finding aid in preparation.

New York (State), Legislature, Joint Committee on Crime, Its Causes, Control and Effect on Society. The Voices of Organized Crime. This cassette contains conversations of actual voices of members of organized crime syndicates taped by various police and prosecutive agencies throughout New York during the years 1963 to 1965. Conversations refer to the activities of organized crime — gambling, loansharking, murder, grand larceny, fraud, extortion — and its methods of operation — mobs, internal security, intelligence, counter-intelligence and discipline. The cassette is accompanied by printed material identifying the voices, transcribing the conversations, and describing their usefulness in obtaining indictments. The published *Report of Legislative Recommendations* by the Committee provides complementary research material.

Police Department Annual Reports. Beginning with the historic Bruce Smith Collection, the library has assembled reports representing some one hundred cities and counties. A significant portion of the reports date from the early part of the century. The library is engaged in a project to update the collection. Access is provided through the public catalog by department name. For ease of research, shelf arrangement is alphabetical within jurisdiction.

Police Department Surveys. The collection of police department surveys not only contains a more detailed description of specific departments than is found in annual reports but also provides recommendations from experts to improve operations. Consultants for these surveys include Bruce Smith, August Vollmer, and Donal MacNamara. Access is provided through the Public catalog by department name and by the subject heading POLICE SURVEYS.

Police Handbooks. A collection of well-worn pocket size handbooks and manuals containing the rules and regulations of forty-five police departments in the United States and Great Britain, 1816-1934.

Public Order, Discontent and Protest in England, 1820-1850. Series I: 1820-1830. A collection of letters, papers, and reports concerning crime and public order from the Home Office manuscript collection held in the Public Record Office. The documents contain information on criminal cases involving persons in the King's service, disturbances in the countryside, turmoil in the cotton mills, and plans to deal with the increased political agitation. This material is particularly useful for the study of public unrest in the years before the Great Reform Bill of 1832. Although no external finding aid is available, a contents list precedes the items on each reel.

Richard Louis Dugdale, 1841-1883. Documents written in Dugdale's hand have recently been received from the New York Correctional Association. Large worksheets from which Dugdale compiled tables for his studies contain raw data on over 800 individuals. The handwritten preface to an early edition of The Jukes describes the preparatory reading and circumstances which led to his conclusions about the relation of family history to crime and poverty. Also included are stray pages discussing criminal characteristics.

Richard O. Hankey, 1915-1979. Recently acquired from the University of Oregon are the correspondence and subject files of this well-known criminal justice educator and past president of the Academy of Criminal Justice Sciences. The files document Hankey's attempts to bridge practical law enforcement experience and the study of law enforcement and police administration. The files contain evidence of Hankey's association with August Vollmer and O.W. Wilson. Also included are documents from the California Peace Officers Training Program which reveal the state of police training in California during the 1950s and 1960s.

State Reports on Corrections and Public Welfare, Prior to 1930. This collection of documents from eleven of the oldest and most populous states contains valuable raw data available in no other sources, the United States census notwithstanding. It consists primarily of annual reports of state departments, boards, and commissions. Although the bulk of the reports focus on the first three decades of the twentieth century, some go back as far as 1837. Not only can social agencies be studied, but trends and attitudes can be traced. Topics covered include prison reform, child abuse, chain gangs, poverty.

State Reports on Corrections and Punishment, Poverty and Public Welfare, Prior to 1930. In Special Collections. Consult Catalog for call numbers of individual reports. This is a collection of over 2,500 microfiche containing reports from state agencies in California, New York, Ohio, and seven other states. Subjects covered include prisons, orphanages, child abuse, rehabilitation, chain gangs, and insanity. Among the reports are: California Board of Charities and Corrections, 1903-22; California Prison Directors Report, 1851-1879; Colorado State Board of Pardons, 1893-1920; Georgia Prison Commission, 1897-1930; Indiana State Probation Department, 1923-30; Massachusetts Agent for Aiding Discharged Prisoners, 1846-1929; Massachusetts State Board of Lunacy and Charity, 1879-1898; New York State Commission to Examine Laws Relating to Child Welfare, 1921-1926; New York State State Prisons, 1848-1926; Pennsylvania Mother's Assistant Fund, 1917-1929.

Theatre for the Forgotten. Theatre for the Forgotten is a non-profit drama group that uses the theatre as a rehabilitation tool in work with prison inmates and troubled youth. Since it was founded in 1967 to perform prison shows, it has grown to include prison acting workshops and inmate productions. In 1975 it initiated children's theatre workshops for youthful offenders and the emotionally disturbed. This collection contains videotapes and printed documentation of TFTF Alternative Educational Drama Program. A manual describes the contents of the tapes and provides suggestions for their use.

United States Census Publications in Microform: Part I, 1820-1945: Section III. Dependent, Defective, and Delinquent Classes. Microfiche Cabinet. Consult the reference librarian. Among the census publications in this collection are: Prisoners, 1904, 1910, 1922, etc.; Crime and Mental Disease, 1933; Juvenile Delinquency, 1933; Dependent and Delinquent Classes, 1933-45; Paupers in Almshouses, 1904, 1910; Insane and Feeble-Minded, 1904, 1910, 1923; Directory of Institutions, 1919; summary of State Laws, 1913.

William H. Bell. Diary. The diary of this New York City policeman and Inspector of second-hand dealers and junk shops chronicles his activities during 1850-1851. From his undercover existence in the city's slum districts he acquired an intimate knowledge of crime and poverty. The text is a stream of impressions with an occasional aside, free of the moralizing which often clutters accounts of the poor. It is accompanied by Sean Wilentz's article from the *History Workshop Journal* which provides background to the daily "jottings."

Indexes to Nineteenth-Century General Interest Popular Periodicals

Among the hundreds of popular general interest periodicals published in the nineteenth century, there were many concerned with issues of crime, justice, and law and order. The keys to locating these articles, including most of those listed at the beginning of this chapter, are these two indexes:

19th Century Readers' Guide to Periodical Literature, 2 vols. New York: H.W. Wilson, 1944.

Covering only the period from 1880 to 1900, this index was actually compiled in 1944 and is identical in format and indexing policies to the *Readers' Guide* with which you are familiar.

Poole's Index to Periodical Literature, 1802-1906. 6 vols. Rev. ed., reprinted. Gloucester, MA: Peter Smith, 1958.

Mr. Poole began compiling his index in 1848. The third edition of the basic volume, covering 1802 to 1881, was published in 1882 and is the basis for the reprint edition. Although not difficult to use, the indexing does not have the consistency or uniformity which we have come to expect in periodical indexes; use with care and imagination.

Nineteenth-Century Criminal Justice Periodicals

Journal of Prison Discipline and Philanthropy. 1845-1920. Wilmington, DE: Scholarly Resources. Microfilm.

Printed in Pennsylvania, this was a substantial and long-lived publication, with close ties to organizations devoted to prison reform. Although a nineteenth-century tone of moral uplift is clearly evident, especially in the early period, the general orientation of this periodical reflects an increasingly professional outlook. It contains complete reprints of many official documents and summaries of others, original articles, and reprints of articles, sermons, and speeches, as well as news reports of interest to its readers. Items are from all over the Old World, as well as the New.

Moral Advocate: A Monthly Publication on War, Duelling, Capital Punishment, and Prison Discipline. Vols. 1-3, March 1821-1824. Ann Arbor, MI: University Microfilms International. Microfilm.

A short-lived publication whose basic tone is reflected in its title, this was largely the work of one man and was published in Mt. Pleasant, Ohio.

National Police Gazette. 1845-1906. Ann Arbor, MI: University Microfilms International. Microfilm.

Originally, a gazette was a government journal reporting official news. The concept of a gazette as a way of officially reporting crimes goes back at least to eighteenth-century England; in the nineteenth century the term *gazette* was adopted by commercial publishers. For some years the *National Police Gazette* did contain official lists of army deserters, but it was part of the sensationalist crime press and never a government document.

The value of this periodical for the researcher is as a picture of popular attitudes toward crime and sensationalism. In the first few years emphasis was placed on violent crime and criminal biographies, but there was a gradual movement toward greater concern with prostitution, and other salacious topics. Occasional appearance of a police blotter and some statistics could be useful in getting a picture of types and numbers of reported crimes.

Some sample headlines give the flavor of the *Gazette*: "A Brutal Assault; A Gang of Grain Laborers Attack One of Their Number; He is Beaten Unmercifully, and His Ear Bit Off; The Perpetrators of the Outrage Still at Large" (December 8, 1866, page 3); "A New York Pugilist Set Upon by Rowdies; He is Beaten and Almost Cut to Pieces in a Brothel; Not Expected to Survive" (September 21, 1867, page 3); "Audacity's Acme; A Wealthy Lady Assaulted, Garroted and Robbed of Her Diamond Earring [sic] on Fifth Avenue; In Broad Daylight; Amid a Throng of People, Who, with Her Companion are Paralyzed by the Bold Attack of the Thief" (March 1, 1879, page 11).

The journal is illustrated with woodcuts, some of which are exceedingly fine.

Indexes to Nineteenth-Century Scholarly Periodicals

The development of scholarly disciplines in the nineteenth century and the related development of publications written exclusively by and for academics have been briefly described in the introduction to this book. Many of these early academic periodical articles can be located through use of the sets described below. Articles written during the period you are researching can be considered primary sources if they document contemporary events; secondary sources if they describe events of earlier periods.

CRIS: Combined Retrospective Index to Journals in History, 1838-1974. 11 vols. (Washington, DC: Carrollton Press, 1977).

CRIS: Combined Retrospective Index to Journals in Political Science, 1886-1974. 8 vols. (Washington, DC: Carrollton Press, 1977).

CRIS: Combined Retrospective Index to Journals in Sociology, 1895-1974, 6 vols. (Washington, DC: Carrollton Press, 1978).

Special Libraries

There are several state and federally supported libraries that maintain special or unique collections of criminal justice literature. The most famous of these is the Library of Congress, as it is probably the largest library in the world, with comprehensive collections of literature and other materials in all fields of knowledge. The services of the Library of Congress are described below, followed by an alphabetical listing and brief summary of the holdings of other libraries having comprehensive, special, or unique collections of criminal justice materials.

THE LIBRARY OF CONGRESS

The Library of Congress was established in 1800 as a reference library for members of Congress, and although its primary role is to serve Congress, it is available for public use as well.

The Library's holdings include over 74 million items on virtually every subject known to man, and new items come in at the rate of more than 7,000 per working day. This vast collection consists of 18 million books, 33 million manuscripts, 3.5 million maps and atlases, 4 million pieces of music, 9 million prints and photographs, one half-million sound recordings, 250,000 reels of motion pictures, and 3 million pieces of microforms. Rare books, prints and maps, and Stradivarius violins are among the items on display.

For those who cannot visit the Library in person, a number of special, no-charge services are offered. The use of books and other academic materials are made available to public and academic libraries through interlibrary loan. There is also the *Photoduplication Service,* which allows the public to purchase photographs, photostats, facsimile prints, and microfilms of research materials not subject to the copyright law by mail. Written requests should be sent to: General Reading Room Division, Library of Congress, Washington, D.C. 20540.

Computer printouts of sources pertaining to a given subject, and searches for new titles and legislative histories can take only a few minutes when the computer terminals are used. Anyone can request a computer printout by writing: Correspondence Section, General Reading Room Division, Library of Congress, Washington, D.C. 20540.

The Library can assist in locating literature or direct the request for information to an organization or agency that can provide the specific answers. The *National Referral Center,* sponsored by the Library of Congress, provides this type of service. The Center refers those who need answers to specific questions to resources or agencies that have the information and are willing to share it with others. A subject-indexed computerized file of 13,000 organizations is used by the referral service. Requests for this service should describe clearly and precisely the information needed. Inquiries should be directed to: Library of Congress, Science and Technology Division, Washington, D.C. 20540.

The Library of Congress has many divisions, including the copyright office, division for the blind and physically handicapped, general reference and bibliography division, geography and map division, law library, microfilm reading room, music division, prints and photographs division, among several others.

16

BOOKS AND DIRECTORIES OF LIBRARIES

American Library Directory, 43rd ed. Biennial. "A classified list of libraries in the United States and Canada, with personnel and statistical data, plus a selected list of libraries around the world." Lists 24,100 libraries in the United States, and 2,285 in Canada. (New York: R.R. Bowker, 1990/1991).

The Bowker Annual of Library and Book Trade Information, 35th ed. Annual. Statistical and directory information for United States and other countries; also covers library and book trade developments and trends during preceding year. Index. (New York: R.R. Bowker, 1990/1991).

Darnay, Brigitte T., ed. *Directory of Special Libraries and Information Centers*, 13th ed. Lists more than 13,000 libraries and information centers. Semiannual supplements. (Detroit, MI: Gale Research Co., 1989).

Library and Information Science Abstracts. Bimonthly. Supersedes *Library Science Abstracts*, 1950-68. International coverage; abstracts in English from about 200 journals in field of library science and technology. Classified arrangement; author-subject index cumulates annually. (London, UK: Library Ass'n, 1969-date).

Library Literature. Bimonthly with annual and biennial cumulations. Subject index to domestic and foreign materials on library and information science. (New York: H.W. Wilson, 1934-date).

World Guide to Libraries, 9th ed. Gives addresses, indicates subject specialties and size for 36,000 public, academic, and special libraries in 158 countries. Subject index. (New York: R.R. Bowker, 1989).

Catalogs of Other Libraries

Los Angeles Public Library. Municipal Reference Library. *Catalog of the Police Library of the Los Angeles Public Library.* (Boston: G.K. Hall, 1980).

The Information Resources Center. American Society for Industrial Security. Information Resources Coordinator, 1655 North Fort Myer Drive, Suite 1200, Arlington, VA 22209.

University of Cambridge. Institute of Criminology. The Library Catalogue of the Radzinowicz Library. Boston: G.K. Hall, 1979. 6 Vols.

National Archive of Criminal Justice Data. Inter-University Consortium for Political and Social Research, P.O. Box 1248, Ann Arbor, MI 48106.

New York Public Library. Research Libraries. *Dictionary Catalog of the Research Libraries;* A cumulative list of authors, titles and subjects representing books and book-like materials added to the collections since January 1, 1971. New York, 1971 to date.

CRIMINAL JUSTICE INFORMATION EXCHANGE

The National Institute of Justice/NCJRS is the sponsor of the Criminal Justice Information Exchange (CJIE) Group, an informal, cooperative association of libraries serving the criminal justice community. It aims to foster communication and cooperation among member libraries and enhance user services.

Member libraries improve services in the criminal justice area through information exchange and interlibrary loan. In addition, group members furnish criminal justice patrons with information about CJIE collections, policies, and services.

The National Criminal Justice Reference Service (NCJRS), a CJIE member, coordinates the group and produces the CJIE Directory. NCJRS is an international clearinghouse of justice information sponsored by the National Institute of Justice (NIJ), a research arm of the Department of Justice. NCJRS also maintains or supports data bases for other Department of Justice agencies and operates their clearinghouses. These include the Juvenile Justice Clearinghouse, the Justice Statistics Clearinghouse, the National Victims Resource Center, the NIJ AIDS Clearinghouse, and the Bureau of Justice Assistance Clearinghouse.

For more information about participation in the Criminal Justice Information Exchange Group, contact:

CJIE Coordinator
NCJRS
Box 6000
Rockville, MD 20850
(800) 851-3420
(301) 251-5500

Abt Associates, Inc. Library
55 Wheeler Street
Cambridge, MA 02138
(617) 492-7100, ext. 5535

Alberta Solicitor General Library Services
10th Floor
John E. Brownlee Building
10365 97th Street
Edmonton, Alberta, Canada
T5J 3W7
(403) 427-3421

American Bar Association Information Services
1800 M Street, NW
Suite 200 South
Washington, DC 20036-5886
(202) 452-9250

Arizona Department of Public Safety Library
2310 North 20th Avenue
P.O. Box 6638
Phoenix, AZ 85005-6638
(602) 223-2301

Arizona Law Enforcement Training Academy Library
5601 West Trails End Road
Tucson, AZ 85745
(602) 792-9934

Arizona State University
Hayden Library
Tempe, AZ 85287
(602) 965-5167

Armed Forces Institute of Pathology, Ash Library
Bldg. 54, Room 4077
Washington, DC 20306
(202) 576-2983

Baltimore Police Department Library
601 East Fayette Street
Baltimore, MD 21202
(301) 396-2518

Benedictine College Library
Second and Division
Atchison, KS 66002
(913) 367-5340, ext. 510

Bowling Green State University Libraries
Jerome Library
Bowling Green State University
Bowling Green, OH 43403
(419) 372-2362

California State University, Los Angeles
Government Publications Section, Library
5151 State University Drive
Los Angeles, CA 90032
(213) 343-3960

Canadian Police College Law Enforcement
Reference Centre
P.O. Box 8900
Ottawa, Ontario, Canada K1G 3J2
(613) 993-3225

Center for Law and Justice
Mail Stop DK-40
University of Washington
Seattle, WA 98195
(206) 545-2043

Drug Enforcement Administration Library
Washington, DC 20537
(202) 633-1369

Erie Bureau of Police
City of Erie, Pennsylvania
626 State Street
Erie, PA 16501

FBI Academy Library
Quantico, VA 22135
(703) 640-1135

Federal Judicial Center Information Services
1520 H Street NW
Washington, DC 20005
(202) 633-6365

Federal Prison System Library
320 First Street NW
Washington, DC 20534
(202) 724-3029

George Mason University
Fenwick Library
4400 University Drive
Fairfax, VA 22030
(703) 323-2392

Georgia Department of Corrections
Reference Resource Center
Two Martin Luther King Drive SF
Atlanta, GA 30334
(404) 656-4582

Governmental Reference Library
602 County Administration Center
1600 Pacific Highway
San Diego, CA 92101
(619) 531-5787

Governors State University Library
University Park, IL 60466
(312) 534-5000

Harvard Law School Library
Langdell Hall
Cambridge, MA 02138
(617) 495-4516

Harvard University
John F. Kennedy School of Government Library
79 John F. Kennedy Street
Cambridge, MA 02138
(617) 495-1302

Hastings College of Law Library
200 McAllister Street
San Francisco, CA 94102
(415) 565-4767

Hennepin County Law Library
C-2451 Government Center
Minneapolis, MN 55487
(612) 348-3022

Indiana Law Enforcement Academy
David F. Allen Memorial Learning Resources Center
Box 313
Plainfield, IN 46168
(317) 839-5191

Jenkins Memorial Law Library
Suite 1220
841 Chestnut Street
Philadelphia, PA 19107
(215) 592-5693

John Jay College of Criminal Justice, Library
899 Tenth Avenue
New York, NY 10019
(212) 237-8265

Justice Institute of British Columbia
Resource Centre
4198 West 4th Avenue
Vancouver, British Columbia, Canada V6R 4K1
(604) 228-9771 ext. 200

Juvenile Welfare Board Library
4140 49th Street North
St. Petersburg, FL 33709

Kansas State Library
State Capitol
Third Floor
Topeka, KS 66612
(913) 296-3296

Lamar University, Gray Library
LU Station
Box 10021
Beaumont, TX 77710
(409) 880-8130

Law Library of Louisiana
Supreme Court Building
301 Loyola Avenue
New Orleans, LA 70112
(504) 568-5705

Maryland Criminal Justice Resource Center
3085 Hernwood Road
Woodstock, MD 21163
(301) 442-2733

Maryland State Law Library
Courts of Appeal Building
First Floor
361 Rowe Boulevard
Annapolis, MD 21401-1697
(301) 974-3395
DC metro area: 858-8041 x3395

Maryland State Police Academy Library
Department of Public Safety and Correctional Service
201 Reisterstown Road
Pikesville, MD 21208-3899
(301) 653-4370

Mercyhurst College, Hammermill Library
501 E. 38th St.
Erie, PA 16546
(814) 825-0234

Michigan Department of State Police
Law Enforcement Resource Center
7426 North Canal Road
Lansing, MI 48913
(517) 322-1976

Ministry Library and Reference Centre
Ministry of the Solicitor General
340 Laurier Avenue W., 11th Floor
Ottawa, Ontario, Canada K1A OP8
(613) 991-2780

Minnesota Criminal Justice Library, State Planning Agency
658 Cedar Street
St. Paul, MN 55155
(612) 296-5973

Missouri State Library
2002 Missouri Blvd.
P.O. Box 387
Jefferson City, MO 65102
(314) 751-3615

Municipal Reference Library, Police Branch
c/o Room 1004
City Hall
Chicago, IL 60602
(312) 744-4992

National Center for State Courts Library
300 Newport Avenue
Williamsburg, VA 23187-8798
(804) 253-2000

National Institute of Corrections Information Center
Suite 130
1790 30th Street
Boulder, CO 80301
(303) 939-8877

National Institute of Justice/NCJRS
Box 6000
Rockville, MD 20850
(800) 851-3420; (301) 251-5500

Nebraska Legislative Reference Library
Legislative Research Division
7th Floor, State Capital
Lincoln, NE 68509

Nebraska Library Commission
1420 P Street
Lincoln, NE 68508
(402) 471-2045

New York Police Academy Library
235 E. 20th Street
Room 639
New York, NY 10003
(212) 477-9723; (212) 477-9742

New York State Division of Criminal Justice Services
Library/Resource Center
8th Floor, Executive Park Tower
Stuyvesant Plaza
Albany, NY 12203
(518) 457-6113

North Carolina Justice Academy
Learning Resource Center
P.O. Drawer 99
Salemburg, NC 28385
(919) 525-4151

North East Multi-Regional Training
Instructors' Library
1 Smoke Tree Plaza
Suite 111
North Aurora, IL 60542-1718
(708) 896-8860

Northeast Louisiana University
Sandel Library
Monroe, LA 71209
(318) 342-2194

Northeastern University Library
360 Huntington Avenue
Boston, MA 02115
(617) 437-2356

Oakland County Governmental Reference Library
1200 North Telegraph Road
Pontiac, MI 48053
(313) 858-0738

Oklahoma State University Library
Stillwater, OK 74078
(405) 744-6540

Prison Fellowship Ministries
Information Center
P.O. Box 17500
Washington, DC 20041
(703) 478-0100

Provincial Police Academy Library
Provincial Police Academy
Queen St. West & McLaughlin Road
P.O. Box 266
Brampton, Ontario, Canada L6V 2L1
(416) 459-4193

Public Information Representatives
Oklahoma Department of Libraries
200 North East 18
Oklahoma City, OK 73105

Rutgers University—NCCD Collection
S.I. Newhouse Center for Law & Justice
15 Washington Street
4th Floor
Newark, NJ 07102
(201) 648-5522

St. Louis Police Library
315 South Tucker Boulevard
St. Louis, MO 63102
(314) 444-5581

Sam Houston State University
Newton Gresham Library
Sam Houston State University Library
Huntsville, TX 77341
(409) 294-1614

South Carolina Criminal Justice Academy
Learning Resource Center
5400 Broad River Road
Columbia, SC 29210
(803) 737-8400, ext. 362

State Library of Florida
R.A. Gray Building
Tallahassee, FL 32399-0250
(904) 487-2651

State Library of Louisiana
P.O. Box 131
Baton Rouge, LA 70821
(504) 342-4920

State Library of Ohio
65 South Front Street
Columbus, OH 43215
(614) 644-7051

State Library of Pennsylvania
Library Services Division
P.O. Box 1601
Harrisburg, PA 17105
(717) 783-7014

SUNY/Buffalo, E.H. Butler Library
1300 Elmwood Avenue
Buffalo, NY 14222
(716) 878-6314.

Tiffin University, Pfeiffer Library
139 Miami Street
Tiffin, OH 44883
(419) 447-6442

Troy State University Library
University Avenue
Troy, AL 36082
(205) 566-8112 ext. 3256

University at Albany, State University of New York
Governor Thomas E. Dewey Graduate Library for Public
    Affairs and Policy
135 Washington Avenue
Albany, NY 12222
(518) 442-3690 or 442-3698

University of Alberta
Weir Memorial Law Library
Law Centre
Edmonton, Alberta, Canada T6G 2H5
(403) 492-5560

University of Central Texas Library
P.O. Box 1416
Highway 190 West
Killeen, TX 76540
(817) 526-1244

University of Detroit Library
4001 West McNichols
Detroit, MI 48221
(313) 927-1072 or 927-1071

University of Iowa Law Library
College of Law
Iowa City, IA 52242
(319) 335-9016

University of Maryland
McKeldin Library
College Park, MD 20742
(301) 454-2916

The University of Mississippi
Room 106, Old Gym
Government Publications Department
John Davis Williams Library
University, MS 38677
(601) 232-5857

University of Nebraska—Lincoln
Don L. Love Library
Lincoln, NE 68588-0410
(402) 472-2525

University of New Haven
Peterson Library
300 Orange Avenue
West Haven, CT 06516
(203) 932-7189

University of North Carolina at Charlotte
J. Murray Atkins Library
Charlotte, NC 28223
(704) 547-2243 or (704) 547-2242

University of Southern Mississippi
Cook Memorial Library
Southern Station, Box 5053
Hattiesburg, MS 39401
(601) 266-4241

University of Tennessee at Chattanooga, Library
Chattanooga, TN 37403
(615) 755-4510

University of Toronto
Centre of Criminology Library
John P. Robarts Research Library
Room 8001
130 St. George Street
Toronto, Ontario, Canada M5S 1A5
(416) 978-7068

Virginia Commonwealth University
James Branch Cabell Library
P.O. Box 2033
901 Park Avenue
Richmond, VA 23284-2033
(804) 367-1104

Virginia Department of Criminal
Justice Services Library
8th Street Office Building
805 East Broad Street
Richmond, VA 23219
(804) 786-8478, 786-4000

Virginia Department of Corrections
Academy for Staff Development
P.O. Box 2215
Waynesboro, VA 22980
(703) 943-3141

Washington State Library
Mail Stop AJ-11
Olympia, WA 98504-0111
(206) 753-4027

Westfield State College Library
Westfield, MA 01086
(413) 568-3311 x234

Other Libraries

Many other libraries throughout the United States and Canada that maintain special holdings of criminal justice materials are presented below.

American Association of Handwriting Analysts, Inc.
AAHA Library
Librarian
420 Rogers Street
Downers Grove, Illinois 60515
Phone (312) 969-0292

Books are available to members and non-members of the American Association of Handwriting Analysts, Inc. A ten-dollar ($10.00) security fee is required of all active members of this association and a twenty-five-dollar ($25.00) security fee is required of all non-members of this association. The security fee must be on deposit at or prior to the time of borrowing. Professional members of this association, in good standing, are not required to deposit a security fee, but must abide by all other applicable rules.

Any person, member or non-member, may visit the library housed at 420 Rogers Street, Downers Grove, IL 60515, upon advance notification and arrangement. Requests for appointments may be made by telephoning the librarian at (708) 969-0292 or by writing the librarian at the above address.

Books listed may be borrowed by writing or telephoning the librarian, indicating the catalogue number, the title and the complete mailing address to which such publications are to be mailed. A charge of one dollar and twenty-five cents ($1.25) per title must accompany all such requests to cover the increased cost of postage and insurance. All material *must* be *insured* for an equal amount when returned to the library.

All inquiries to the librarian must be accompanied by a stamped, self-addressed envelope when necessary to facilitate handling.

No more than two books may be borrowed at any one time. The normal lending period is one month, although certain publications in demand may be limited to a two-week period.

American Police Academy Library. (1100 NE 125th Street, North Miami, FL 33161, P.O. Box 15350, Chevy Chase, MD 20815, (202) 293-9088 Washington DC or (305) 891-1700 Miami, FL.)

Boston College — Law School Library. (885 Centre Street, Newton Centre, Massachusetts 02159, (617) 332-6700.) Holdings include Anglo-American law, international law and relations, foreign and comparative law, Common Market materials, plus special collections of crime and delinquency materials.

California State Health and Welfare Agency — Interdepartmental Library. (714 P Street, Room 1800, Sacramento, California 95814, (916) 445-8975.) Holdings include literature concerned with adult corrections.

California State Medical Facility — Staff Library. (1600 California Drive, Vacaville, California 95696, (707) 448-6841.) Holdings contain research material relating to criminology and case work as well as psychiatry, medicine, and penology.

Chicago State University — West Center Library. (500 North Polaski Road, Chicago, Illinois 60624, (312) 826-3456.) Holds literature on criminology, corrections, counseling, and black history.

Connecticut Police Academy — Library. (285 Preston Avenue, Meriden, Connecticut 06450, (203) 237-5571.) Holdings include books, films, filmstrips, and other materials relating to criminal justice.

Correctional Service of Minnesota — Education Center on Crime and Delinquency. (1427 Washington Avenue, S. Minneapolis, Minnesota 55454, (612) 339-7227.) Holdings on crime and delinquency, law enforcement, corrections, including films, cassette tapes, games and posters.

Criminal Justice Archive. (Criminal Justice Archive and Information Network (CJAIN), P.O. Box 1048, Ann Arbor, Michigan 48106.) Within the Inter-university Consortium for Political and Social Research. Its goal is to facilitate and enhance research, planning, and policy development in the field of criminal justice. Researchers are encouraged to use these resources.

Criminal Justice Reference and Information Service. (University of Wisconsin, Madison, Wisconsin 53706, (608) 262-1499.) Holds current criminal justice literature and bibliographies in the areas of police, courts, corrections, juvenile justice, evaluation, community crime prevention, advanced technology and drug abuse. General bibliographies are sent to addresses on a general mailing list as they are developed.

Franklin and Marshall College — Fackenthal Library. (Lancaster, Pennsylvania 17604, (717) 393-3621.) Contains the *Judge Paul N. Schaeffer Collection on Criminology* (300 volumes dated 1729-1957). It is open to the public for reference use only.

Handwriting Analysis Research Library (HARL). (Robert E. Backman, Curator, 91 Washington Street, Greenfield, Massachusetts 01301, (413) 774-4667.) This library has a collection of 80,000 items related to handwriting analysis and document examination. It serves as a permanent archive and repository for graphological information and literature, continually develop and maintain extensive reference collections on all aspects of graphology, supplemented by other special collections dealing with history and teaching of handwriting, penmanship, and questioned documents. This includes continual adding to collections, keeping them available to on-the-spot users under specified rules for their use.

To provide informational help and services, including conferences, consultations, discussions, meetings, seminars, tutorials or workshops on Library premises where reference collections form on-the-spot informational backup for these activities. Primary emphasis is to motivate participants toward enriched knowledge, insight and understanding while providing informational help for their particular inquiries, researches or studies.

In all ethical ways, maximize use of our reference collections.

Indiana University/Purdue University at Indianapolis — University Libraries. (420 Blake Street, Indianapolis, Indiana, (317) 264-4101.) Contain holdings on social work, business, child welfare, community organization, criminology and penology, and public welfare.

International Reference Organization in Forensic Sciences. (The Milton Helpern International Center for the Forensic Sciences, Box 95, Room 204 Liberal Arts Building, Wichita State University, Wichita, Kansas 67208, (316) 689-3707.) Serves as a reference resource center to forensic scientists, students, and law enforcement authorities of over 100 countries. Holdings include textbooks, monographs, periodicals, reports and cases, and video and audio tapes of meetings pertaining to forensics.

Los Angeles Public Library — Municipal Reference Department — Police Department Library. (150 North Los Angeles Street, Room 503, Los Angeles, California 90012, (213) 485-3288.) Over 10,000 volumes relating to criminal justice, particularly in the law enforcement area.

Massachusetts State Department of Correction — Central Office Staff Library. (State Office Building, 22nd Floor, 100 Cambridge Street, Boston, Massachusetts 02202, (617) 727-3312.) Contains holdings on criminology, sociology, social work, and psychology.

National Council on Crime and Delinquency — Library. (Continental Plaza, 411 Hackensack Avenue, Hackensack, New Jersey 07601, (201) 488-0400.) Contains materials on crime and juvenile delinquency, prevention, control, and treatment of delinquency, criminology and corrections. Consists of books, bound periodical volumes, unpublished and published reports, monographs, letters, clippings, and pictures.

National Crime Prevention Institute. (University of Louisville, Shelby Campus, Louisville, Kentucky 40292, (502) 588-6987.)

American Association for Protecting Children. (9725 East Hampden Avenue, Denver, Colorado 80231-0811, (303) 695-0811, (800) 227-5242.)

New York City — Department of Correction — New York City Adolescent Remand Shelter Library. (1414 Hazen Street, East Elmhurst, New York 11370, (212) 274-2400.) Holdings deal primarily with penology, criminology, and psychology. The library is not open to the public.

St. Louis Metropolitan Police Department — Police Library. (1200 Clark Avenue, St. Louis, Missouri 63103, (314) 231-1212.) Contains materials on police science, criminology, crime detection, sociology, juvenile delinquency, traffic, criminal law, narcotics, and alcoholism. It is open to the public for reference use only.

United States Army Military Police School — Library. (Ramsey Hall Building 38705, Fort Gordon, Georgia 30905, (404) 791-6528.) Contains over 15,000 books, 30,000 military publications on military science, penology, international affairs, and criminology.

United States Department of Justice — Bureau of Prisons. (Central Office Library, 117 D Street, N.W., Washington, D.C. 20534, (202) 739-2276.) Archival material of the Bureau as well as holdings on corrections, criminal psychology, and criminology.

United States Federal Judicial Center — Information Service. (1520 H Street, N.W., Washington, D.C. 20005, (202) 393-1640.) Holdings on judicial administration, court management, crime and criminals, probation, and constitutional law.

University of Missouri School of Law Library. (Tate Hall, Columbia, Missouri 65211, (314) 882-4597) Among the special collections of this library is a crime and criminology collection.

Wisconsin State Governor's Office/University of Wisconsin Law School — Criminal Justice Reference and Information Center. (University of Wisconsin, L 140 Law Building, Madison, Wisconsin 53706, (608) 262-1499.) Holdings on the criminal justice system, police science, corrections, drug abuse, delinquency, and alcoholism.

DEPOSITORY LIBRARIES

Depository libraries are libraries that are designated to receive government publications. In return, the libraries must keep and care for the materials they receive. Each congressional district in the United States can have two depository libraries, most of which were designated as such years ago. Also, all land grant colleges are depository libraries, regardless of whether there are already two in that congressional district. Subject matter of the government documents available varies from library to library because each one is designated to receive materials from certain subject categories. However, there are also regional depository libraries in addition to those described above, and each regional depository library receives copies of all materials distributed. Thus, any regional depository library would have a wealth of government publications in criminal justice, or any other subject in which one might be interested. The following is a list of 50 regional depository libraries.

Auburn University at Montgomery
Library, Documents Department
Montgomery, AL 36193
(205) 271-9650

University of Alabama Library
Documents Department
Box S
University, AL 35487
(205) 348-6046

Arizona State Library
Department of Library Archives and Public Records
State Capitol Building
1700 W. Washington
Phoenix, AZ 85007
(602) 255-4121

University of Arizona Library
Government Document Department
Tucson, AZ 85721
(602) 621-4871

Arkansas State Library
Documents Service Section
One Capitol Mall
Little Rock, AR 72201
(501) 371-2090

California State Library
Government Publications Section
914 Capitol Mall
Sacramento, CA 95814
(916) 322-4572

University of Colorado Library
Government Publications Library
Campus Box 184
Boulder, CO 80309
(303) 492-8834

Connecticut State Library
231 Capitol Avenue
Hartford, CT 06106
(203) 566-4971

Denver Public Library
Government Publications Division
1357 Broadway
Denver, CO 80203
(303) 571-2346

University of Florida Libraries
Documents Department
Library West
Gainesville, FL 32611
(904) 392-0367

University of Georgia Libraries
Government Documents Department
Athens, GA 30602
(404) 542-8949

University of Hawaii
Hamilton Library
Government Documents Collection
2550 The Mall
Honolulu, HI 96822
(808) 948-8230

University of Iowa Libraries
Government Publications Department
Iowa City, IA 52242
(319) 335-5926

University of Idaho Library
Documents Section
Moscow, ID 83843
(208) 885-6344

Illinois State Library
Government Documents
Centennial Building
Springfield, IL 62756
(217) 782-5012

Indiana State Library
Serials Section
140 North Senate Avenue
Indianapolis, IN 46204
(317) 232-3686

University of Kansas
Spencer Research Library
Documents Collection
Lawrence, KS 66045
(913) 864-4660

University of Kentucky Libraries
Government Publications Department
Lexington, KY 40506
(606) 257-8400

Louisiana State University
Middleton Library
Government Documents Department
Baton Rouge, LA 70803
(504) 388-2570

Louisiana Technical University
Prescott Memorial Library
Documents Department
Ruston, LA 71272
(318) 257-4962

Boston Public Library
Documents Receipts
Copley Square
Box 286
Boston, MA 02117
(617) 536-5400 X 226

University of Maryland
McKeldin Library
Documents Division
College Park, MD 20742
(301) 454-3034

University of Maine
Raymond H. Fogler Library
Tri-State Regional Documents Depository
Orono, ME 04469
(207) 581-1680

Detroit Public Library
5201 Woodward Avenue
Detroit, MI 48202
(313) 833-1409

Library of Michigan
Government Documents
P.O. Box 30007
735 E. Michigan Avenue
Lansing, MI 48909
(517) 373-0640

University of Minnesota
Wilson Library
Government Publications
309 19th Avenue South
Minneapolis, MN 55455
(612) 624-5073

University of Mississippi
J.D. Williams Library
Documents Department
University, MS 38677
(601) 232-5857

University of Montana
Maurene & Mike Mansfield Library
Documents Division
Missoula, MT 59812
(406) 243-6700

University of North Carolina at
Chapel Hill Library
BA/SS Documents Division
Chapel Hill, NC 27514
(919) 962-1151

North Dakota State University Library
Government Documents Department
Fargo, ND 58105
(701) 237-8352

University of Nebraska
D.L. Love Memorial Library
Documents Department
13th and R Streets
Lincoln, NE 68588
(402) 472-2562

Newark Public Library
U.S. Documents Division
Five Washington Street
P.O. Box 630
Newark, NJ 07101
(201) 733-7812

University of New Mexico General Library
Government Publications and Maps Department
Albuquerque, NM 87131
(505) 277-5441

New Mexico State Library
325 Don Gaspar Avenue
Santa Fe, NM 87503
(505) 827-3826

University of Nevada—Reno Library
Government Publications Department
Reno, NV 89557
(702) 784-6579

New York State Library
Documents Control
Sixth Floor
Cultural Education Center
Empire State Plaza
Albany, NY 12230
(518) 474-5563

State Library of Ohio
Documents Section
65 South Front Street
Columbus, OH 43266
(614) 644-7051

Oklahoma Department of Libraries
Government Documents
200 Northeast 18th Street
Oklahoma City, OK 73105
(405) 521-2502 X 252

Oklahoma State University Library
Documents Department
Stillwater, OK 74078
(405) 624-0489

Portland State University Library
P.O. Box 1151
Portland, OR 97207
(503) 229-3673

State Library of Pennsylvania
Government Publications Section
Box 1601
Walnut Street & Commonwealth Ave.
Harrisburg, PA 17105
(717) 787-3752

Texas State Library
Public Services Department
P.O. Box 12927
Capitol Station
Austin, TX 78711
(512) 463-5455

Texas Tech University Library
Documents Department
Lubbock, TX 79409
(806) 742-2268

Utah State University
Merrill Library and Learning
 Resources Center, UMC-30
Documents Department
Logan, UT 84322
(801) 750-2682

University of Virginia
Alderman Library
Government Documents
Charlottesville, VA 22903
(804) 924-3133

Washington State Library
Documents Section
Olympia, WA 98504
(206) 753-4027

State Historical Society of Wisconsin Library
Government Publications Section
State Library Bldg.
816 State Street
Madison, WI 53706
(608) 262-2781

Milwaukee Public Library
Documents Division
814 West Wisconsin Avenue
Milwaukee, WI 53233
(414) 278-3065

West Virginia University Library
Government Documents Section
P.O. Box 6069
Morgantown, WV 26506
(304) 293-3640

Wyoming State Library
Supreme Court and Library Building
Cheyenne, WY 82002
(307) 777-7509

SPECIALIZED CRIMINAL JUSTICE LIBRARIES IN CANADA

Alberta Solicitor General Library Services
10th Floor, John E. Brownlee Building
10365 97th Street
Edmonton, Alberta, Canada T5J 3W7
(403) 427-3421

British Columbia Co-ordinated Law Enforcement
Unit Library
2588 Cadboro Bay Road
Victoria, British Columbia, Canada V8R 5J2
(604) 598-4545

Canadian Police College
Law Enforcement Reference Centre
P.O. Box 8900
Ottawa, Ontario, Canada K1G 3J2
(613) 993-3225

Centre of Criminology Library
University of Toronto
John P. Robarts Research Library
Room 8001
130 St. George Street
Toronto, Ontario, Canada M5S 1A5
(416) 978-7068

Justice Institute of British Columbia
Resource Centre
4198 West 4th Avenue
Vancouver, British Columbia, Canada V6R 4K1
(604) 228-9771 X 200

Ministry Library and Reference Centre
Ministry of the Solicitor General
340 Laurier Avenue W.
11th Floor
Ottawa, Ontario, Canada K1A 0P8
Reference: (613) 991-2780
ILL: (613) 991-2787

Ontario — Ministry of Correctional Services
2001 Eglinton Avenue, E.
Toronto, Ontario, MIL 2M9
Holdings pertain to the subjects of penology and
    criminology.

Provincial Police Academy Library
Provincial Police Academy
Queen St. West & McLaughlin Road
P.O. Box 266
Brampton, Ontario, Canada L6V 2L1
(416) 459-4193

Royal Canadian Mounted Police
Law Enforcement Reference Center
St. Laurent Blvd., N. and Sandridge Rd.
P.O. Box 8900
Ottawa, Ontario, Canada K1G 3J2
(613) 993-9500 X 233
Joan Beavis, Librarian

University of Alberta
Weir Memorial Library
Law Center
Edmonton, Alberta, Canada T6G 2H5
(403) 432-5560
Ann Rae, Assistant Law Librarian

Legal Research

Legal research is conducted for a variety of purposes but is not generally undertaken to an extensive degree by undergraduate students. The highest trained legal researcher may possess a law degree and a master's degree in library science, or may hold a Doctor of Jurisprudence degree. The researching of legal subjects can take the form of determining what a specific statute may state or may be as complex as a Ph.D. dissertation to determine the ramifications and impact of a landmark Supreme Court decision.

The quality of legal research will depend upon many factors including the legal holdings of the library used. A small junior college will usually at least have a copy of the state's general statutes and perhaps a copy of *Black's Law Dictionary*, while a major university with a law school may have a separate building containing only law books.

The student at the smaller school should not become discouraged. Nearly every county courthouse or district court will have a library of law books adequate to meet the needs of most criminal justice students. In addition, students near a federal courthouse may be able to use those excellent holdings, although it may be necessary to obtain permission from one of the judges or clerks.

There are a number of books, bibliographies, dictionaries, and legal encyclopedias available to help students conduct legal research. Sources of assistance are provided below, but this description is not intended to be comprehensive in nature, for that would require an entire text in itself. It should, however, provide the basic foundation necessary to undertake legal research. In addition, students should not hesitate to request the assistance of the librarian, since legal research is sometimes intricate and time-consuming.

There are a number of books that have been written on how to research law in the library. The one that I have found to be the easiest to use as well as being thorough and comprehensive is *Find the Law in the Library: A Guide to Legal Research*, by John Corbin and published by the American Library Association, Chicago, 1989.

The next section of this chapter will explain the different sources of law.

FEDERAL STATUTES

Session Laws

U.S. Statutes at Large. The official edition. Laws and amendments in chronological order for each session of Congress.

U.S. Code Congressional and Administrative News, 1944-date. Despite its title, this set does not consist of codified laws. It contains the laws as passed at each session of Congress, plus a good deal of additional material, including full legislative histories.

Codified Laws

> *United States Code* (U.S.C.) Updated with bound annual supplements.
> *United States Code Annotated* (U.S.C.A.) West Publishing Co.
> *United States Code Service* (U.S.C.S.) Lawyers Co-operative Publishing Co.

STATE STATUTES

When researching the law of state crimes, or of a state judicial system or process, always begin your search with the state statutes or code for your state. Ask your reference librarian for the volume on criminal laws or other topics. Always check the current status of state laws in the pocket-part supplement to each volume.

COURT DECISIONS

In order to understand the process of legal research, one must be familiar with West Publishing Company's National Reporter System (see steps to Legal Research at the end of this chapter). The decisions of the federal and state courts are reported as follows:

United States Supreme Court: Decisions are found in the *Supreme Court Reporter* (West Publishing Co.), *United States Reports* (U.S. Government Printing Office) and in the *U.S. Supreme Court Reports, Lawyers' Edition* (Lawyers Co-operative Publishing Co.).

For example, *Miranda v. Arizona* could be found in any of the following volumes:

Volume	Page Number	Year of Decision
384 U.S.	436	(1966)
86 S. Ct.	1602	(1966)
16 L. Ed. 2d	694	(1966)

Weekly updates of recent Supreme Court decisions are found in *United States Law Week* (Bureau of National Affairs, Inc., Washington, D.C.).

United States Courts of Appeal: Selected decisions for all circuits are found in the *Federal Reporter* or *Federal Reporter, Second Series,* and should be cited as follows: _____F.2d_____(circuit number and year)

United States District Courts: Selected decisions are found in the *Federal Supplement*. A case would be cited as follows: _____F. Supp._____(district and year)

State Courts

The decisions of the highest courts of each state appear in the National Reporter System according to the state's geographic location, as follows:

Reporters for State Decisions

The first seven reporters described below are results of the National Reporter System, a system that was developed to facilitate legal research. This system grew out of a successful attempt by West Publishing Company to provide the legal profession of the state of Minnesota with reliable and quick sources of information in 1876. This endeavor grew, and as one Reporter after another was added, the entire country was eventually covered. The following seven Reporters now comprise the National Reporter System.

Atlantic Reporter. Contains select decisions of the appellate courts of Connecticut, Delaware, District of Columbia, Maine, Maryland, New Hampshire, New Jersey, Pennsylvania, Rhode Island, and Vermont.

Northeastern Reporter. Contains select decisions of the appellate courts of Illinois, Indiana, Massachusetts, New York, and Ohio.

Northwestern Reporter. Contains select appellate court decisions from Iowa, Michigan, Minnesota, Nebraska, North Dakota, South Dakota, and Wisconsin.

Pacific Reporter. Contains select appellate decisions of Alaska, Arizona, California, Colorado, Hawaii, Idaho, Kansas, Montana, Nevada, New Mexico, Oklahoma, Oregon, Utah, Washington, and Wyoming.

Southern Reporter. Contains select decisions of appellate courts of Alabama, Florida, Louisiana, and Mississippi.

Southeastern Reporter. Contains selected appellate decisions of Georgia, North Carolina, South Carolina, Virginia, and West Virginia.

Southwestern Reporter. Contains select decisions of the appellate courts of Arkansas, Kentucky, Missouri, Tennessee, and Texas.

FEDERAL ADMINISTRATIVE AGENCIES

While the rulings of state and federal administrative agencies have had only limited application in researching the law of traditional crimes or criminal procedure, their regulations are becoming more and more important in today's world. Remember, the rules and regulations of administrative agencies have "the force and effect of law."

United States Code of Federal Regulations (cite as *C.F.R.*). The *CFR* is an annual compilation of federal rules and regulations in force at the time of publication. The rules and regulations are arranged by broad subject areas into 50 titles, some of which correspond to the titles of the *United States Code*. The *CFR* includes a number of special volumes which aid in its use. These are:

(1) The *General Index* volume which provides access to the rules by both subject and issuing agency.

(2) The *Finding Aids* volume serves as a general guide to *CFR* by providing a number of specialized finding tools. In addition to a detailed table of contents for the entire *CFR* set, the *Finding Aids* volume includes

Federal Register (cite as Fed. Reg.). The *Federal Register* serves as a daily supplement to the *CFR*, updating the *CFR* by publishing the texts of all new federal rules and regulations. To determine the current status of a particular *CFR* rule, consult the latest issue of the *CFR*'s *Cumulative List of CFR Sections Affected* and the "List of CFR Parts Affected" in the most recent daily issue of the *Federal Register*. These lists refer the researcher to the *Federal Register* citations which modify the *CFR* rules.

In addition to new rules and regulations, the *Federal Register* includes the texts of proposed rules and regulations, presidential orders and proclamations, and notices concerning modifications in the structure and function of government agencies.

Each issue of the *Federal Register* contains a subject/agency index. These indexes are then cumulated on a monthly, semiannual and annual basis.

Federal Rules Decisions. 1941 to date. (cite as: F.R.D.). Publishes opinions, decisions and rulings concerning only one field of federal administrative law: that relating to the Federal Rules of Civil and Criminal Procedure. These Rules, although generally thought of as part of administrative law, have actually been enacted and are therefore included in the *U.S. Code*. (References to FRD cases are included in the annotations to the *U.S. Code Service*.)

ANNOTATED ARTICLES

Although few college libraries contain the *American Law Reports* annotated series (A.L.R., A.L.R.4th, A.L.R. Federal), published by Lawyers Co-operative Publishing Co., all law libraries and many law offices will have them available. Many lawyers find this tool indispensable. It gives citations and commentary to many cases that have been decided on the particular point of law that you are researching.

LEGAL ENCYCLOPEDIAS

American Jurisprudence 2d ed. (Am. Jur. 2d) (Lawyers Cooperative Publishing Co.) A standard encyclopedia of American law. It will be a helpful place to begin your legal research, particularly to gain a better understanding of your topic. It is the easiest to read of the legal encyclopedias.

Corpus Juris Secundum (C.J.S.) (West Publishing Co.) A comprehensive legal encyclopedia which is frequently cited as authority by federal and state appellate courts. It is a very exhaustive work which purports to restate all American law based upon all reported cases since 1658.

LAW JOURNALS AND PERIODICALS

Courts often cite the articles contained in law journals and law reviews as persuasive authority for their decisions. For the student, these articles and case notes, written by legal scholars and law students, are helpful in building an understanding of the legal, social, economic, and public policy issues surrounding important court decisions. (Also see Chapter 5, titled "Journals.")

Index to Legal Periodicals (I.L.P.) Index to Legal Periodicals provides thorough indexing of articles in 500 leading journals, yearbooks, institutes, bar association organs, university publications and law reviews, and government publications originating from the United States, Great Britain, Ireland, Canada, Australia, and New Zealand.

Law schools, bar associations, legal aid societies, law firms, attorneys, judges and jurists at all levels, business people, librarians, and other researchers use *Index to Legal Periodicals* for access to information on developments in all areas of jurisprudence including recent court decisions, precedents, new legislation, and original scholarship. Also, such topics as International Law, Constitutional Law, Malpractice Suits, Securities and Antitrust Legislation, Labor Law, Criminal Law, Latest Developments in Takeovers, Multinational Corporations, Discrimination, and Environmental Law are covered.

In addition to the single alphabetical subject-author index which forms the main body of *Index to Legal Periodicals*, it also offers: Table of Cases arranged alphabetically by name of plaintiff and defendant; Table of Statutes arranged by jurisdiction and listed alphabetically by name; Book Reviews of current books relevant to the legal profession, indexed by author's name. (Bronx, NY: H.W. Wilson).

Index to Periodical Articles Related to Law. Four volumes cumulated indexes from 1958 to 1988. This index covers selected journals which are not included in the *Index to Legal Periodicals*. (Dobbs Ferry, NY: Glanville Publishers, Inc.).

Current Law Index. This has more comprehensive journal coverage than the *Index to Legal Periodicals*, more specific subject headings and is generally the preferred index to law review articles. There are subject, author/title, case, and statute indexes. It began in 1980. (Foster City, CA: Information Access Co.).

Index to Foreign Legal Periodicals. 1960 to date. (Quarterly, with annual and triennial cumulations.) Covers law reviews from all over the world, except those from English speaking countries. It therefore excludes all countries with legal systems based on principles of common law. (Berkeley, CA: University of California Press).

Ritz, Wilfred J. *American Judicial Proceedings First Printed Before 1801: An Analytical Bibliography.* Attempts to list "every law report, trial, or separate event of judicial significance occurring in or relating to what was the United States in 1801, and for which there was something *printed* prior to that date (other than a newspaper account.)"— *p.xvii.* Arranged by geographical area and subject. Citations include library locations and references in early American imprints bibliographies and microform projects. (Westport, CT: Greenwood Press, 1984).

National Indian Law Library. Catalogue; an index to Indian legal materials and resources. Cumulative eds. issued at irregular intervals. Publ. with the Native American Rights Fund. The 1982 cumulative ed. includes about 3,400 items relating to "tribal existence, protection of tribal resources, promotion of human rights, advancement of tribal self-determination; and to the accountability of the dominant society."—*Introd.* A subject section, plaintiff/defendant, defendant/plaintiff table, and author/title table refer user to the numerical listing where complete bibliographic and file contents information are given. (Boulder, CO: 1974-date).

Checklists of Basic American Legal Publications. Meira G. Pimsleur. Sec. 1 covers *State statutes, revisions, compilations.* Sec. 2 covers the *Session laws of the various states of the United States.* Sec. 3 is a *Checklist of reports and opinions of the attorneys-general.* Sec. 4 (1974-) lists reports of state judicial councils and conferences. Sec. 5 (1976-) lists American Law Institute restatements of the law and codifications. (South Hackensack, NJ: Rothman).

Legal Looseleafs in Print 1981- . Arlene L. Sterne. (N.Y., Infosources Publ., [1981}- . Annual.) A title listing of legal looseleafs published in the United States which are currently in print. Each entry provides title, publisher, year of original publication, number of volumes, price, frequency and annual cost of supplements. Detailed subject index. Annual. (New York: Infosources, 1981-date).

Supreme Court of the United States, 1789-1980; An Index to Opinions Arranged by Justice. Linda A. Blandford and Patricia Russell Evans. Sponsored by the Supreme Court Historical Society. (Listed chronologically), opinions are organized by category, indicating majority, plurality, concurring, separate, or dissenting opinions, statements, or opinions as circuit judges; each listing provides name of case and citation to its appearance in the *United States reports.* Appendixes provide some biographical data and a chronology of succession of Justices from 1789 to 1980. (Millwood, NY: Kraus International Publications, 1983).

Hein's Legal Periodical Check List. William S. Hein, Kevin M. Marmion and Ilene N. Hein. (Buffalo, NY: W.S. Hein, 1977-date).

Legal & Law Enforcement Periodicals: A Directory. Over 3,800 periodicals published in the United States and Canada are listed in 50 subject categories. (New York: Facts on File, 1981).

Bibliographic Guide to Law. Successor to the *Law Book Guide* (1969-74). Includes all material cataloged by the Library of Congress within each year; full cataloging information. Annual. (Boston: G.K. Hall, 1975-date).

Law Books, 1876-1981: Books and Serials on Law and Its Related Subjects. Contents: v.1-3, Books—Subject index; v.4, Books—Author and title indexes, Serials—Subject and title indexes, Publishers, Online database producers and vendors. (New York: R.R. Bowker, 1981).

Citations to about 130,000 books and 4,000 serials titles drawn from the *American book publishing record* database, *National union catalog,* and MARC tapes. Updated by:

Bowker's Law Books and Serials in Print. Contents: v.1, Books—Subject index; v.2, Books—Author index; v.3, Books—Title index; Subject index to cataloged titles; Serials—Subject index, Title index; Publishers and distributors abbreviations. Annual. (New York: R.R. Bowker, 1984-date).

Law Information (1982-83) and *Law Information Update* (1983-84). Lists English-language legal materials drawn from the Bowker databases, MARC tapes, and the Government Printing Office Publications Reference File; Updated by:

Bowker's Law Books and Serials in Print Update: materials on law and related topics recently published and to be published. (New York: R.R. Bowker, 1984-date).

Law Books Published. v.1- . A quarterly record of books published in English during the year. The fourth quarterly issue is an annual cumulation. Quarterly. (Dobbs Ferry, NY: Glanville, 1969-date).

National Legal Bibliography. Recent acquisitions of major legal libraries v.1, no.1- , Jan. 1984- . (Buffalo, N.Y., W.S. Hein, 1984- . Monthly.) Includes books, serials, government and other documents, theses and dissertations cataloged by about 15 university and public libraries. Broad topical arrangement (U.S. and general; international; foreign jurisdiction by country). Monthly. (Buffalo, NY: W.S. Hein, 1984-date).

BOOKS AND DIRECTORIES

Books, like law journal articles, are not considered sources of law. However, they are exceedingly helpful in understanding the development of legal doctrines and in explaining leading court decisions. The following texts are commonly available and highly recommended for general reading.

Basic Text on Administrative Law, Third edition. K. Davis. (St. Paul, MN: West Publishing, 1972).

Bar Admission Rules and Student Practice Rules, Fannie J. Klein, Steven H. Leleiko, and Jane H. Mavity. (Ballinger Publishing Co., Cambridge, MA, 1978.) This book is the result of an ambitious project: to complete the only comprehensive source of state and federal bar admission and student practice rules...a convenient, ready reference tool—an excellent source for beginning research in practice rules. (Cambridge, MA: Ballinger, 1978).

Barron's Guide to Law Schools, Profiles of ABA approved schools, ratings, and samples of LSAT. Also includes practical advice on applications, funding and job search. (Woodbury, NY: Barron's Educational Series, 1990).

Criminal Law. Rollin M. Perkins and Ronald N. Boyce. (Mineola, NY: Foundation Press, 1989).

Effective Legal Research. Miles O. Price and H. Bitner. Includes chapters on legislation, statutes, law reports, digests, legal periodicals, dictionaries, encyclopedias, and also addresses citations and citation style. (Boston: Little, Brown, 1979).

Effective Legal Writing. A style book for law students and lawyers, Third edition. Gertrude Block. Offers a method to improve legal writing through coverage of basic grammatical rules, legal style and organization, and various other expository techniques. Samples of unclear writing are shown and corrected. Writing assignments and legal problems with model answers are included. Materials are the appropriate teaching solution to courses on legal writing and legal research and writing. (Mineola, NY: Foundation Press, 1986).

Finding the Law: A Guide to Legal Research. David Lloyd. Written in non-technical language, designed to assist first year law students and others unfamiliar with legal research, in using the law library. Appendices on common legal citations and abbreviations are included. (Dobbs Ferry, NY: Oceana, 1974).

Fundamentals of Legal Research and Legal Research Illustrated: Assignments. J. Myron Jacobstein and Roy M. Mersky. An assignment workbook in which each chapter corresponds to a chapter in *Fundamentals of Legal Research* (or *Legal Research Illustrated*). The book is divided into three parts. Part I introduces the reader to legal bibliography problems which are used to demonstrate how research on the same set of facts is accomplished in different types of index and research books. Part II provides the opportunity for the reader to apply the knowledge gained from working the exercises in Part I. The final section, Part III, is concerned with descriptions of sources of federal tax law and methods for locating these sources. (Mineola, NY: Foundation Press, 1983).

How to Find the Law, Ninth edition. Morris L. Cohen (ed.) (St. Paul, MN: West Publishing, 1989).

International Law and Organization: General Sources of Information. Jacob Roginson. Lists reference works and periodicals on an international basis. (Leiden, Netherlands: Sijthoff, 1967).

An Introduction to the Legal System of the United States, Second edition. Farnsworth. Designed for the foreign student, this introductory text also serves the American student with chapters on the judiciary, legislature, state laws, statutes and sections on civil and criminal procedure, contracts, torts, and many types of law. (New York: Oceana, 1983).

Law Books Published. A quarterly publication since 1960 that includes English language law books published during the year. (Dobbs Ferry, NY: Glanville).

The Law in the United States of America, A Selective Bibliographical Guide. Andrews, et al. Describes basic sources that should be included in the holdings of any law library. (New York: New York University Press, 1965).

Legal Problem Solving: Analysis, Research, and Writing. Rombauer. A basic text on conducting legal research. Contains chapters on briefing a case, analyzing opinions, interpreting legislation, conducting computer-assisted research, writing memorandums, and arguing a case orally. (St. Paul, MN: West Publishing, 1983).

Legal Research in a Nutshell. Morris Cohen. An introductory manual to the main areas of legal literature (judicial reports, case finding, statutes, legislative histories, international law, etc.) (St. Paul, MN: West Publishing, 1988).

Legal Research Illustrated. J.M. Jacobstein and Roy M. Mersky. A beginner's text which takes the legal researcher step by step into the legal research process. Contents include information on the legal process, court reports, federal and state court decisions, the national reporter system, annotated law reports, constitutions, federal and state legislation, administrative law, Shepard's citations, legal encyclopedias and periodicals, and many other research aids. (Mineola, NY: Foundation Press, 1990).

Legal Research and Education Abridgment, A manual for law students, paralegals and researchers. Edward Bander with the assistance of David F. Bander. (Cambridge, MA: Ballinger Publishing Co., 1978).

Legal Research and Writing (1986), and *Case Analysis and Fundamentals of Legal Writing* (1989). William P. Statsky. These books provide clear introductions on subjects such as using the law library, types of law materials, principles of legal research, reading administrative regulations, and case law. (St. Paul, MN: West Publishing).

The Living Law: A Guide to Modern Legal Research, 1990-91. Designed to assist the legal researcher achieve an organized, systematic approach to legal research. Various publications which are incorporated into a legal research system known as the Total Client Service Library (TCSL) are described. The TCSL was created by the Lawyer's Cooperative Publishing Company and the Bancroft-Whitney Company. (New York: The Lawyer's Cooperative Publishing Company, 1979).

Supreme Court of the United States 1981-1986: An Index to Opinions Arranged by Justice. 2v. Linda A. Blandford and Patricia Russel Evens (eds.) Sponsored by the Supreme Court Historical Society. (Millwood, NY: Kraus International, 1983).

Using a Law Library; A Guide for Students in the Common Law Provinces of Canada. Margaret A. Banks. (London, ON: University of Western Ontario, School of Library and Information Science, 1971).

Using American Law Books, Third edition. Alfred J. Lewis. (Dubuque, IA: Kendall/Hunt, 1990).

West's Law Finder: A Research Manual for Lawyers. Describes law finder aids which are published by West Publishing Company. Publications and services described include the National Reporter System, West Key Number Digests, Key Number System Law Chart, *Corpus Juris Secundum, United States Code,* methods of search for *United States Code, Words and Phrases, Federal Practice Procedure,* Westlaw (West's computer law retrieval system) and sources of legislative and session law services. (St. Paul, MN: West Publishing, 1990).

LAW DICTIONARIES

Legal dictionaries will give the user a precise definition of law-related terms. The most widely used are *Black's Law Dictionary* and *Ballentine's Law Dictionary.*

Ballentine's Law Dictionary With Pronunciations, Third edition. James A. Ballentine. (Rochester, NY: Lawyer's Cooperative, 1969).

Dictionary of Legal Abbreviations. Doris M. Bieber. (Buffalo, NY: William S. Hein, 1979).

Black's Law Dictionary; Definitions of Terms and Phrases of American and English Jurisprudence, Ancient and Modern, Sixth edition. Henry C. Black. (St. Paul, MN: West Publishing, 1990).

The Law Dictionary. Wesley Gilmer, Jr. (Cincinnati, OH: Anderson Publishing Co., 1986).

Law Dictionary for Laymen. John C. Howell. (Leesburg, VA: Citizens Law Library, 1979).

Law Dictionary for Non Lawyers. Daniel Oran. (St. Paul, MN: West Publishing, 1984).

The Oxford Companion to Law. David M. Walker. (New York: Oxford University Press, 1980).

You may also want to check Chapter 6, "General Reference Sources," under the heading "Dictionary" for definitions of general criminal justice terms.

COMPUTERIZED LEGAL RESEARCH

There are several computer data bases in the field of legal research. The most widely used are listed below.

Westlaw. This data base, produced by West Publishing Co. is the largest data base of its kind. Included in this legal data base are summaries and citations for reported cases that were heard in state courts since 1965. The data base also contains information on federal cases dating back to 1790.

The Westlaw computer holds a vast store of information important to lawyers, a national full text case law library, a specialized Federal Tax Library, the text of the U.S. Code, and Shepard's Citations.

Westlaw provides the entire text of the U.S. Code, giving the researcher electronic access to the federal statutes. Special search methods make it easier to find the exact section or subsection you need as well as to scan related sections whenever needed. Also included are Supreme Court Reporter, from 1932 to date; Federal Reporter 2d, from 1945 to date; Federal Supplement from 1950 to date.

Westlaw has a 50-state data base. It provides the text of the Code of Federal Regulations, giving the researcher access to current federal administrative regulations and offers the capability of addressing commands based on fundamental units of ordinary English: sentences and paragraphs.

LEXIS, along with Westlaw, ranks as one of the top two legal data bases.

Shepard's Citations. All Shepard's case law citators are included in LEXIS: federal, state, and regional reporter series. Shepard's provides parallel citations, case history, subsequent treatment of the case, and all cases that cite the cited case. Shepard's is a product of Shepard's/McGraw-Hill.

Auto-Cite offers a virtually instantaneous verification of a citation. Auto-Cite provides the name of the case cited, the date and place of decision, official and parallel citations, and the citation to any case that directly affects the official status of the case as precedent. Auto-Cite is a service of the Lawyers Co-operative Publishing Company and its affiliate, Bancroft-Whitney.

LEXIS finds cases by name, citation, or both. *LEXIS* as a citator can prove invaluable when only the name of the case is known, as when an important case is to be relied upon before it has been given a citation. Thousands of recent slip opinions are available only through *LEXIS. LEXIS* also contains thousands of cases that never appear in the reporters. You will find it a considerable advantage to perform a citation search by name as well as by citation. You will also appreciate the fact that *LEXIS* can find citations in documents other than cases, such as statutes, regulations, or Supreme Court briefs.

LEXIS can also be used for a variety of legal research tasks: *Locating cases involving specific fact patterns.* LEXIS permits searching for specific fact patterns independent of the legal concepts and principles involved. Fact pattern searches are particularly useful in areas of law in which principles are well defined and cases are decided on nuances of fact. *Locating cases involving specific legal principles,* such as res ipsa loquitur and mens rea.

Identifying opinions written by a particular judge, or in which particular counsel appeared. *Locating cases or statutes* containing particular terms or phrases (e.g. de facto segregation, unconscionable, short swing profits). *Retrieving cases* that discuss the language contained in a standard contract. *Finding cases* that construe particular statutory provisions or contain definitions of statutory language or discuss several statutory provisions. *Locating a case* when only the name of a party, or docket number, or other limited information is known. Using LEXIS as a citator to locate the most recent cases citing an earlier decision, statute, treatise, or article. *Obtaining the text* of a recent opinion that is not yet available in the advance sheets or of U.S. district court decisions that was not included in any case law reporter. *Determining how federal circuit or district courts* have applied a U.S. Supreme Court decision in subsequent cases. *Double checking other research.* LEXIS can be used to examine the accuracy of previously prepared work or of a brief submitted by opposing counsel. Along with general federal and state law, LEXIS offers a comprehensive collection of specialized law libraries. Among these are Tax, Securities, Trade Regulation, Bankruptcy, Patent, Trademark, and Copyright, Communications, Labor, Public Contracts Law, Delaware Corporation Law, United Kingdom Law, French Law.

Index to Legal Periodicals. This Index is now computerized. For a complete description see the section of this book entitled *Indexes.*

Legal Resource Index: This is the data base of the "Current Law Index." This data base is searched by putting into the computer the same subject headings that would be used if you were using the printed version of the "Current Law Index." This data base can also be searched to find a particular court case, a statute or an article by an author. It also gives bibliographic information in the field of law.

Additional computer data bases that will contain law related information can be found by consulting the section of this book entitled: *Computerized Literature Searches.*

STEPS TO LEGAL RESEARCH

I. *Always Check Federal and State Statutes as Primary Sources of Criminal Law First.*
Most state codes are annotated, meaning that at the end of each section on the criminal laws or court procedures there will be a list of reported court decisions which might have interpreted, applied or ruled on certain aspects of that particular law. Begin your research here and follow through by reading the cited cases in the reporter which pertain to the offense or topic which you are researching.

II. *The Key Number System*
West Publishing Co. has developed a system of researching court decisions that is unique. It is based on a system of "Key Numbers," whereby every legal topic is referenced according to certain key words, and is assigned a key number. Find the key words, and your search for the law begins. Common key words in the criminal field might include "criminal law," "criminal procedure" or "constitutional law." These are then broken down into more specific topics for reference. Each topic, or point of law, is then assigned a key number. Find your key words and numbers in the Digest to the Supreme Court Reporter, or to the reporter of the state whose law you are researching.

III. *The Digests*
Every reporter, *the Supreme Court Reporter, the Federal Reporter*, and each of the regional state reporters (i.e., *Atlantic Reporter*) of *the National Reporter System* has a Digest of Cases. Open your digest to the appropriate Key Word and begin your search. You will find "digests," or short paragraphs summarizing many case decisions. By reading these summaries you can determine if one of these is important enough, or relevant enough, to read in its entirety. If so, find the case in the bound reporter and read it carefully. Be certain to check the pocket-part supplement at the back of each Digest to be sure you have found the latest court decisions on that topic.
West's General Digest. Eighth series through 1992. This Digest contains all state and federal cases included in the National Reporter System. The sixth series covers 1982 to present. The fifth series covers cases from 1977 to 1981; earlier series, published in 10-year intervals, and called Decennial Digests, contain cases as far back as 1658. Digests are available for each of the Federal Reporters, the Regional Reporters and the State Reporters. Digests for state court cases may be found in either the Regional Digest or the State Digest.

IV. *Advance Sheets*
These paperback supplements are published monthly as updates to the digests and to the reported decisions. In the front of the advance sheet you will see the Digest of Cases. Check this digest for recent cases (if any) on your key word and key number. Remember, once you have found the key word (your topic) and key number (your subtopic), you can go through the advance sheets quickly by looking only for your word and number. Then turn to the rear of the advance sheet to read the actual case in its entirety.

V. *Shepard's Citations* (Publishers)
These volumes allow a researcher to take a previously decided court case (or a federal statute), and look at the history of that case and to find every single case in which that earlier case has been cited. For example, in the federal system, U.S. District Court cases *(Federal Supplement)* may have been overruled or upheld on appeal to the U.S. Court of Appeals for that Circuit *(Federal Reporter)* or to the U.S. Supreme Court *(Supreme Court Reporter)*. If so, this history will be shown in *Shepard's Citations*. Cases often remain "the law" for many years, until changed circumstances call for a court to reverse the precedent. If this happens to a case which you are reading, go to *Shepard's Citations* and look up the case by volume and page number, and it will give you the complete history of the case. It will indicate whether the case has been mentioned by courts and what action they took that might influence or alter the precedential value of the case.

HOW TO BRIEF A CASE

Unlike a lawyer's brief, a student's brief is intended to be a concise summary of a decided case for use in classroom discussion and for study purposes. The brief should contain the following sections:

1. *Case Name and Citation.* It is difficult to tell the type of case or relationship of the parties from the name of the case. Generally speaking, civil cases will contain the names of the plaintiff and defendant, while criminal cases will contain the names of the State, People, or United States and the name of the defendant.

   Be certain to give a complete and proper citation to the case, including its year of decision.

2. *Summary of Operable Facts.* Begin this section with a one-sentence statement on the type of case being briefed or the type of offense involved. You may also want to add a summary of the actions taken by lower courts and how (i.e., certiorari) this case came before the present court.

   The facts are usually given in the beginning of the reported case, although concurring and dissenting opinions often give very concise statements of facts. In drafting your summary, be sure to include only the *operable* facts; that is, facts pertinent to the resolution of legal issues in the case. Do not get caught up in extraneous details unless you feel they have a bearing on how and why the court decided the case as it did.

3. *Legal Issues or Questions of Law.* This is often considered the most important section of your brief, although it should rarely be longer than a few short sentences. It can often be phrased as a question that could be answered with "yes" or "no." Remember, the question should ask what is the question of *law*, not fact. For example, do not ask "Did the defendant commit burglary?", because that is a question of fact. Instead ask the legal question with which the court is faced. You might ask, for example, "Under the laws of the state of Mississippi, did the defendant commit the crime of burglary, when the required intent to commit a felony was not formed until after the defendant had already gained lawful entrance to the dwelling?"

   Do not be frustrated if you fail to correctly state the question of law in your first few briefs. Listen to your professor's instructions and your ability to brief a case will begin to improve.

4. *Court's Decision.* Once you correctly identify the legal issues involved, this section should be easy. Many times you will find the explicit holding of the court identified as such by the author of the court's opinion. In any event, you may wish to phrase this as an answer to your Question of Law, with slightly more elaboration. Be careful here. Look to see if the court has developed a judicial doctrine in the case that could be used to resolve the legal issues. This is the Court's Decision, not merely who won or who lost.

5. *Court's Reasoning.* Many case decisions result from the historical development of the common law. Other decisions will turn to an interpretation of a particular statute (legislation) or of the United States or state constitution. Furthermore, cases are often decided on the basis of the social, economic or political issues underlying the case. Be sure to discuss these issues to determine why the court decided the case in the way it did. Try to develop an understanding of the difference between law and policy.

6. *Concurring or Dissenting Opinions.* You may wish to indicate that there were concurring opinions. In a concurrence, a judge may vote with the majority of the court, but feel compelled to set out his individual reasons for doing so.

   In a dissent, the judge (or judges) may set forth his reasons for disagreeing with the majority decision. While these opinions are not the law per se, they do serve to sharpen the legal or policy issues involved in the case. They help us see different points of view and often give clues as to how the court might decide future cases.

When you become weary of reading judicial opinions, and you most surely will, remember this: We live in a nation in which justice is not meted out behind closed doors. We are fortunate to have a judiciary that feels compelled to publicly justify its decisions. That justification serves not only as notice to the parties and their lawyers as to why the case was decided the way it was, but as justification and accountability to each and every member of our society. Further, it serves as a basis of precedent upon which future cases can be decided.

Glossary

As you read through and use this handbook, you may come across some words with which you are not familiar. Although each concept is normally explained in every section, a brief glossary is offered for the following terms.

Abstracting Services. Publications that list books, articles, or other literature by subject while also providing summaries of their contents.

Annotated. Containing notes or short descriptions about a particular publication that are supplied so that a reader may have knowledge of the nature of that literature.

BBS. Bulletin board system.

Bibliography. Compilations of references pertinent to a given subject, used to give suggestions for further reading and also to acknowledge the contributions of other authors.

Biennial. A term used to describe works that are published every two years.

Biography. Written account of an individual's life.

CD-ROM. Compact disk read only memory.

Computerized Literature Searches. A method of gathering literature on a particular topic by searching a machine-readable file of references.

Cumulative. A term used to describe a work that has been combined with several other works. For example, a cumulative periodical index will contain subject and/or author listings for several issues of that periodical, as with quarterly or yearly cumulative indexes.

Data base. A set of interrelated data records stored on a direct access storage device, attempts to provide all the data allocated to a subject and to allow programs to use only those items needed.

GPO. The official abbreviation for Government Printing Office, which indicates the literature is a publication of the United States Government.

GPO Stock Number (#). A number which appears with the bibliographical information (author, title, publisher, location of publisher and date) of government documents. Indicates that copies of the literature can be purchased from the Government Printing Office.

Index. Publications that list books, articles, and other materials by subject and/or author, and provide other bibliographical information about the literature so that it can be found within the library quickly and easily.

Journal. A term generally reserved for periodicals whose content is solely scholarly.

Magazine. A periodical containing miscellaneous articles and stories.

Microforms. Greatly reduced photographic reproductions of printed matter on film, usually 4" x 6" microfiche cards, which contain the approximate equivalent of 98 book pages. Microforms may also be available as roll film. A special microform reader must be utilized to read microform material.

NCJ Number (#). The unique identifying number assigned to books and other materials in the NCJRS collection of 65,000 items. Documents in the NCJRS collection are arranged by this accession number.

NCJRS. An abbreviation for the National Institute of Justice/NCJRS (National Criminal Justice Reference Service).

On-line. Information is introduced into the data processing system as soon as it occurs, is directly in-line with the main flow of the transaction processing.

Periodical. Published with a fixed interval between issues or numbers.

Selected Bibliography. A collection of references that have been compiled on the basis of selected criteria, such as year of publication, form, etc., as opposed to a comprehensive bibliography on a given topic.

Topical Bibliographies. Refers to bibliographies arranged according to subject or topics of specialty.

Abbreviations

AFL-CIO	American Federation of Labor and Congress of Industrial Organizations		FMC	Federal Maritime Commission
ATF	Bureau of Alcohol, Tobacco and Firearms		FRS	Federal Reserve System
BBB	Better Business Bureau		F&S	Funk & Scott
BIBL	Bibliographic Citation File		FSLIC	Federal Savings and Loan Insurance Corporation
BPD	Bureau of the Public Debt		FTS	Federal Telecommunications System
CCH	Computerized criminal history		GAO	U.S. General Accounting Office
CFDA	Catalog of Federal Domestic Assistance		GAODOCS	U.S. General Accounting Office, Documents Retrieval System
CG	Congressional Status Files		GPO	Government Printing Office
CID	Criminal Investigation Division		GSA	General Services Administration
CMIR	Currency or Monetary Instruments Report		HHS	U.S. Department of Health and Human Services
CPA	Certified Public Accountant		HUD	U.S. Department of Housing and Urban Development
CTR	Currency Transaction Report			
D&B	Dun & Bradstreet		ICC	Interstate Commerce Commission
DBA	Doing business as		INS	Immigration and Naturalization Service
DD	U.S. Department of Defense		INSING	Immigration and Naturalization Service Integrated Network Communications System
DEA	Drug Enforcement Administration			
DOC	U.S. Department of Commerce			
DOD	U.S. Department of Defense		INTERPOL	International Criminal Police Organization
DOE	U.S. Department of Education		IRS	Internal Revenue Service
DOJ	U.S. Department of Justice		JURIS	Justice Retrieval and Inquiry System
DOL	U.S. Department of Labor		LCCC	Library of Congress Computerized Catalog
DOS	U.S. Department of State		MIN	House Member Information Network
EPIC	El Paso Intelligence Center		NACJD	National Archive of Criminal Justice Data
FAA	Federal Aviation Administration		NADDIS	Narcotics and Dangerous Drugs Information System
FBI	Federal Bureau of Investigation			
FCA	Farm Credit Administration			
FCC	Federal Communications Commission		NASA	National Aeronautics and Space Administration
FDA	Food and Drug Administration			
FDIC	Federal Deposit Insurance Corporation		NCB	National Central Bureau
FERC	Federal Energy Regulatory Commission		NCIC	National Crime Information Center
FHA	Federal Housing Administration		NCJRS	National Criminal Justice Reference Service
FHLBB	Federal Home Loan Bank Board			

NCRM	National Referral Center Master File	SEC	Securities and Exchange Commission
NCUA	National Credit Union Administration	SIC	Securities Information Center
NLETS	National Law Enforcement Telecommunications System	S&P	Standard & Poor
		SSA	Social Security Administration
NNBIS	National Narcotics Border Interdiction System	SSN	Social security number
		TECS	Treasury Enforcement Communications System
NTP	National Texts and Periodicals Data Base		
OCC	Office of the Comptroller of the Currency	TFLEC	Treasury Financial Law Enforcement Center
ORBIT	Online Retrieval of Bibliographic Information, Timeshared	USCG	U.S. Coast Guard
		USCS	U.S. Customs Service
OSI	Office of Special Investigations, U.S. General Accounting Office	USDA	U.S. Department of Agriculture
		USNCB	U.S. National Central Bureau
PAIS	Public Affairs Information Service	USPS	U.S. Postal Service
R&A	Research & Analysis, Office of Special Investigations, U.S. General Accounting Office	USSS	U.S. Secret Service
		VA	Veterans Administration
		WALES	Washington Area Law Enforcement System
SBA	Small Business Administration		